*The Gilded Gutter Life of Francis Bacon*

*Books by Daniel Farson include*

MARIE LLOYD AND MUSIC HALL
JACK THE RIPPER
OUT OF STEP
A WINDOW ON THE SEA
THE MAN WHO WROTE DRACULA (biography of his great-uncle, Bram Stoker)
HENRY (biography of Henry Williamson)
THE DAN FARSON BLACK AND WHITE PICTURE SHOW

*With photographs by the author*

SOHO IN THE FIFTIES
SACRED MONSTERS
ESCAPADES
LIMEHOUSE DAYS

*Fiction*

THE DOG WHO KNEW TOO MUCH (by Matilda Excellent)
SWANSDOWNE

*Art*

GALLERY (based on his TV series)
WITH GILBERT & GEORGE IN MOSCOW

*For children*

THE CLIFTON HOUSE MYSTERY
THE HAMLYN BOOKS OF HORROR/GHOSTS/MONSTERS

*Travel*

WANDERLUST (anthology of the travel writings of Negley Farson)
A TRAVELLER IN TURKEY
THE INDEPENDENT TRAVELLER'S GUIDE TO TURKEY
A DRY SHIP TO THE MOUNTAINS (climbing the Caucasus)

# THE GILDED GUTTER LIFE OF FRANCIS BACON

Daniel Farson

CENTURY

LONDON SYDNEY AUCKLAND JOHANNESBURG

First published in Great Britain in 1993 by Century
Random House UK Limited
20 Vauxhall Bridge Road, London SW1V 2SA

Century Hutchinson South Africa (Pty) Ltd
PO Box 337, Bergvlei 2012, South Africa

Random House Australia Pty Ltd
20 Alfred Street, Milsons Point, Sydney, NSW 2061
Australia

Random House New Zealand Ltd
18 Poland Road, Glenfield, Auckland 10
New Zealand

British Library Cataloguing in Publication Data

ISBN 0 7126 5725 8

Typeset by Deltatype Ltd, Ellesmere Port
Printed in Great Britain by
Mackays of Chatham plc, Chatham, Kent

For
Francis Bacon and John Edwards

# Contents

# Acknowledgements

The respect in which Francis Bacon is held, and the devotion felt towards him, have been amply demonstrated by the generosity of his many friends in helping me. With only a few exceptions, who had particular reasons of their own, they have provided me with more support than I had dared to expect. Above all, I am grateful to Valerie Beston of the Marlborough Fine Art Gallery for her patience, which has been exemplary. However, I should stress that this is not an authorised biography but a personal memoir. Francis did consider collaborating on a book with me but changed his mind on three occasions, writing to me finally on 14 October 1982: 'I would rather not have any book about my life. I was a bit drunk the other day but I really don't want one until I'm dead. . . .' I respected this sentiment while he was alive, but knowing Francis's reluctance I value Miss Beston's trust and tolerance very highly; also, the personal encouragement given to me by Francis's closest companion, John Edwards.

I am grateful to the Earl of Gowrie and Sir Robert Sainsbury for sparing time to see me, and to David Sylvester for his letter of goodwill. Helen Lessore and Robert Medley welcomed me to their homes; so did Michael Wishart in Hove and Paul Danquah and Peter Pollock in Tangier, who were among the first to convince me that I should go ahead and offered me their unique material and memories. Peter Beard in America was remarkably generous in telling me of his experiences with Francis both as an artist and as a close friend, as was Robin Cook.

Leading figures in the art world have been kind in their assistance: Nicholas Serota, the Director of the Tate Gallery; Bryan Robertson, the former Director of the Whitechapel Art Gallery; Roy Miles; Tobias Meyer; the critics Giles Auty and Richard Cork; the artists Maggi Hambling, Richard Hamilton and Victor Pasmore. Also, my warm thanks to my old friend George Melly for putting me in touch with Mollie Craven, who gave me a new insight into Francis's early years in London; to John Moynihan; to Ian Board and Michael Wojas in the old Baconian stamping-ground of the Colony Room; and to Noel Botham and Lesley Lewis of the French pub down Dean Street.

I received invaluable help in my research from Sara Waterson, and from Mathew Floris of the Miles Gallery who spent hours in the Witt Library on my behalf and came up trumps. Patrick McKenna proved indispensable in his picture research. Finally, though particularly, I should like to express my gratitude to my agent, Bill Hamilton, who has been supportive throughout, and to my editor, Mark Booth, for his sympathy and acceptance from the outset that this would not be a conventional biography.

# 1

## The Violence of the Rose

*When I'm dead, put me in a plastic bag and throw me in the gutter.*
*Francis Bacon to Ian Board*

With a final flourish and a sleight of hand, Francis Bacon died on the morning of 28 April 1992 in Madrid. He was eighty-two. This was what he had hoped for: no fuss, no discovery of his body in an empty room a day or two later, not even a funeral. It was not so much a death as a disappearance.

Francis had been in hospital for six days with heart trouble aggravated by the asthma which dogged him throughout his life. He was no longer painting when he died, but by then he had the love of a young Spaniard. In his way, he was triumphant to the end.

He treated death with the same disdain as he treated life. On 14 July 1989 we had met in Soho to honour the departure of Gaston Berlemont from the French House, a pub Francis had visited in 1930 at the age of twenty and the pub where I had met him on my first visit to Soho. Abruptly he spoke to me of suicide.

'After all, when we're dead we're no good, we're finished. When I go, I hope to drop dead working!'

I said that as he fell with brush in hand one last accidental stroke might leave a masterpiece.

'I'm not talking as romantically as *that*,' he said scornfully. 'Just drop dead working – that's all. Otherwise I would commit suicide.'

'Would you commit suicide?'

'*Well*' – he always drew out that word to its fullest extent – 'if I knew how to do it really properly, having a doctor to give me the right thing. I see so many people do it wrong – haven't succeeded, brain is gone – and end up like vegetables. If you *do* it,' he declared emphatically, 'you've got to do it right.'

'Don't you think it's an insult to life?'

'Bollocks!' he said, angry now. 'It's not! What do you mean: "an insult to life"? Have you gone religious or something, then?'

'I love life, but I think perhaps I talk pretentiously.'

'I certainly think you do. What do you mean: "an insult to life"?'

I tried to explain, though nervousness rendered me half-articulate. 'Life is of such glorious vibrance, and I have known many friends who killed themselves and have thought since how much they would have enjoyed this or that . . . It seems such a waste,' I concluded lamely.

'But it doesn't *matter*,' he said. 'You just do yourself in. Why can't we get those things the Germans had? Cyanide – it just takes two minutes of agony.'

'But in that last moment of agony, if . . .'

'Well, you can't change your mind after that!' he laughed. 'It's too late. You can't waffle about it!' He poured another glass of champagne – 'Cheerio!' – with that inimitable smile.

As he approached his eightieth birthday he was so 'trim', as one woman described him, his stamina so intact, that talk of suicide was perhaps a game.

Yet his friends were shocked by the news of his death. In Soho there was a tangible sense of loss even though at the age of eighty-two death was hardly a cause for surprise. I knew it would be an important event, but had not grasped the extent of it. At first, I experienced the inexplicable thrill that comes when you learn that someone famous has died. Almost an elation. The phone rang incessantly for the next twenty-four hours – largely newspapers demanding obituaries. I had written mine for the *Daily Telegraph* four years earlier; though people are frequently surprised that obituaries are prepared in advance, this is normal practice. I had to refuse other requests, since I was committed to the *Mail on Sunday* for whom I worked as art correspondent. I did, however, contribute a few lines to a general round-up in the *Sunday Times*:

He was unlike anyone else in life, as in his art. He was a true original, as if he had descended from another era. Everything he did was different: the deliberate way he walked; the particular way he talked; his particular emphasis on words, which made his conversation irresistible. When he entered a room it was an occasion. What I shall miss is his sense of fun and that disarming laughter.

In Soho there was almost revelry. Members climbed those dingy stairs in Dean Street to the Colony Room, an afternoon drinking club which will figure prominently in this book. 'It's been electrifying,' the owner, Ian Board, told me. 'The fucking worms have crawled out of their holes – I thought many of them were dead – but the extraordinary thing is that the younger generation came in full fucking bloom.' The singer Lisa Stansfield, close to tears, told an intrusive journalist to 'Fuck off!'

Nearby, in a late-night gay bar called the Toucan, several of the members raised their glasses dramatically and toasted 'Eggs', a nickname occasionally used for Bacon, claiming a friendship that scarcely existed – though a rent boy told me privately that he had gone back with Francis: 'He didn't give a damn, did he?'

His death received massive publicity, outstripping any contemporary British figure I can think of, including Graham Greene. The *Times* broke precedent with a haunting colour photograph on the front page beside the headline: 'WORLD OF ART PAYS TRIBUTE TO BACON'; *Paris Match* ran several pages; and I was phoned from Moscow by James Birch, who had arranged the Bacon exhibition there in 1988, to tell me that the Union of Soviet Artists was in mourning.

My own sense of loss overwhelmed me a few days later when I knew, finally, that I should never see that disarming smile, nor hear his inimitable laughter again. He was so intensely alive it was hard to accept that he had gone. I realised, too, that I had known him for forty years, in other words for most of my life, during which we had had furious arguments for his mood could be as variable as an English summer sky, and I am seldom placid myself. 'I have always thought of friendship as where two people tear each other apart,' he said. 'That way you learn something from each other.' When the film director Gavin Millar described him to me as 'nice' I echoed the word incredulously. He could be nice but he could be monstrous too – though a sacred monster.

One letter I received gave me particular pleasure, for it came from David Sylvester, Britain's most distinguished art critic and one of Bacon's closest friends. Their *Interviews* are still the finest insight into Bacon's art, but he too remembered Bacon as the man:

Since he died, I've not thought about him as a painter. I've only thought about the qualities which have long made me feel he was probably the greatest man I've known, and certainly the grandest. His honesty with himself and about himself; his constant sense of the tragic and the comic; his appetite for pleasure; his fastidiousness; his generosity, not only with money – that was easy – but with his time; above all, I think, his courage. He had faults which could be maddening, such as being waspish and bigoted and fairly disloyal, as well as indiscreet. But he was also kind and forgiving and unspoiled by success and never rude unintentionally.

I liked that 'unintentionally'. David Sylvester's personal consideration was touching: 'May I send you *my* sympathy on Francis' death. You played a terribly important part in his life. I can think of few people who were as enviably close to him as I have always felt you were.'

Once when I asked Francis if it gave him pleasure to realise that his work would be remembered, that he had secured his place in the history of art, he brushed any such suggestion aside. 'Oh, don't talk such rubbish!' he exclaimed impatiently. His reaction was genuine. Others might have nurtured a secret satisfaction, but he had little time for posterity and none for the trappings of fame. When I asked why he had refused the honours offered him – first a knighthood, then the Order of Merit – he said he had no wish 'to be cordoned off from existence', laughing a moment later as he added: 'And they're so *ageing*!' Characteristically, he asked me not to publish his refusal as he had no wish to cause embarrassment to the Lord Chamberlain. No one was more dismissive of his work than Francis.

If Picasso and Bacon stand apart from other artists in the twentieth century it is because of a strength which never allowed fashion to encroach. Both were men of exceptional single-mindedness, selfishness and determination. They were both obsessed by personal sexual fantasy, though their tastes were opposed. As Bacon said in 1991, to the critic Richard Cork, 'If we [Picasso and himself] were both compelled by the erotic impulse, it would be a different eroticism as I'm homosexual.' Homosexuality dominated his life. The savagery of his work related directly to those around him in the gilded-gutter milieu which he preferred.

He insisted he had never been inspired by anybody else but in this he dissembled, for there were undeniable influences. One he was prepared to acknowledge, especially in his later years, was Picasso's. Francis's first experience of Picasso's work, in Paris, at the Paul Rosenberg Gallery in 1928, encouraged him to paint. The first work of his own that Francis regarded as important, the triptych of *Three Studies for Figures at the Base of a Crucifixion* shown in London in 1944, echoed one of Picasso's drawings in that Paris show sixteen years earlier.

Rightly, he detested labels, disliked being 'pinned down'. When Richard Cork reminded him in 1967 that one celebrated triptych was 'inspired by T. S. Eliot's poem "Sweeney Agonistes" ' he complained, 'It was not pinned down by me, it was pinned down by the gallery.' The gallery labelled it after he happened to mention that he had been reading Eliot's *Waste Land*. When asked if he was unhappy about this, he replied, 'I certainly am.'

Bacon paid tribute to three artists in his paintings: Van Gogh carrying his easel on the road to Tarascon; his series of popes produced in 1953, based on Velasquez's *Pope Innocent X* – work he subsequently disowned; and *Oedipus and the Sphinx after Ingres* of 1983. His over-riding debt, however, was perhaps due not to other artists but to photography, especially the *Studies* by Eadweard Muybridge, an American born in London in 1830 who died in 1904.

Muybridge was interested in photography as a form of scientific proof rather than as art. He experimented with sequences which showed the movements of a horse's legs while galloping, proving that these differed from the previous preconception in which they were splayed. Bacon, who was allergic to dogs, used one of Muybridge's *Animals in Motion* for his studies of dogs in 1952 and 1953, and you sense the animal panting from exertion. Muybridge also appealed to Bacon because of his preoccupation with the unusual – *Chicken Scared by a Torpedo*, *Man Walking after Traumatism of the Head*, and the *Paralytic Child Walking on All Fours*, closely copied by Bacon in the stark painting which now hangs in the Gemeentemuseum in The Hague.

When his friend, the painter Denis Wirth-Miller, told him that Muybridge's *Studies for the Human Figure in Motion*, made in 1887, could be seen at the Victoria and Albert Museum, close to where he lived, Bacon had ample opportunity to borrow the images.

The most famous, or infamous, was the *Two Figures* of 1953, known to friends as 'The Buggers', based on the Muybridge study of two naked wrestlers. The different activities may be obvious, but their positions are similar. 'Of course we don't know what the wrestlers were *thinking*,' Bacon pointed out with careful emphasis. He used this athletic/sexual embrace in further versions, notably *Two Figures in the Grass* in 1954, the following year; but the first is the most tremendous, rarely seen today because it is owned by Lucian Freud, who refuses to loan it for exhibition. He is entitled to do so, but one day it deserves to be released as one of the most provocative homosexual images of our time.

People caught in motion in film stills had an obvious appeal, and the greatest of these was the one from Eisenstein's 1925 masterpiece *Battleship Potemkin* of the nurse shot on the Odessa Steps, her glasses shattered by a bullet, blood running from her eye, her cavernous mouth open in a scream. Referring to the scream which dominated so much of his work, as it did Edvard Munch's, Bacon made the surprising admission: 'I always thought that I could make the scream as beautiful as a late Monet landscape, but I never succeeded.'

I assumed this was mock modesty until Peter Bradshaw asked me to deliver a picture to Bacon's studio when I came to London from North Devon, where Bradshaw, an old friend, lived next door. Though Bacon used the *Potemkin* image for a full-length *Study for the Nurse* in 1957, he had not painted a portrait of the face, and this Bradshaw had done as a form of affectionate homage. Knowing Bacon's detestation of material possessions, especially paintings and particularly those by friends, I flinched from the encounter – though I could hardly refuse. Yet when I climbed those steep, narrow stairs at the mews cottage he took the package wrapped so carefully and tore off the brown paper with the glee of a boy on his birthday. I realised, with a shock, that because he had so much, people seldom gave him anything. Even so, when he saw the picture I expected a dismissive 'Oh yes, very nice indeed' in his mocking voice. Instead, he studied it intently in total silence while I held my breath. Almost a minute must have passed when he gave an emphatic gesture and exclaimed: 'That's what I've always wanted to achieve – the colour of the mouth.'

Though I knew him so well, I was startled, for this revealed a modesty I had not suspected, or, as I recognised a moment later, the strength of a man who knows his genius and his limitations too. He sent Peter Bradshaw a handwritten letter, remarkable in its generosity:

London S.W.7 2/9/86

Dear Peter, I love the painting I think it is beautifully done and it is marvellous to see it in colour Thank you so much for giving it to me it is something I really love to have – do hope to see you soon and thank you again for such a marvellous present – All very best wishes Love Francis [he rarely used punctuation].

From the outset Bacon appreciated the impact of painting on massive canvases; he used the reverse side when he needed to do so for economy, and found that this provided the ideal texture. These paintings were mounted in sumptuous gold frames, protected by glass which enhanced the effect of the 'railed enclosure' which he created by using horizontal and vertical lines with which to confine his figures. When Adolf Eichmann was put on trial for war crimes, caged in a glass box in the court room, people were quick to note the resemblance to Bacon's portraits – though these were made as early as 1949, the date of *Head VI* which the late Sir Lawrence Gowing praised so powerfully:

The cubicle reveals itself as a veritable cube, of plate glass perhaps. The curtains of light, unless they are shadow, stream down like rain round and through the box, drenching it more than ever. Suspended in it, the ironic tassel now hangs against the nose between invisible unseeing eyes (which shadow and fate have washed away) of a figure who is both a prisoner and a ruler, nothing less than a Prince of the church in a violet satin cape, which evokes the biretta on his unseen head. Under the satin with excruciating refinement he wears white lace. The tassel teases him, tickles or tortures. In a huge grimace, a Pope is screaming.

This was the picture chosen for the poster for the first great Bacon retrospective at the Tate Gallery in 1962. It provided the climax to a sequence of *Heads* in 1948 and 1949, among his most disturbing work. Lawrence Gowing was a perceptive critic and a painter of the old school himself, and his reaction to the *Heads* at the Hanover Gallery, and *Head VI* in particular, confirmed the previous triumphs of the *Three Figures at the Base of a Crucifixion* four years earlier. Writing of *Head VI*, Gowing said:

> It was an outrage, a disloyalty to the existential principle, a mimic capitulation to tradition, a profane pietism, like invented intellectual snobbery, a surrender also to tonal painting, which earnestly progressive painters have never forgiven. It was everything unpardonable. The paradoxical appearance at once of pastiche and iconoclasm was indeed one of Bacon's most original strokes. The picture remains one of his several masterpieces, and one of the least conventional, less predictable pictures of the twentieth century. Like the really important pictures of our time, it inaugurated a dimension that we could not have imagined, and still cannot wholly describe.

Much has been made of Bacon's manipulation of the creative accident and the way the paint landed on the canvas, giving him the inspiration to continue in a direction not previously intended. In his interviews with David Sylvester he said: 'If anything ever does work in my case, it works from that moment when consciously I don't know what I'm doing.' Admitting the strong element of risk in such an approach, he described a portrait he attempted in 1962 in which the eye sockets, the nose and mouth, had no reality though the paint, twisting from contour to contour, suddenly achieved a likeness. However, when he tried to take this further the following day he lost the image completely. In this way he walked a tightrope between abstraction and figurative painting.

As an artist who disliked abstraction, he invariably fell off the tightrope whenever he veered too far in that direction. Equally there was the determination to avoid illustration, stressing that the moment the narrative story emerged it led to boredom. He claimed that in his despair he used a big brush and great deal of paint and sloshed it on very freely, and sometimes the thing clicked and became the exact image he was aiming for. In this respect, as in his life, Francis was the master magician, a conjurer of paint.

When he claimed that he threw paint on the canvas with his hand without knowing what would happen, though he hoped for 'the creative accident', he reminded me irresistably of Tony Hancock in the film of 'The Rebel' who was asked by a group of sophisticated art critics in a Paris gallery how he mixed his paint – 'In a bucket, with a big stick!'

He told me frequently, 'If you can *say* it, why bother to *paint* it?' and numerous words to that effect, yet he spoke on this theme with surprising regularity, returning to the same phrases, such as 'unlock the valves of feeling', repeatedly over the years. Ironically, he came closest when writing about someone else. In a rare commendation of another artist, he paid this unexpected tribute in the Tate Gallery's catalogue for the 1953 Matthew Smith exhibition:

> He seems to me to be one of the very few English painters since Constable and Turner to be concerned with painting – that is, with attempting to make idea and technique inseparable.
>
> Consequently, every movement of the brush on canvas alters the shape and implications of the image. That is why real painting is a mysterious and continuous struggle with chance.
>
> I think that painting today is pure intuition and luck and taking advantage of what happens when you splash the stuff down, and in this game of chance Matthew Smith seems to have the gods on his side.

I have no doubt that Bacon had himself in mind.

The creative accident, the very daring of 'splashing the stuff down' and seeing how it lands, is attractive. The unpredictability signifies so much of Bacon as the artist and the man. He was a compulsive gambler, and this gambling – at which he sometimes won huge sums of money – grew out of his heightened awareness of the role of chance in our lives and our vulnerability to it. He used accident in his painting with the *calculation* of the gambler. Often the movement of the brush created a more interesting image than he intended, thus 'one is attempting to keep the vitality of the accident yet preserve a continuity'; for, conversely, he was the most controlled and disciplined of artists. Towards the end his work was almost clinical in its dissection: 'I never think of my work as convulsive,' he told Richard Cork in 1991. 'I love very ordered work.'

With the justification of experience, Francis may have felt that the element of chance enhanced the mystery in which he wrapped himself, making his art appear as hazardous as his life when both were highly controlled. Francis was disciplined to an extent I have known in few other people, and in this he was selfish as all great artists are and need to be. Most of us have inadequacies, but he was never inadequate in the sense of shortcomings. His faults were

9

fearful and in his perverse way he manipulated them, often at the expense of those around him. In trying to understand him in retrospect, I have been shocked to remember the extent of this crueller side. A savage single-mindedness commandeered his life in the name of art – and excused it.

He exploited the sensation of despair, turning it into exhilaration. He explained that he never believed one should have security and never expected any for himself – 'Existence is in a way so banal, you may as well try and make a kind of grandeur of it.'

Ultimately, what was his achievement? He told me once: 'It's necessary to reinvent the language of paint,' and this is what he did. *That* was his great achievement. In conversation he referred to the *neurosis* of our time, and in his painting he caught it on the wing. Though he was personally a masochist, his art had little to do with physical violence or the violence of war as so many assume. He said: 'It's to do with an attempt to remake the violence of reality itself. And the violence of reality is not only the simple violence meant when you say a rose or something is violent, but it's the violence also of the suggestions within the image which can only be conveyed through paint.'

The violence of the rose! – now there's a thought. As for the violence of reality, here we come close indeed. Where others sought an impression or a moral statement, Bacon gave the fact stripped of comment, unlike Picasso's *Guernica* which he believed reeked of propaganda.

In a sense he went a stage further than Picasso's conception of reality, and his version of the truth struck a chord in the latter half of this century. He talked admiringly of Buñuel, and suggested that if he had not been fascinated by the use of paint he might have become a film director, for while the Impressionists veered away from the formal representation of the new art of photography, Bacon was drawn to the split second captured on film. Film makers were fascinated by him, too. Bernardo Bertolucci used Bacon's images for the opening titles of his 1972 movie *Last Tango in Paris*, noted for its 'sexual explicitness and savagery', and when the set designers started work on *The Silence of the Lambs* they too turned to Bacon and his 'railed enclosure' to create the hellish cell of Hannibal Lecter.

His view of life could hardly be harsher. He did not believe in

10

God, in morality, in love or in worldly success – only in, as he put it, 'the sensation of the moment' locked into her strange, masturbatory fantasies. Bacon, above all, conveyed twentieth-century man in his various states of loneliness.

To understand Bacon the man it is necessary to accept that he was contradictory. He was a loner, though he relished company. His work is seen as pessimistic, yet he had an innate optimism which helped him to survive. He was the best company, the funniest and most humorous. He could be kind and generous as I knew from experience, yet capable of sudden anger, even petulance.

He betrayed many of his close friends, especially if they were rival artists, and some did not forgive him. He was totally amoral. He had little time for weakness in others and no patience with human foibles or small vanities, the qualities that fascinate me. He was easily bored. Lucian Freud once called him the wildest and wisest man he had ever met. Even if he had not become a painter his personality was so original that he would have made an impression on his time. Like Wilde, he poured his genius into his life as much as his art.

Apart from their homosexuality, he was the antithesis of David Hockney, an artist whom he dismissed and even ridiculed privately. Hockney's photographic Californian cleverness was everything he despised – though it could be said that he despised everything when it came to contemporary British art. With his calculated mock modesty, he protested to Richard Cork that he was not liked in the way that Hockney was liked.

'You're saying that he cannot deal with the darker side of life?' asked Cork.

'Am I?' Francis exclaimed. 'What is the Hockney side of life?'

'Celebration?' ventured Cork.

'I would like to celebrate it too. Well, happiness and love is a wonderful thing to paint also. I always hope I will be able to do it. After all,' he gave a shrug, 'it's only the reverse side of the shadow, isn't it?' Such self-deprecation was uttered with a radiant, disconcerting smile.

The point is that he preferred the shadows cast by the fiercest light outside: 'If you really love life you're walking in the shadow of death all the time. . . . Death is the shadow of life, and the

11

more one is obsessed with life the more one is obsessed with death. I'm greedy for life and I'm greedy as an artist.'

I doubt if he was the greatest man I have known, but he was the most extraordinary. He was the most magical, also the most ruthless.

He could not have been otherwise.

# 2

## The Blood-bespattered Cells

The sill old cunt.

*Francis Bacon on his father*

Francis Bacon was born on 28 October 1909 of English parents in a Dublin hospital, and was brought up at 63 Lower Baggot Street. John Deakin, the photographer, teased him for inverted snobbery: 'You don't fool me. I bet it was *Upper* Baggot Street!' When I visited the birthplace in 1990, I found that Deakin was closer to the truth than he realised. I was astonished to find it a grand Georgian house. Allowing for the splendid renovation of Francis's home by the firm of solicitors who occupy it today, 63 Lower Baggot Street was elegant, in the heart of fashionable Dublin with the Shelbourne Hotel and St Stephen's Green nearby. Oscar Wilde was born around the corner on 16 October 1854 at 1 Merrion Square, which is shabbier today, with fainter echoes of its former splendour. In tracing the scenes of Francis's childhood I am not sure what I expected, for in all the years of our friendship there was scarcely a passing reference to Ireland, as if there were something to hide and certain things to forget. The subject seemed unmentionable.

Consequently, as I drove out of Dublin in search of Bacon's early homes, I became increasingly bemused by the discovery that he had been brought up in luxury and style. This cast him in a different light, as a man whose background conditioned him to expect the best. It explained something about the grand style of his personality. People who are *déraciné* never entirely break free.

How Irish was he? The Rt Hon. the Earl of Gowrie, the former Arts Minister, who is known more succinctly as Grey Gowrie, understood Bacon's background – they shared the same roots, indeed the same village in County Kildare where Francis's father trained racehorses. Though Lord Gowrie does not consider him

13

an Irish painter, he told me that Francis was in many respects Irish and his memories of Ireland had a traumatic effect upon his paintings largely because of the Civil War.

Francis remembered listening to the army's night manoeuvres. Gunshots could easily be heard. 'You mustn't forget that I was born in Ireland,' he told Richard Cork in a *Times* interview of 16 March 1991,

> where my father trained horses very unsuccessfully. I grew up there at a time when the Sinn Fein was going around. All the houses in our neighbourhood were being attacked. I'll always remember my father saying, 'If they come tonight, say nothing.' He expected to be attacked, and on all the trees you'd see the green, white and gold of the Sinn Fein flags.

At the age of five Francis heard the British cavalry galloping up the drive to their home: 'I was made aware of what is called the possibility of danger even at a very young age,' he told David Sylvester.

Roy Miles, who became London's most ebullient art dealer, saw Francis in a Chelsea restaurant when he was a very young man and sent him a glass of champagne as a tribute. 'Are you being fucking rude?' said Francis – but he ended up as Miles's dinner guest. Miles dared to admire his art's 'painterly quality' but expressed reservations about the violence of the subject matter. 'Francis told us at dinner that this was due to his experience as a young man in a house called Mereworth in Ireland when he felt "the shadow of the hangman's noose" across his country. When he passed the prisons he felt he could hear the screams of the Irish prisoners as they were lashed by the cat o' nine tails in their blood-bespattered cells. Francis hated the British hypocrisy and thought that the English had been saved by the Irish and the Scots, that it was the Celts that made Britain great.' Miles suggests that this was one reason why he refused a title. Also, the midnight alcohol could have heightened Francis's early recollection of screams and cat o'nine tails.

Francis's father, Edward Anthony Mortimer Bacon, was a major in the British Army, and later he moved to Ireland to run a racing stable. He was twenty-five years older than his wife, born Christina Winifred Firth, by whom he had two daughters and three sons. He made the grand claim of being descended from the philosopher and statesman Francis Bacon, the 1st Viscount St Albans, described by Alexander Pope as 'the wisest, brightest, meanest of mankind'. This Francis Bacon was a pederast who died in 1626 leaving debts of £22,000, a pedigree that his namesake was proud of. Allegedly, Queen Victoria urged Francis's grandfather to resume the title, but he lacked the money. Obsessed by horses, Edward Bacon took the family to stay in a series of houses outside Dublin. Francis's earliest memory was of himself as a five-year-old 'walking up and down a pathway lined with cypresses at my Irish home, dressed in a bicycling cape which I used to borrow from my brother.'

County Kildare is horse-training country, and Cannycourt near Kilcullen remains a comfortable house with outbuildings and stables: ideal for a child who was fond of horses and hunting. Francis liked neither, and he detested the countryside for the rest of his life. The only attempt his parents made to give him a formal education was to send him to Dean Close School at Cheltenham in England, but he stayed there for just a few months. Partly because of his asthma, his education amounted to little more than private tutorials with the parish priest. 'I had no upbringing at all,' he once said. 'I used simply to work on my father's farm.' His closest companion was his nanny, a commonplace relationship in an upper-class family when the parents were wayward, and she alone remained a constant in his life.

Edward Bacon was nomadic for reasons of necessity as well as temperament. Having served in the army, he volunteered for the War Office and worked in London for most of the First World War. 'We lived near Hyde Park, in Westbourne Terrace,' recalls Francis, 'and after the bombing started they sprayed the park with phosphorescence from watering-cans so that zeppelins would mistake the glow for the lights of the city and drop their bombs there.' With the threat from the Sinn Fein in Ireland and the bombs in London, he said he was brought up 'to think of violence'.

After the war his father bought a property called Farmleigh, near the mansion of Abbey Leix in County Leix, from his maternal grandmother. Apparently a beautiful house with curved rooms at the back which, it has been suggested, may have inspired the curved backgrounds in the triptychs, Farmleigh was destroyed.

15

Always on the move, Edward Bacon then set up home at Straffon Lodge near Naas, an attractive mansion in open grounds not far from Dublin. This could have been a sympathetic home for an ordinary child, but not for Francis. His father had little time for his awkward son. Though an intelligent man, it seems he never developed his intellect. 'He just fought with people,' Francis told David Sylvester. 'He really had no friends at all . . . because he had this very opinionated attitude. And he certainly did not get on with his children.' Yet Francis admitted that he was sexually attracted to him, even if he scarcely understood his feelings at the time, and recognised the truth only after he had been 'broken in' by his father's grooms and stable lads.

'How many of them?' I asked, amazed, for Francis could not have been older than fifteen.

'Several.'

With her own Irish background as a member of the Guinness family, Lady Caroline Blackwood encouraged him to speak of his 'unlikely and horsey Irish upbringing'. He responded with surprising passion. Though he denied his 'Irishness' vehemently, it seems this was partly a reaction to his 'traumatically painful' childhood.

Lady Caroline, who knew him in the fifties after she married Lucian Freud, says that Francis found it impossible to return to Ireland. 'He developed a neurotic attack of asthma on the plane whenever he tried to get there. He could fly to any country in the world without physical mishap, but any flight to his homeland always proved disastrous.'

Francis liked Caroline and praised her novel *Great Granny Webster*, which I bought on his recommendation for it was unusual for him to admire anything contemporary. He found her so sympathetic that he was able to confide in her. 'My father was a horse trainer,' he told her with a shudder. 'A *failed* horse trainer.' She says that he stressed the word 'failed' with such disgust and anger that he made his father's occupation sound utterly repulsive. When he was a little boy his parents had put him astride a pony and had forced him to go fox-hunting. He loathed the brutality of the 'Sport of Kings' and developed a violent allergy to horses. Once he found himself on the hunting field he turned blue and started to choke with asthma. His parents were very soon made to realise that he was never going to be the son they wanted.

He told Caroline – and it is easy to imagine the ringing tones of the declaration – 'Surely there's nothing worse than the dusty saddle lying in the hall.'

Coming from Ireland herself, Caroline longed to hear more, but the subject made him freeze. 'He became agitated whenever I broached it. He started to tug at the collar of his shirt as if he were trying to loosen some kind of noose which he found asphyxiating; for a moment he resembled the agonised figures in his paintings whose faces turn a truly dangerous shade of indigo purple. I always stopped my questioning because it seemed cruel and tactless to upset him.'

Then she made an extraordinary claim. A homosexual friend had told her that Francis admitted that his father arranged for his small son 'to be systematically and viciously horse-whipped by his Irish grooms'. Edward Bacon may have been a remote, stiff, ill-tempered man with no interest in the arts – 'As for pictures,' said Francis, 'I was hardly aware that they existed' – but I find it harder to accept him as the monstrous sadist of Francis's recollection. Yet the very fact that Francis could make such an accusation shows how traumatic his childhood may have been and how far-reaching the consequences.

'With all his horror of Ireland,' Caroline concluded, 'he had the intellectual Irishman's traditional dislike of Catholicism. The popes that he painted were all screaming and distorted. Some of them were sitting on the lavatory. Although he stubbornly denied that he had been influenced by his Irish upbringing, the desolation of his vision was very similar to that of Beckett.'

The comparison with Beckett is one that I shall examine later in greater detail. As for the subject of the popes, David Sylvester asked Francis: 'Do you think your involvement in it had some-thing to do with feelings about your father?'

'I'm not quite sure I understand what you're saying,' Francis replied, and I expect he did so warily. 'Well, the Pope is *il Papa*,' Sylvester explained.

Francis dismissed this. 'I certainly have never thought of it that way,' he said, adding, 'but I don't know – it's difficult to know what forms obsessions. The thing is, I never got on with either my mother or father.'

On another occasion he said of his parents: 'They didn't want me to be a painter – they thought I was just a drifter, especially my mother. It was only when she began to realise that I was making some money out of it – and that was very late in her life and not so long before she died – that we made any contact and she altered her attitude.' By then she had remarried twice and was greatly changed.

His happiest times were spent with his mother's eccentric family. Francis's wealthy grandmother was half French, married to the owner of a colliery in Northumberland, and she bore him seven children. According to the art critic John Russell, his aunts and great-aunts gave Francis his first taste of 'human strangeness'. One of his great-aunts married into a family called Mitchell and lived in a castle, Jesmond Towers, near Newcastle where the work of a relation, Charles Mitchell, who painted in the style of the Pre-Raphaelites, hung in the ballroom. He remembered, too, her London house in Hill Street as one of the smartest in Mayfair, because she gutted it and replaced everything with black marble. Years later he would laugh when he recalled another aunt who went to dinner at the Berkeley only to realise as she sat down that her dress was on back to front.

Such simple, touching human failings were not part of life with his family. The only time Francis saw his father openly show emotion towards a human being was on the death of his fourteen-year-old brother, Edward's favourite. No such tears were shed for Francis unless in impotent rage. His father's exasperation reached breaking point when he discovered the boy dressing up in his mother's clothes. 'One day my father caught me trying on some of my mother's underwear. I must have been fifteen or sixteen at the time. He threw me out of the house.' His father decided it was time for Francis to leave home and live independently in London on a weekly allowance of £3, to be paid by his mother. Doubtless everyone breathed a sigh of relief – with the possible exception of the stable boys and the nanny.

What had Ireland taught him? A touch of arrogance and a healthy scorn for convention and religion, tempered by a sympathy for that eccentric minority who entertained in their crumbling mansions, gambling and drinking to excess. Although I hark back constantly to my parents, Francis never spoke to me of his own apart from rare references to his narrow-minded father as an 'absolute bastard' and on one occasion as 'the silly old cunt'. There was no indication that he felt the least affection for his mother, or that she loved him.

Yet his attraction to his father helps to explain his subsequent attachment, when a young man, to elderly toughs; and the kindness of older women, such as his nanny and the aunts, explains his loyalty to elderly retainers even when they were falling apart – when his devotion was saintly. Francis was one of those people who shut out the things which disagree with them. He neither compromised nor rationalised. Usually devoid of sentimentality, he suffered on the few occasions he yielded to it.

Having lacked intimacy in his childhood, he hesitated to accept it afterwards. There would be neither concession nor sacrifice. The young Francis Bacon left Ireland hardened.

# 3

# Queer Berlin and London

I worked on myself to be as unnatural as I could.
                        *Francis Bacon, in an interview with Peter Beard*

Bacon described his early years in London as divided 'between the gutter and the Ritz'. He was at home at either address, and equally himself. Years later he admitted to Miriam Gross (*Observer*, 30 November 1980) that he preferred to rely on stealth rather than work: 'I can't say that when I was young I was at all honest. I used to steal money from my father whenever I could and I was always taking rooms in London and then disappearing – not paying the rent, not being able to.'

Three pounds a week was enough to live on but not enough for fun, so Francis indulged his tastes by petty theft and living off people. After placing a carefully worded advertisement in *The Times* seeking employment as a 'gentleman's gentleman', and presenting himself under the facetious name Lightfoot – oddly enough, his Nanny's name – he was startled by the large number of erotic replies. He chose the home of a respectable solicitor in Mecklenburgh Square. 'I had to be there early to get his breakfast, then I was supposed to "do" the place and come back in the evening to cook the dinner. 'I was a good cook.' When I gave in my notice, as they say, I always remember him saying, "I don't know why he's bothering to go because he never does anything." ' In his next position, he was dining at the Ritz on his evening off when he was spotted by his new 'gentleman' at another table across the room; his employer was so shocked by the proximity of a servant that he sacked him.

Francis said that as an adolescent it had been his ambition to do nothing. Drifting on, in a sort of malaise, he worked in a wholesale shop in Poland Street which sold women's clothes. At least this introduced him to Soho, but the job was bound to end in grief: 'I knew nothing about the business; they more or less employed me just to answer the telephone.' He idled the hours away composing poison-pen letters to the owner, whom he detested, until one afternoon when an abusive missive was included in the post by mistake and he was sacked again.

By now he had accepted his homosexuality. Though he claimed he was 'incredibly shy' until the age of twenty-seven, there is nothing like a stud farm to teach one the facts of life. Homosexuality was his nature, and he had the strength not to wish it otherwise. Another turning-point came when he was eighteen and Edward Bacon made a final, misguided attempt to 'make a man of' his son by placing him in the custody of a tough, no-nonsense horse trainer who was a close friend: 'He handed me over to a friend of his for him to educate me.' This man, sometimes referred to as an 'uncle', though I suspect that was an honorary title, promptly took his charge to Berlin where all pretences were flung aside as the 'uncle' revealed a similar zest for decadence and for sporting activities which had little to do with horses. 'We settled in Berlin for a time,' said Francis. 'It must have been in 1926. And by way of education I found myself in the atmosphere of the Blue Angel.' They stayed at the Adlon Hotel, where young Francis enjoyed the luxury of breakfast in their double bed, served by an unperturbed German waiter. He remembered it as 'one of the great decadent years of Berlin. The night was very exciting to me, coming from a very puritanical society like Ireland. . . . Every night we went round the bars and cabarets. I didn't question what we were doing – it was wonderful and I was enjoying myself. Without my realising it, it must have had a profound effect on me.'

This was the decadence of the Weimar Republic recorded by Otto Dix. Francis told me, too, of the street theatre outside the bars and clubs, performed by touts who encouraged the customers to go inside with a tantalising glimpse of the particular treat in store. A cabaret in miniature. An early photograph shows him in profile and, though the features are strong, the effect is effeminate. This was taken during the visit to Berlin, and John Russell remembered another taken at the same time, in the gardens of Schloss Nymphenburg, with 'dark London hat, the formal striped suit, the tall collar and the neatly tied tie', which sounds like the delightful affectation of a young man trying to appear grown-up. Russell added that this image was soon discarded and went for ever.

Russell saw Francis's visit to Berlin as a 'continuation of Ireland', as a city which reinforced his scorn for convention. The artistic turning-point came neither in Berlin nor in Munich, where he moved after two months, but in Paris on the journey home in 1927. More than either of the German cities, Paris was instantly sympathetic. 'I think Paris is the most beautiful and marvellous city in the world,' he told me in 1988, and he found it so congenial on this first acquaintance that he returned to spend three months with a family in Chantilly in order to learn the language. He was fluent, though, speaking it with the exaggerated accent of the Englishman and his own careful emphasis – 'Par-der-too, sherree!'

It was at Chantilly that he saw Poussin's *Massacre of the Innocents*, which he described as probably the best human cry in painting. The impression which this image made on him, and which was to become such an important feature of his paintings, was reinforced back in Paris, where he bought a secondhand book with beautiful hand-coloured plates of diseases of the mouth.

He said of his experience of the drawings by Picasso in the Paul Rosenberg Gallery – 'I thought, "I'll try and do it too." ' When you see a reproduction of one of Picasso's charcoal sketches, the inspiration is undeniable, particularly for the *Three Studies at the Base of a Crucifixion* of 1944 which would mark his arrival as a painter. They have been described as 'abstract' shapes, but this is misleading: one is an upright figure which could be dancing, with a face composed of a chin, a similar protuberance as a breast-like nose with a tiny nipple at the end, and a similar breast for the dome of the head. The figure has one slender leg and arm, a larger limb which serves both as leg and torso, and another limb as the second arm. Years later he would say: 'Why not be influenced by Picasso, who has been the greatest artist of the twentieth century?'

After staying in Paris for several weeks, his guardian tired of his precocious ward and vanished, without leaving him the money to stay on. Forced to survive by his wits – already something of a habit for Francis – he lingered until even his charms ran out and he was forced to return to London and try his luck there instead –

'When you're young, you're always taken out . . . if you're easy-going!'

Even when I met him many years later, homosexual London was very different in atmosphere from what it is now. For us it was a fact of life rather than a statement. However, it was against the law. Francis confided that one of his closest friends from those early days, a painter, had been sent to prison, but we never referred to this publicly. Others became 'victims' after local police indulged in witch-hunts in the provinces, culminating in the arrest, trial and scandal of Lord Montagu, Michael Pitt-Rivers and the writer Peter Wildeblood, who were accused of seducing three chaps in the RAF. I met Pitt-Rivers soon after his release and he told me of Montagu's bravura throughout, putting his shoes out to be cleaned while he was on remand, eyeing up one of the policemen in court, turning to the others as the gates of Pentonville clanged behind them – 'Well, dears, just one of those things!' Today, Montagu is a respectable married man and one of the most respected peers of the realm. Others suffered, too. Lives could be destroyed by exposure and blackmail, and a few 'victims' preferred to kill themselves rather than face a public trial.

Some found solace in the anonymity of 'cottages' (public lavatories), a furtive underworld of sideways silence with the constant danger of arrest from the man in the next cubicle who might be an *agent provocateur*. Francis preferred the more gregarious atmosphere of pubs and clubs to chance encounters in urinals and Turkish baths. He also made the occasional retreat to clubs which were wholly queer, with no need for pretence despite the threat of being raided; here one encountered a gauntlet of looks which were just as sideways as they were in the cottages, and the raised-eyebrow scrutiny of T.B.H.? – 'to be had?'

I have depended on the kindness of policemen, but they were unsympathetic towards us then because this was the official mood of the time. Like any dissident, I lived in fear of the knock on the door. Francis, too, had an ambivalent relationship with the police. Soon after I met him he startled a group of us one afternoon in the Kismet Club, a seedy basement bar used by policemen, villains and 'resting' actors, with the revelation that one of the 'coppers' had 'a thing' about him after discovering that Francis wore fishnet stockings and suspenders under his trousers – though we had to take his word for that.

The point is that Francis had no nerves. He felt no reservation whatsoever. He was the embodiment of all that was advantageous in being homosexual, and it has to be admitted that it frequently enhanced as well as shadowed our lives. Though he might have appeared effeminate as a youth, this was the effeminacy of leather. In spite of his exaggerated mannerisms, no one ever called him a queen. He moved alone, cutting his particular swath of calculated chaos, and his homosexuality was an irreversible part of both his life and his art.

# 4

# The Australian Entourage

*It's all so meaningless we might as well be extraordinary.*
*Friedrich Nietzsche often quoted by Francis Bacon*

When Francis returned to London in the late twenties, there was no thought of art school even though his admirers would have paid. Just as well. If he had studied under one of the masters of the time like Professor Tonks, who encouraged Stanley Spencer, he could have become a finer and possibly more versatile artist, but he would have lost that imperious solitude which stamped his greatness.

He regretted not having learned ancient Greek; otherwise he does not seem to have missed a formal education and, though a lack of training delayed his development as an artist, he thought this could have been an advantage: 'I don't think art schools can do anything for artists today. One sees the people who have been taught. What are they doing? After all, they never make anything new, they just go back to a kind of academic drawing which was much better done by artists in the past.' Unlike Lucian Freud, who established himself originally as a draughtsman, hardly any drawings by Bacon exist. In the course of research for this book I have found only two.

To start with, his interest lay with interior decoration rather than painting. Encouraged by commissions gained in Paris, he moved into a studio in 7 Queensberry Mews, South Kensington, where he showed the rugs and furniture he designed in 1929. The concept of Francis Bacon as a furniture designer seems bizarre and the thought of him weaving is highly comic. In fact, the rugs were manufactured by Wilton, and I suspect that craftsmen helped with the furniture too. His work was striking enough to be bought by the politician R. A. Butler and his wife, among others. The monstrous but knowledgeable art collector Douglas Cooper kept the pieces of furniture he bought in order to make fun of them in front of his guests. The writer Patrick White, though, was so fond of the desk he commissioned, with wide shallow drawers and a red linoleum top, that, when he was forced to auction it before he returned to Australia, he employed a local carpenter there to reproduce it. Though the copy was a cruder version, it reminded him of the lost original and became his writing desk.

Characteristically, Francis later dismissed his designs as un-original, influenced by contemporary French design, but even if this was an experimental interlude it contributed to his future as an artist. In August 1930, *The Studio* included his studio in a spread on 'The New Look in British Decoration', with tantalising clues to what lay ahead: the bareness of the room emphasised by white rubber curtains, a glass and tubular dressing table, and particu-larly the Art Deco rug. This bleak austerity foreran the lonely figures in their empty rooms of the later paintings. John Russell recognised a rug as 'almost a straight paraphrase of a synthetic cubist painting by Picasso', so that influence lingered too.

In 1933, Francis abandoned interior decoration to concentrate on painting. Though self-taught, he had some excellent teachers. Foremost in the early years in London was Roy De Maistre, an Australian painter whose work is scarcely known today but who was one of the few men whom Francis spoke of with unreserved affection.

De Maistre had a ground-floor studio in Ebury Street, a sparse white-boarded room with a minimum of furniture which appealed to Francis's taste and preceded the greater austerity of his own studio a few years later, where the two of them exhibited. De Maistre's method of working encouraged Francis to discipline himself as an artist, he told me later, for the older man was ruthless in forbidding interruptions, shutting his door in the face of callers who dared to 'drop in'.

When De Maistre relaxed, however, especially after his move to another studio at 13 Eccleston Street, he held a salon which was predominantly, and I suppose naturally, Australian. Apart from Henry Moore and Graham Sutherland, who became Francis's closest friend, the attendants included Douglas Cooper and Patrick White.

Though he was four years older than Francis, White was shy and unsure of himself: 'I was pretty well tongue-tied, I could feel myself behaving like the complete leaden bore, while he [De Maistre] tried drawing out of me ideas which might have persuaded me they were worth expressing. He was very patient, more than kindly; Roy's relationships with either sex began as courtships, of which he was often unconscious. I fell in love very quickly.'

De Maistre was twenty years older than White, a short, thick-set, genial, bald-headed, avuncular man, described as 'more like a banker than an artist', which was very much Francis's type at that time. Was he some sort of father figure for Francis? Certainly neither he nor Patrick White found the age difference inhibiting. De Maistre was recovering from an unrequited love affair at the time. While he was doing so and after the 'initial skirmishes', as White described them, 'the relationship for which I had been hoping developed instead into a fruitful, lasting friendship. He became what I most needed, an intellectual and aesthetic mentor. He taught me how to look at paintings, to listen to music.'

From what Francis told me, his own experience was similar. Plainly, De Maistre was a dominant personality with exceptional charm. His influence artistically is the more remarkable and seldom recognised. I was under the impression that De Maistre 'churned out' flower pieces in order to survive, and that though these were anathema to Francis their sales allowed the older man to entertain his young friends. This begrudging assessment could hardly be further from the truth.

LeRoy Leveson Laurent Joseph De Maistre (it is not surprising that he shortened his name) was born on 27 March 1894 and brought up in a colonial-style house in New South Wales. He received no schooling until he went to Sydney at the age of nineteen to study music and painting. Ten years later, in 1923, he won the Society of Artists' Travelling Scholarship, which he used to go to Paris where he exhibited in the Salon of 1924. On returning to Australia, he gave his first one-man show in Sydney in 1927 around the time that Francis was experiencing his first taste of Picasso. De Maistre went back to the livelier scene in Europe and another one-man show, at the Beaux Arts in London in 1929. Afterwards he settled there, with frequent visits to St Jean de Luz and Paris. Like many other artists, he stopped painting in wartime and produced nothing between 1939 and 1942.

In his eighties the painter Robert Medley told me: 'Francis learned a lot off Roy, who was terrifically complicated and at times a total fraud, claiming to be related to the royal family through the Earl of Athlone, with an allowance paid to his family by Queen Victoria to keep quiet about a liaison with a royal cousin. Complete fabrication – but rather fun! That side of Roy would not have appealed to Francis. Roy was a good painter, very intelligent and extremely ambitious. He was most interested in the sado-masochism of the Crucifixion.'

Bryan Robertson, who gave De Maistre a retrospective exhibition at the Whitechapel Art Gallery in 1960, told me that Francis did not see him often in the fifties and sixties but always kept in touch. 'They dined together at intervals, usually at Roy's. They never quarrelled. It must be remembered that Roy was "insecure" about money. He leaned on the Church for commissions, and on rich patrons – he'd known Rab Butler since long before the war – and connections of this kind reassured him. Roy had an exceptionally benign disposition – friendly, and capable of many kindnesses for his friends. He had humour, also, and was endlessly entertained by the eccentricities of English social life. According to Roy, Francis looked like a somewhat dubious choirboy, and although very young when they first met – about twenty-one – already often in a pickle.'

Writing of the De Maistre retrospective John Rothenstein emphasised De Maistre's 'singular position' in art: 'Ever since his work was first seen in London . . . in the South Kensington studio of his friend Francis Bacon, his work has been held in high respect by a number of painters, mostly his juniors, and a few writers.' But even Rothenstein under-rated the extent of De Maistre's importance outside his small, mainly homosexual coterie. Certainly there were flower pieces to pay the bills, and they look very attractive even in black and white reproductions – a still life was acquired by the Tate. He was a portraitist, too, and painted such sitters as R. A. Butler, who nearly succeeded Harold Macmillan as Prime Minister; Camilla, Lady Keogh; and the former Countess of Harewood, whom I knew later as Marion Thorpe. The retrospective also included an extraordinary portrait of Francis Bacon done in 1935 (Collection of the Artist), in which, caked in make-up, he looks like a Firbankian dandy; and a painting of Francis Bacon's studio, painted in the same year (Collection of Mrs H. MacDermot). Other eye-openers are the paintings on such religious themes as the Pietà, Noli Me Tangere, and the sado-masochistic Crucifixion, a remarkable interpretation which today hangs in the Leicester Museum.

Rothenstein wrote that De Maistre was moved by the images of the Crucifixion not as 'dramatic' subjects or symbols, but because of the truth they represent, and he quoted De Maistre's remark that the painter is not so much attracted by the content of certain subjects, 'simply that he recognises them as occasions for the exercise of this urge'. That could be Bacon talking, and even though many of the religious themes were painted by De Maistre after those ready days in Chelsea, his studies for the Stations of the Cross destined for Westminster Cathedral were executed as early as 1932. One painting suggests that both De Maistre and Bacon were, at the very least, aiming in the same direction – De Maistre's *Figure and Bath*, sold at Sotheby's in 1982. The figure has a lizard-like head, a beak and a bloated body. It would be an exaggeration to describe it as Baconian, but the thought does occur. Certainly it is an odder image than De Maistre's reputation led me to expect.

Just as I was fortunate in meeting Francis in my early twenties, so was he in his friendship with De Maistre. For a young man starting to find his way after the initial inspiration of the Picasso exhibition in Paris, the presence, if not the actual guidance, of the older Australian provided the support which he would otherwise have forfeited when he refused to go to art school. De Maistre's example as a 'living painter', Picasso, and the Old Masters seen in art books or galleries were the training he chose instead, and they gave the young Francis Bacon the confidence that even he must have needed at this moment.

Patrick White remained too gauche to speak to Moore or Sutherland but relaxed with Francis, describing his 'beautiful pansy-shaped face, sometimes with too much lipstick' in his autobiography, *Flaws in the Glass*, written fifty years later. One afternoon in Battersea they crossed a temporary footbridge while the permanent bridge was under repair.

Francis became entranced by the abstract graffiti scribbled in pencil on its timbered side. Alone, I don't expect I would have noticed the effortless convolutions of line he pointed out for me to admire. To discover something as subtle as it was simple made me feel quite elated. In those days Francis was living at the end of Ebury Street, across the Pimlico Road, within a stone's throw of the Mozart-Sackville brothel. He had an old nanny who used to go shop-lifting whenever they were hard up, and as lover there was an Alderman.

It is a measure of Francis's attraction that servants did not hesitate to abandon their employers and follow him into a world that was fraught with risk and bohemian squalor.

In 1933 Francis's *Crucifixion* was published in the book *Art Now* by the critic Herbert Read, whose affection for Roy De Maistre did not extend to a similar compliment. Ahead of its time, the *Crucifixion* was included in a mixed show at the Mayor Gallery that same year and was bought by telegram by Sir Michael Sadler. This was a sensational beginning, to be recognised by a leading critic, collector and gallery, and belies the general claim that nothing of this period mattered – though Francis himself went out of his way to encourage this misrepresentation. Considering that he was untrained and no more than twenty-three or twenty-four, it revealed an astonishing talent at an earlier age than has generally been realised. Everything Baconian was there, in life, philosophy and aesthetics. Of course there were developments in technique to come, but the idea that he was little more than a dilettante throughout this period could not be more misleading.

In 1934, Francis tried to build on this success in *Art Now* with his first one-man show; it was organised by himself in the basement of Sunderland House, occupied by an admirer called Arundell Clarke. It was not a success and he subsequently destroyed most of this work. Later he admitted regret over the loss of one of the paintings exhibited, *Wound for a Crucifixion*, which was a precursor to the *Three Figures* ten years later. It was of a clinical ward painted dark green to waist height and cream above, with a typical horizontal black line in between and the 'very beautiful wound', which referred to the piece of human flesh on a sculptor's armature. It sounds 'Baconish', and John Russell, the crucial source for these years, saw two comparable paintings dated 1933, confirming that Bacon was already marked out as 'a painter of figures in rooms': 'The sense of enclosure, of situations pushed to

30

their extreme between four walls, is powerful enough to offset all shortcomings of assurance in the way those situations are handled. One or two people sensed that he could become a painter of real consequence.'

These people included Eric Hall, a wealthy businessman and reputedly the mayor of some northern city – probably the 'Alderman' referred to by White. He was a dominant influence for many years, who at one point left his wife and children to live with Francis. Robert Medley says: 'Eric Hall was indeed Francis's lover. A conventional, well-off, tallish businessman who made no impression but was very important to Francis. The relationship lasted for seven or eight years. Eric paid Francis's bills in Monte Carlo on one of their visits, and the family objected more to the gambling than to the relationship, which merely gave an edge to their objection. Eric adored Francis and worked tremendously hard for him. He laid everything out on the carpet for him. Francis, a gambler, basically didn't care if he had money or not, but he was pretty ruthless. He didn't allow anything to get in the way of his artistic ambitions.'

In an interview with Michel Archimbaud Francis said of Eric Hall: 'I met a man who lived in Chelsea with his wife and his two children. One day he came to find me, he had been very interested by my work and from that moment he began to come to my aid without ever letting me down . . . during almost 15 years! He gave me money. He was a man of wealth.' Francis talked to me of Eric Hall as someone who had greatly influenced and encouraged him, as an intelligent man with a lot of sensibility. 'He taught me the value of things – decent food and so on.' Good food and good wine were to be tremendously important to Francis – he never compromised in this any more than in anything else.

Well known as a 'benefactor', Eric Hall 'got on terribly well' with the working classes, as someone said disparagingly of his snobbery, and also with young people. He helped to organise a group exhibition called *Young British Painters* at Thomas Agnew and Sons in 1937 as part of 'a scheme to provide a permanent gallery for the constant display of works by Contemporary Painters and Sculptors'. Robert Wellington, who ran the Zwemmer Gallery in Charing Cross Road, and Roy De Maistre, who had 'connections', were involved as well. This was a noble venture, and Henry Moore responded with the assurance that he could abandon teaching to concentrate on sculpture if he was guaranteed as much as £400 a year. As idealistic schemes tend to do, this one started with a flourish and fizzled out, Wellington and De Maistre going their separate ways. Eric Hall, on the other hand, was supportive throughout: not only did he secure, for less than forty guineas, the loan of Agnew's, which before the scheme fizzled out was where thirty-three pictures were exhibited, but he also helped to choose them, as Victor Pasmore confirmed in a letter of 3 July 1992 from his home in Malta. 'The Agnew's exhibition in 1937 was selected by Francis Bacon together with his friend Eric Hall; they both came to my studio to choose my contribution.' In fact they chose four paintings by Pasmore, two by De Maistre and four by Sutherland. The Agnew's exhibition was a failure at the time, but in retrospect it can be seen as an important moment in contemporary British art, particularly for Francis, exhibited in the company of such promising artists as Robert Medley, Ivon Hitchens, Ceri Richards, Julian Trevelyan and John Piper, quite apart from Pasmore and Sutherland.

Francis contributed three paintings and was singled out for attack in such papers as the *Daily Mail* of 14 January, under the headline: 'NONSENSE ART INVADES LONDON'. 'It is a pity', wrote Pierre Jeannerat,

that the nonsense art or pseudo-art of today conquers and invades more and more of the leading dealers' galleries of London. Messrs Agnew, of 43 Old Bond Street, with a long-established reputation as sponsors of much that is great in painting (their old masters shows are well known) have lent their galleries for an exhibition of contemporary pictures which include the representation of a set of false teeth on a tripod. *No, it is not a pity. The more we see of such absurdities the more we shall realise their emptiness and ugliness.*

Dismissing Trevelyan's work as 'no better than the scribbles made on his blotting paper by a tired businessman', Jeannerat turned to *Abstractions from the Human Form*, by Francis Bacon, which 'describe the human form as a distorted toy balloon'.

'A set of false teeth'? This echoes a claim by Patrick White that Bacon was painting false teeth obsessively, but destroying almost every canvas. When in the course of researching this book I saw the *Abstractions* reproduced in the *Referee* of 17 January that year, I experienced the delicious shock of recognition: unmistakably, these were preliminary skirmishes for the *Three Studies for the Figures at the Base of a Crucifixion* of 1944, which was finally to establish him in the British art scene seven years later. The early 'abandoned' pictures are convincing evidence of his hard work and experiment, ultimately fulfilled in 1944. They include *Man in a Cap* (1941–2), inscribed F. Bacon, Petersfield, where he had a cottage at the time, the open mouth exposing the teeth which echo the previous version of *Landscape with Car*, where the shape is remarkably similar to the *Three Studies*.

Throughout these years he was blessed in knowing Graham Sutherland. Whenever I think of Graham in relation to Francis I feel a pang of remorse. His role in Francis's ascendancy is poignant. Though they had so much in common, there were some important differences. Graham was only six years older but he was married, converting to Catholicism a year before his marriage to Kathleen Barry in 1927. Graham was, as far as anyone knew then, heterosexual, though he was so intrigued by the ramifications of Francis's love-life that he enjoyed the role of an honorary homosexual. He was a close friend of the framer Alfred Hecht and the wealthy American art collector Arthur Jeffress. Relishing the role of go-between in every walk of life, Graham was an unashamed gossip, fiercely interested in the lives of other people. It is hard to believe that Francis did not in some way benefit from Graham's longer experience, as he did with De Maistre, especially as Graham was starting to be recognised as Britain's foremost young painter. Few friends were so unselfish as Graham in his support, though he must have known that this could be to his detriment. He was a man of outstanding charm, courtesy and generosity, and if he became envious of his protégé towards the end this is understandable.

For both artists, painting was the be-all of existence, but for Graham it was more than that, a compensation for a terrible personal tragedy. Graham called it 'our trouble', confiding in only a few close friends. I reveal it here, for Graham and Kathy are dead and the tragedy shows their courage. Their first child was not stillborn but so deformed that there was little more than a stump and a heart, no arms or legs; for a week it lived, and then, mercifully, died. The doctors told Graham and Kathy that their blood groups were so disastrously opposed that they should never attempt to have a child again. From that time they lived in enforced celibacy, sleeping in separate beds. I am sure the medical profession would find a solution today, but his Catholicism, which Graham embraced with all the passion of the convert, may have provided solace in his celibacy – while at the same time confirming it. One can imagine their feelings, and still not get near to them: the guilt, the frustration, the anguish, the temptations, the bitter sadness of regret. This is one reason why Francis's role in Graham's life was pivotal – Graham needing Francis's friendship, offering his guidance unreservedly. For Graham, friendship and painting were everything apart from Kathy. In private, they referred to his pictures as 'our children'.

On 22 April 1962, a profile published in the *Observer* referred to the 'faintly cloistered atmosphere' of the Sutherlands' home, with 'no children, no dogs'; the writer had no concept of this unwitting cruelty, but I am sure that Francis knew. Even if he did, this would not have made him kinder. He would have shrugged it off as an act of vengeance by the fates, always so keen to punish those they deem successful. He was to suffer this himself.

Graham's biographer, Roger Berthoud, discovered that it was Francis's *Crucifixion* which proved the most heavily thumbed page in his subject's copy of Herbert Read's book – from which Graham, like Roy De Maistre, was excluded. This did not prevent Sutherland's constant encouragement, recommending Francis's work to his own patrons, Sir Kenneth Clark, and Sir Colin Anderson, the shipping millionaire, who eventually acquired the 1933 *Crucifixion*. It was Graham who persuaded Clark to visit Francis's studio. Outwardly a glacial man, the Director of the National Gallery looked at the available work, commented, 'Interesting, yes,' and left.

'You see,' said Francis angrily, 'you're surrounded by cretins.'

That evening Clark told Graham, 'You and I may be in a minority of two, but we will still be right in thinking that Francis Bacon has genius.'

Piecing a life together is like a jigsaw puzzle except that a fragment is discovered unexpectedly which does not fit. A girl called Mollie

Craven left college in 1937 and rented a small semi-basement flat in a three-storey house in Chelsea, 1 Glebe Place, which she describes as 'one of the less impressive Victorian streets' and 'architecturally miserable' – though it is fashionable now. She went down a few steps to her basement, which extended to a back courtyard; a retired headmistress lived above; and her landlord, a young and 'slightly eccentric artist', occupied the top floor where he had his studio. This was Francis Bacon.

The concept of Francis as landlord is startling. Mollie Craven says she was young and naive and took it for granted then that the house belonged to Francis, though she suspects now that it was rented. The dates suggest that it was owned by Eric Hall. Every weekend she climbed the communal staircase to pay her rent to Francis, for in those days this was a personal business, almost a social occasion compared to the automatic debit and credit by the banks today.

As a late teenager Mollie gave parties in the basement, with music and singing which the 'stuffy' headmistress objected to. She did not invite Francis because he 'lived his own life' and was cut off in the attic, 'though we used the same stairs and the same big bathroom. It was not his sort of thing. He seemed to be working all the time but he must have had a wide circle of friends for there were constant deliveries of fruit and game at the door. In some ways he was a bit like a good elder brother and pointed out to me how much my public school education had left out. He gave me the thin original copies of poems by T. S. Eliot and Wystan Auden and a ticket for *The Dog Beneath the Skin*. A top public school doesn't equip one for that. I was grateful to him for taking my schooling in hand.'

In the summer, Francis occasionally called down to offer her tickets to Hurlingham or the Regent's Park Zoo which he had been given by friends but could not use himself. Apart from the weekly formality of 'Here's my cheque' and 'Thank you' when he was working, he was welcoming when not so busy and they 'struck up quite a friendship'.

Apart from his unaccustomed roles as landlord and 'elder brother', here is interesting confirmation of the continuation of his work; this belies the idea, put about by himself, that after 1933 he just 'enjoyed' himself. Doubtless he did that too, but in the

35

daytime he worked hard perfecting the promise shown in the *Crucifixion* of 1933.

Mollie Craven does not remember his drawing at an easel, but she has a clear memory of Francis leaning over a pile of paper making charcoal 'sketches', simply 'roughing them out'. He dropped the heavy, expensive paper on the floor and tore up reams of it, which distressed her. Once a week it was gathered together and dumped.

She describes him as a 'vivid' personality, never relaxed. His painting was surprisingly Impressionist, and happier – he was working things out in an optimistic mood, with sunshine and colour. She remembers particularly a picture of the Upper Thames with sunlight through the leaves, pale yet bright and luminous; 'subjects which I liked very much. You would be happy to live with them. You couldn't with the later screaming mouths which looked impressive in a gallery, but not on a living room wall. When his pictures became so thunderous and savage, I recalled the earlier work with nostalgia and thought: "Poor Francis, he's going through an awful time!" '

Did he destroy as many as we are told? 'I assumed he sold them all. I am very sorry if he destroyed them.' He told her he had rejected an invitation to exhibit in Paris at a recent Surrealist exhibition – 'No way would I accept.' (In fact his submission to the International Surrealist Exhibition was rejected as 'not sufficiently surreal'.) He also said he was planning a large exhibition of his own, complaining that the gallery owners insisted on titles for each one, rejecting his suggestion of numbers one to a hundred. 'One Sunday in the brilliant light of June he was putting them on an easel in turn and we thought up the fanciful titles they would like . . . some of river-and-leaves subjects. I dared to suggest that, far from being a Surrealist, he was a Post-Impressionist. My recollections are scrappy at such a huge distance of time. I recall standing in his studio window and looking across Glebe Place at the large windows of some studio buildings, and we watched the ballet star Anton Dolin working on his parallel bars in his window, while we discussed ballet. On one occasion the stink in his studio was tremendous, quite overwhelming the usual pleasant smells of the oil and paint. Francis was busy at his easel so I prowled round, at his request, trying to trace the origin of the pong. His table down the middle of the room was an enormously high-heaped affair with a mountain of papers and magazines, and I saw a long bird-tail projecting from it. This turned out to be a pheasant, distinctly off-colour, which he had forgotten completely.'

There was one painting which forecast the later work. Mollie Craven saw it on a winter Saturday when she went up to his studio and heard him coughing dreadfully. She followed his voice into the bedroom – 'a truly frightening room with dark blue walls and ceiling, with a vast mural of a crucified arm across the opposite wall – enough, I felt, to induce a fever'. She had the feeling it was based on Dürer's *Crucifixion*, though, it may have been inspired by Grünewald's *Crucifixion* of 1515 from the Isenheim altarpiece, which had a strong influence both on Francis and on Graham's *Crucifixion* for St Matthew's church in Northampton. 'The whole was an enormous left arm with the nails in it, and just a hint of torso, pointing towards the window. The body was virtually cut off by the chimneypiece. A tortured bedroom if there ever was one.'

She fetched a doctor and for a few days kept Francis supplied with broths and 'uninspired kinds of invalid diet'. He rallied from his illness 'and began painting again with tremendous vigour'.

# 5

# Stalking the Blitz

Death can be life-enhancing.

*Francis Bacon*

Francis Bacon had a deplorable war. After his death, a few obituaries stressed his contribution to Civil Defence in the Blitz, and one writer described him as an ambulance driver – a ludicrous concept. Yet old men forget and have the right to embellish, and he gave Richard Cork the impression that his experiences in the London Blitz had a traumatic effect on his work. 'He wasn't very willing to talk about it,' Cork remembers, 'pulling dead bodies out of the debris.' In his obituary in the *Guardian*, entitled 'Genius formed in the blackness of the Blitz', Tim Hilton referred to Bacon's 'relish for the darkness and the Blitz. As he later said, "We all need to be aware of the potential disaster which stalks us at every moment of the day." It is a neat encapsulation of his personal muse, born as he stalked bombarded London in search of places to gamble.'

If Francis had been chosen as a war artist, like Graham Sutherland and Henry Moore, his scenes of the carnage might have been unsurpassed, but he remained virtually unknown as an artist. The truth is Baconian and louche. When he received his call-up papers, he hired an Alsatian dog from Harrods and slept beside it in order to aggravate his asthma. Reporting for his medical the next morning, he was in such a streaming state that he was granted an immediate exemption and the unfortunate animal was returned to Harrods – or so one hopes.

Certainly he 'stalked' the 'sexual gymnasium of the city', as he described the streets of London. The atmosphere invited it, for no one gave a damn as to who did what to whom, and in addition to the vital element of risk the darkness of the blackout provided convenient cover as you went in search of trade. Of course the

Blitz was notoriously a time of great promiscuity for all sorts of people. Asked later if he liked rough trade, Francis said, 'Yes, and married men too.' He also stalked in order to gamble. Throughout the war, when he refused to exhibit – although it is doubtful if many opportunities arose – he survived by gambling, partly from his winnings but mainly from his own gambling sessions which he held illegally at night, usually once a week.

In 1943, after a year in the cottage at Petersfield in Hampshire, he moved to the studio once used by Sir John Everett Millais, the founder of the Pre-Raphaelites. I remember that studio at 7 Cromwell Place, close to South Kensington Tube Station, with its high ceilings and bare boards and, if my memory is reliable, a faded velvet sofa and some paint-stained scraps of carpet. Otherwise it was suitably stark and Francis loved it. Selling this studio to the painter Robert Buhler seven years later was one of his few regrets. Graham and Kathy Sutherland dined there at least once a week: 'It was a large, chaotic place,' she recalled, 'where the salad bowl was likely to have paint on it and painting to have salad dressing on it, but the wine and food were good and the conversation was marvellous' – as it always was with Francis.

When Francis met Michael Wishart in a Soho pub he asked him to have a drink, followed by dinner in the Millais studio of spaghetti with garlic and walnuts, a speciality which he cooked for me in my grandmother's house in nearby Pelham Place a few years later. Wishart is now an established writer – his autobiography *The High Diver* is one of the wittiest of the century – and a painter who showed early promise so that when he was a fourteen-year-old schoolboy at Bedales he sold his first picture to Eric Hall, the ubiquitous patron, who owned a cottage in the school grounds. Wishart's first impression of the studio suggested that Francis was poor, though he poured his guests lavish dry Martinis in large Waterford tumblers filled to the brim. He recalled him then as

a striking young man, resembling strongly David's self-portrait in the Louvre, or pictures of a youthful Beethoven. I was struck by the intensity of his gaze; it was as though he had X-ray eyes. I succumbed at once to his romantic charm, which was allied to a caustic wit. Within the same sentence he could pursue an idea into the darkest corners of human endurance and withdraw with an observation as hilarious as it was tragic.

By the time I came to know Francis his humour was blunter and more modern than it seems to have been in those rather mannered days. I have traced just one saying from this period: 'Physical attraction is destroyed the moment the man shows the faintest aspiration towards intelligence.' In this again we return to Dublin, for there is surely some aspiration to Wilde here?

The Millais studio resembled a dowdy cavern of diminished grandeur – 'a certain forlorn sense of Edwardian splendour', in Wishart's words. There were three paintings stacked against the wall, for the triptych of *The Studies for the Three Figures at the Base of the Crucifixion*. He had never seen a Bacon before, apart from the *Crucifixion* reproduced in *Art Now*.

What did he make of that mysterious figure so essential to Francis's life, the nanny who slept during the day on the kitchen table? He remembers her as considering Edward VIII a disgrace because he failed to become king, and as a fervent advocate of capital punishment – 'as I suppose all nannies are'. Apparently she looked forward to the re-erection of the gibbet at Marble Arch, and the first offender to be hung, drawn and quartered would be the Duchess of Windsor. She was 'very like a nanny, a Victorian spinster', and half-blind (though it was said that she could tell the difference between a ten shilling and a pound note instantly). When acting as an unlikely hat-check girl at the illegal gambling sessions she augmented their income with tips from the clients.

Once, when Wishart rashly went banco at one of the gaming parties, he lost 'a packet – not that the wheel was fixed'. On such evenings Wishart had the chance to observe Bacon closely as he 'made himself up'.

> He applied the basic foundation with lightning dexterity born of long practice. He was more careful, even sparing, with the rouge. For his hair he had a selection of Kiwi boot polishes in various browns. He blended them on the back of his hand, selecting a tone appropriate for the particular evening, and brushed them through his abundant hair with a shoe brush. He polished his teeth with Vim. He looked remarkably young even before this alchemy.

Wishart found the atmosphere *fin-de-siècle*, reflecting the touch-and-go *richesse* and weary glamour of the hotels in Monte Carlo where Francis gambled whenever he (or Eric Hall) could afford it. The china was embellished by a Bacon family crest, and two large and exquisite chandeliers formed the dominant decoration. But apart from these and 'Nan', there was no other sign of Francis's family except for the rare appearance of a brother who was a hypochondriac and died of tetanus after cutting his finger with a potato peeler. 'My God,' he apparently exclaimed, 'they're South African potatoes and the soil is full of tetanus!' and in this case his hypochondria was justified.

One afternoon Francis asked Wishart to take some money to the painter Anne Dunn, guessing that he would like her. Michael Wishart knew of her beauty and intelligence and was not disappointed, nor discouraged by her menage of an Australian fruit bat which hung upside down munching oranges while squirting a fountain of diarrhoea into the air, and an ageing night club hostess christened Edomie, known as Sod, who rose late, drank all the available gin, went shoplifting at lunch, and slept in the afternoon. 'Catatonic, snoring quietly, her large body unclothed, she lay upon or near a divan. At times her eyes were open though glazed, resembling those of a fish. Inquisitive blue-bottles, profiting from her total lack of self-consciousness, whiled away the summer afternoons in exploring what had long ceased to be her private parts.'

Wishart described her as extraordinarily kind and generous, and even I, a naive young man just down from Cambridge, knew of Sod Johnson as a legendary character whose drinking club was a refuge for homosexual servicemen on leave in the war. During air raids she used the downstairs bar of the Ritz, where she was known, according to Wishart, as 'the buggers' Vera Lynn'.

Within a few days Anne and Michael were engaged. Though she was the youngest daughter of the Canadian banker Sir James Dunn, who bequeathed a million pounds to each of his daughters, that prosperity lay in the future. Their wedding displayed the extravagance of those accustomed to enjoying wealth without possessing it themselves. The party was held at the Millais studio, where Francis painted his chandeliers crimson and his face a pale shade of pink. Sod was maid of honour. Wishart bought two hundred bottles of Bollinger for the two hundred guests, but the gate-crashers invaded and he had to ask my friend Ian Board to bring more supplies from the Colony Room – the drinking club run

41

by Muriel Belcher, who was one of the guests. Others included the Sutherlands and Brenda Dean Paul, the famous drug addict of the twenties, who danced in a scarlet trouser suit on high silver heels, her pageboy hair dyed platinum. At midnight she disappeared with her friend Jean in a hired Daimler, and returned refreshed by the white powder which they distributed with a thimble to revive the wearier guests.

A piano was played by the artist Ruskin Spear and Leonard Blackett, also known as Granny and described by Muriel Belcher as 'a brave little woman in the Somme', who trilled:

> You stepped out of a train
> With your tiara on
> And your mascara on . . .

They danced for two days and three nights, and carried on to Wivenhoe in Essex for a two-day regatta given by Dennis Wirth-Miller and his friend Dickie Chopping. After five nights of non-stop celebration, Michael and Anne continued to Paris – 'un-exhausted'. Francis had given them his hundred Waterford glasses, which they divided between them on their divorce – Michael's have since been smashed – and was so broke after the party that he had to sell his chandeliers. David Tennant, who ran the Gargoyle nightclub, hailed it as 'the first real party since the war'.

By this time the years of preparation for the *Three Studies for Figures at the Base of a Crucifixion* had been realised. Described as a triptych, a form also used by De Maistre, the central panel with grinning teeth and a bloated body on a tripod, it is instantly reminiscent of the *Abstractions* shown at Agnew's in 1937; but now the images are perfectly worked out, perfectly fulfilled. Even the title is calculated – 'Studies' and '*a* Crucifixion' to avoid any identification with *the* Crucifixion.

Shown at the Lefevre Gallery in April 1945, when the end of the war was just a month away, the *Studies* were part of a group exhibition which included the work of Matthew Smith, Henry Moore and Graham Sutherland. But these artists were already eclipsed. 'Visitors tempted by the already familiar name of Graham Sutherland,' wrote John Russell, were brought up short by images so unrelievedly awful that the mind shut with a snap at the sight of them. Their anatomy was half-human, half-animal, and they were confined in a low-ceilinged, windowless and oddly proportioned space. They could bite, probe, and suck, and they had very long eel-like necks, but their functioning in other respects was mysterious. Ears and mouths they had, but two at least were sightless. One was unpleasantly bandaged. . . . Set down on what looked like a metal stool, the [left-hand] figure was thrashing round as if to savage whatever came within biting distance. The central figure, anatomically like a dis-feathered ostrich, had a human mouth, heavily bandaged, set at the end of its long, thick tubular neck. . . . Each was as if cornered, and only waiting for the chance to drag the observer down to its own level. . . . They caused a total consternation.

Francis Bacon was established.

# 6

## Addicted to Soho

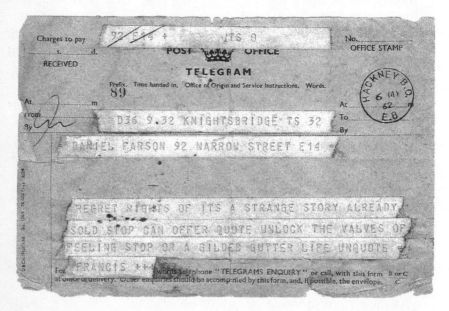

Francis told my agent at the time, Irene Josephy, 'You know, Soho is only part of my life.' He said this when he changed his mind after we discussed our possible collaboration on a book. Once, in 1962, after a boozy night which I can hardly remember, he sent me the joke telegram reproduced above which suggests that we had discussed various titles for such a book. Another time he sent me this letter:

> I would rather not have any book about my life. I was a bit drunk the other day but I really don't want one until I'm dead – I have had a bit of luck gambling – enclose cheque for £500. I do hope you understand, do hope I will see you next time you are in London. . . .

I could hardly asked for a more gracious rejection. In 1982, I was commissioned by Macdonald to write his biography and he agreed. I left for a working holiday in Turkey with a light heart but I was not wholly surprised when I discovered on my return that he had changed his mind again. His reluctance was understandable and confirmed at a later date when both Lord Gowrie and myself approached him again, giving the same reply to us both – that he did not wish such a book while he was alive, with the implication that he did not wish to embarrass the children of former partners, though this objection is not so valid today. I hope that Lord Gowrie may write the definitive life of Francis Bacon in the future: meanwhile, he was extraordinarily generous in wishing me luck with my own book, saying that he could only have described Francis's rumbustious life in Soho with Francis's collaboration, abandoning the project on Francis's death.

It was true that Soho was only a part of Francis's life: Tangier and Paris were crucial too, as was Monte Carlo in the early days, but I am certain that Soho and its characters in the 1950s and 60s witnessed the most exhilarating period of his life and work, which is why I am describing it in detail, for I had the luck to be an eyewitness. If the spirit of a place can stimulate an artist, as I am sure it can, Soho did so for Francis.

Although I had no way of knowing it in the spring of 1951, I was about to enter a remarkable twelve-year period covering Francis in his ascendancy, a period in which he disregarded conventional standards in his painting as he continued to do in his life.

At the risk of seeming more self-obsessed than usual, I should explain why entering Soho, and meeting Francis in particular, meant so much to me. At the age of twenty-three my naivety was almost obscene. Paradoxically, this could have been due to my over-worldly upbringing, travelling around Europe in the whisky-wake of my father, Negley Farson, the American foreign correspondent and one of the legendary figures of that vanished breed. I suspect that his alcoholism, which I never resented, blinkered me to life, seeing only what I wished to see – rather like Francis himself. My father's guilt made *me* guilty, with the irony that his addiction to drink is one of the few traits I have inherited.

Jostling around the world led to a certain insecurity: I was evacuated to Canada in the war, spending my vacations in America; in England I became the youngest Parliamentary Correspondent until I enlisted in the American Army Air Corps.

When my dual-nationality came to an end at the age of twenty-one, I chose to be British while taking full advantage of the G.I. Bill of Rights which enabled me to go to Cambridge where I started a magazine with my old school friend Anthony West, called *Panorama*. A satirical feature which made fun of *Picture Post* resulted in a summons to the office of the Managing Director who had just sacked Ted Castle for the Socialist policy I had lampooned. I emerged from the building, not as the new wonder-boy-editor but a staff photographer, and it was while I was killing time before I started working for the magazine that I drifted accidentally into Soho.

In spite of all this experience, I remained an innocent in the ways of the world, unsure of myself in many ways, including sexually, a mould waiting to be cast. Soho cast me. All too quickly, I made up for the lost time. Francis Bacon was the crucial mentor; later, completely by chance, I had the good fortune to coincide with Kathy and Graham Sutherland at the Voile d'Or Hotel in Cap Ferrat. For the next few days we were inseparable as we drove around the South of France in search of a place where they could settle, eventually finding a bungalow in the hills above Menton. To have two such friends at this threshold was an influence not to be denied, though there were to be moments when I yearned to escape from my addiction to Soho. Writing to my mother from the Voile d'Or, I admitted:

> away from the perils of Soho, I feel saner than I have done for years. I realise it would be mad, now that I've got somewhere, to throw up photography. Sutherland and Bacon are really so extraordinarily enthusiastic about my photography and so keen to boost it that I feel most bucked . . . Sutherland says I should paint, and it is fascinating talking to him about painting, especially as I have done so often with Bacon and I suppose they are the two leading British painters working today. I have been lucky in making such interesting friends and, in Sutherland's case, such charming ones. They have warmly invited me to stay in England. I do think, fantastic though it is, that they quite like me.

Before that momentary disillusionment with Soho, for that never lasted, Soho had become my second home – often my first. I had move out of my father's shadow into Bacon's. Soho was a revelation, with the discovery of people who behaved outrageously

46

without a twinge of guilt and drank so recklessly that when they met the next morning they asked each other if they needed to apologise for the day before. Friends who had fought the previous night returned to the pub arm in arm. The camaraderie of the morning after has never been better.

'When I first knew Soho,' Francis told me, 'the prostitutes were all over the streets. The streets were more fun, more amusing. The prostitutes gave a living sense to the streets.'

Across the parallel streets ran alleys like the branches of a tree. Old Compton Street at the base led into Brewer Street, lined with restaurants and food and wine stores such as Randall and Aubin, where Roma G ler looked after the till, decade after decade, and the Lena Stores two doors away with sacks of risotto rice beside the door.

Blocks of ice outside the shuttered restaurants started to dribble across the pavements, and kept the fish fresh at Richards, noted for such rare delicacies then as Mediterranean squid and fresh sardines. A few yards away the markets were alive with fruit and vegetables: Rupert Street smaller and posher; Berwick Street, heading north, cheaper, noisier and more crowded. For a young photographer they offered the excitement of a stage set come alive.

A man who wore dark glasses tried the door of the York Minster opposite and waited outside, lifting his face to the sun, missing the beautiful girl who walked past him barefoot. At 11.30, half an hour later than the other pubs, the bolts were drawn back and the doors opened.

'Good morning,' said the barmaid.

'Christ, I feel awful!' said the man in dark glasses, and downed his first drink with a shudder. 'Ah, that feels better.'

The York Minster, which was also called the French pub, was run by Gaston Berlemont and so it was also known as Berlemont's. His father, Victor, was noted for his white moustache which Gaston copied in a darker shade, and was the first foreigner to be granted an English pub licence at the outset of the First World War. Gaston was born upstairs in 1914. Francis, I would learn, first went to the French pub in 1949 when Victor was still there. 'It attracted a lot of artists. It attracted lots of French people. And,' he added with typical acerbity, 'for some reason

French people are much more intelligent than English people.' In the Second World War the French was the natural rendezvous for members of the Free French forces and received an official visit from General de Gaulle. However, rumour claimed that there were such carryings-on in the lavatory downstairs – a further extension of *entente cordiale* – that the licence was transferred, diplomatically, to Victor's son.

Gaston became the doyen of Soho landlords, a man who gave his life to his vocation and deserves to be honoured more than many a civil servant for the happiness he gave. He refused to serve draught beer due to the lack of space in the small bar; also because he made a greater profit from the wine he imported himself, and from such spirits as Pernod. He had a splendid carafe on the counter which dripped water onto a lump of sugar on a perforated spoon into a glass of Pernod or absinthe underneath. The walls were lined with photos of famous stars like Chevalier or Carpentier who had paused there, and more of those who never topped the bill – the forgotten jugglers, acrobats and boxers. With no juke-box or fruit machine there was nothing to interrupt the growl and sometimes the roar of conversation apart from the barking of the house dog, an ill-tempered terrier called Mons (short for Monsieur) who hated the one-armed accordionist who played outside and rushed to the door at the first squeezy note.

I felt at home as soon as I stepped inside. Gaston would become a friend and banker, cashing cheques even when they were returned, though he protested when I felt so guilty that I stayed away. 'It's bad enough that your cheque bounced, worse when you spend your money somewhere else!'

There would be an interlude when I was barred for particularly bad behaviour, though I cannot remember what this was. Usually he gave me a quizzical look, murmured, 'One of us will have to go and it's not going to be me,' and showed me out politely. 'Do me a favour, *monsieur*, and join me tomorrow at opening time for a glass of champagne?' By then I was outside on the pavement. I know of no other landlord who ejected one so charmingly. Francis remembered Gaston's father, too, as being a 'brilliant chucker-outer'.

As the French filled up on that first day I began to identify the principal actors, or regulars, on the stage. One man made an entrance with the gait of a midget wrestler and stood so close that I was struck by the details of his appearance, curiously dishevelled as if he had been rescued at sea and fitted out in clothes donated by the crew: paint-smeared blue jeans whose zip was half-open, and a thick white polo-neck sweater now grey with age, on which blood had fallen from the ridge of congealed gore behind his ear. On top he wore a British officer's 'warm', a tattered sheepskin overcoat which was a graveyard of nostalgic wine stains and cigarette burns as if he had fallen asleep in it on countless nights. He clasped it to him, arms akimbo, like a mandarin. Suddenly, sensing my scrutiny, he turned around with a hideously forced grimace, revealing a broken row of discoloured teeth and a tongue the colour of an aubergine. I was entranced.

I cannot remember how we began to talk, but when he heard I was starting as a photographer he announced in the clipped tones of Noël Coward: 'Child, I am the star photographer – for *Vogue*.' His name was John Deakin and he became my *éminence grise* and the catalyst for the friendship between Francis and myself for the next twelve years and more.

'Good morning, Mr Deakin,' said Gaston when he went behind the bar. 'I hope you don't feel as badly as you look?'

Deakin shook his head grimly. 'I swallowed a raw egg in a glass of milk earlier, but it was halfway down before I realised it was bad.'

Gaston flinched and poured him a Fernet-Branca, charging him three shillings and sixpence.

'For this muck? You must be joking!' Outraged, Deakin searched through his pockets, opening and shutting his mouth like a ventriloquist's dummy. 'I'll have to settle later.'

Glad to gain a foothold in this new territory, I volunteered to pay for it myself. Deakin wandered off with his drink to join people who were more entertaining or useful, and when he returned we were joined by a breathless woman whom he introduced as Henrietta, wildly attractive, fussing over her cigarette, with an arrogant upturned nose which I later learned had earned her the title of 'The Lady Brett of Soho'. Pitching her voice as if she wished to be overheard, she gave me a quick,

49

disappointed appraisal and exclaimed: 'It really is too bad. Tony took us to the Caprice last night but *refused* to give us the money for the taxi fare home. So we had to walk *all* the bloody way!' Her laugh was partly a wail, and she emphasised words like an osprey swooping on fish. 'Could you believe anyone could be so *mean*!'

Not to be outdone, Deakin told her that Tony had taken him upstairs to the restaurant a few days earlier to watch him eat his lunch. 'He didn't even give me a glass of wine.'

'But that's marvellous,' cried Henrietta. 'It's just *so* typical!'

It was nearly one o'clock when Deakin gave a stage whisper: 'I think, kiddo, this is going to be one of the good days. Look who's just come in.' Opening his mouth in that grimace of a well-meant smile, he nodded to a man on the far side of the bar who now came over to join us. He walked with the cautious tread of a first-class passenger venturing out on deck in a high sea, or that of a man who suspects there might be a small earthquake at any moment. This was my first sight of Francis Bacon; he was laughing already. I had no idea who he was.

'What are you all having to drink?' He emphasised his words in a curious mock-cockney whine, a sort of measured Edwardian alto. It was so enchanting that it is difficult to convey in print, making a comment like 'I'm just a simple iddy-ott' sound hilarious, though it looks silly on paper. His appearance was extraordinary too. He wore a well-cut grey suit and an open-necked shirt, with an effect that was simultaneously smart yet casual, which was unusual then. He was the first person I had met with pronounced jowls, and as he talked he habitually tugged at the collar of his lapels as if to conceal the absence of a neck.

Realising I was with Deakin, he swung round with a radiant smile and his laughter was so infectious that I started laughing too as he paid for the drinks and announced: 'Well, the most extraordinary thing has happened to me! I was in the Westminster Bank yesterday and a perfect stranger came up and asked me the way to Harrods. Well, really. . . !' He tugged at his collar and shook with laughter at such absurdity. 'He could have thought of a better excuse for picking me up than *that*. As a matter of fact he was rather good-looking in a fascist sort of way, very sunburnt, and told me he was a colonel in the South African Army, and then he asked me to lunch. He took me to the Ritz.'

50

'The Ritz!' this was greeted by a scream from Henrietta.

'Well,' he continued, gratified by our rapt attention, 'it really was too amazing. At the end of the meal he said that he was going back to South Africa in the evening and would I like to come too. He said he'd pay all my expenses, and do you know, I said "Yes." I thought it might be quite interesting – who knows?' Suddenly serious, he shrugged. 'Well, there you are, I shall never know, shall I? By the time the coffee arrived I'd thought better of it. After all, I knew nothing about him, so I said I'd changed my mind. I was sorry but I couldn't go after all, and invented some excuse. I've forgotten what it was. Well, he made the most fantastic scene! He threw his glass on the floor and shouted. He shouted the most *filthy* things at me. Of course the waiters behaved impeccably and picked up the plates and things again, but he was *really* filthy. He went so far I had to leave. Wasn't that an extraordinary thing to do?'

Having come to the end of his story he lost all interest in it, leaving me open-mouthed, for I'd never heard anyone speak like that before. A few minutes later, he turned to me with the attentiveness reserved for strangers: 'Shall we all go to Wheeler's for something to eat?'

Wheeler's was Francis's favourite restaurant, and I was soon to understand why. It introduced me to oysters – number ones, and number twos which were smaller and more succulent – and to dressed crab unsurpassed ever since. It was posh in the best Edwardian sense. The large green menu made no concessions. There were thirty-two sole dishes, in addition to the turbot and hot lobster – though that was best when served cold with a bowl of home-made mayonnaise. Apart from a few grudgingly boiled potatoes there were no vegetables unless you count salad, and no puddings. 'Not even an ice?' my grandmother asked wistfully when I was able to afford to take her there a few years later.

If the test of a successful restaurant is to leave it happier than when you arrived, Wheeler's was triumphant. The atmosphere was as English as a traditional fish restaurant should be, spartan with bare wood tables, though they glistened with glass and cutlery, with linen napkins and small bowls of olives, radishes and spring onions, and a plate piled with brown bread and butter. A counter ran down the left where waiters in white aprons and with the authority of ex-regimental sergeant-majors opened the oysters with the alacrity born of long devotion. Fish plates and prints hung on the wall behind them, accompanied by a signed cartoon by Walt Disney of the Walrus and the Carpenter and 'all the little oysters waiting in a row'.

Beyond, there was a small back bar with red velvet banquettes; it was run by John Normile, who became a friend of Francis's in particular. In fact all the waiters with the exception of a self-important Pole were our friends, for they were our audience and we were their cabaret. There must have been times when they found us exasperating, but at least we provided a distraction.

Our table that day, and the one which was also to become our usual table for forty years, was at the back, and if there were too many of us a couple of tables would be pushed together. On the right-hand side were smaller tables for two, sometimes too close for comfort.

I was present when Francis's language was so explicit that an American husband and wife asked the waiter to summon the manager. Francis was describing a woman called Doreen who had to keep calling the fire department. The firemen charged round, and burst in, asking: 'Where's the fire?' 'Here,' she'd say, lifting her dress to show her cunt. This story did not not go down well with the Americans. Presumably the nice maître d'hôtel, Peter, was away ill, for Bernard Walsh, the owner, came instead. He listened to their complaints courteously; then he tore up the bill which had just been presented on a plate. 'There is nothing to pay,' he informed them furiously, 'but I must ask you to leave at once. If you return, you will not be served.' With a gesture in our direction, he added: *'These are my friends.'* We were so over-whelmed by this act of loyalty that even Deakin did not dare to cheer as the unfortunate Americans slunk out, mystified.

Bernard Walsh was an ebullient figure who could have played one of the jovial benefactors in Dickens, like Mr Brownlow in *Oliver Twist*. He twinkled. Though a large, florid man he was light on his feet and had been a 'hoofer' in his youth, appearing on stage until he joined his father's oyster business in Whitstable. Until the First World War, oysters provided a diet for the poor of London. Afterwards, reduced to a few hundred thousand due to bad winters and disease, they became a luxury, though Walsh was able

52

to sell them for eight shillings and sixpence a hundred when he set up shop in Old Compton Street in 1929. When he noticed customers consuming them on the spot he opened his oyster bar, with immediate success. By now the upstairs rooms were open too, though we stayed firmly on the ground floor. Strangely, most of the kitchen staff were Chinese. The top chef, Mr Song, would murmur 'Musn't glumble' when Lucian Freud asked how he was as he glided through the customers at the end of the afternoon.

One Sunday morning Francis phoned me to ask, 'Did I see you last night? It's very odd, but when I woke up I found my pockets absolutely stuffed with money. I can't remember a thing, but I don't believe I went gambling.' A few minutes later, someone I knew slightly phoned in a state of dudgeon to say he had asked Francis to a cocktail party the night before, and Francis had apparently been rash enough to invite the host and several of his friends to dinner at Wheeler's afterwards. As soon as he sat down his mood changed, as it was to do so often, especially as the 'friends' proved shrill and not his type at all. In fact he turned against the 'silly queens' with such abuse that the cocktail party host answered back. This in turn prompted Francis to fling his glass of the house Chablis in the man's face. He missed, and the wine landed instead on the strapless back of an elegant woman at the table beyond; she wiped it off with her napkin and admirable aplomb, not even deigning to turn round. Presumably the argument behind her was explanation enough. Outraged, the cocktail party host rose to his feet declaring he would not stay there to be insulted a moment longer. 'I don't know how much this dreadful meal costs, but this should cover my share. I have no intention of being in your debt.' With this he slapped his money on the table and stalked out, followed by his friends who felt duty-bound to do the same, though I suspect they did so reluctantly as they were probably enjoying the fracas and could ill afford the gesture. However, they added their contributions and left Wheeler's with an equal show of umbrage.

'Do you think,' the man on the phone concluded lamely, 'that if you ask him Francis will return the money?'

'I doubt it,' I replied tersely. 'I'm meeting him in a few minutes and we're going to spend it.' I hung up with the satisfaction of someone who had not been invited to his party in the first place.

Throughout the initiation of my first lunch, I had a slight doubt about the bill. Francis had said, 'Shall we all go to Wheeler's for something to eat?' Was that an invitation? I need not have worried, and never did again. When the bill was produced, Francis signed it with a flourish and dug in his pockets for a handsome gift for the waiters. This was his routine and no one opposed him. Even if others were able to afford it, he preferred to pay. He was usually so broke in those early days that he could not buy fish and chips around the corner – so he resorted instead to a diet of oysters charged to his credit at Wheeler's, which Walsh was happy to extend. He was fond of Francis, and had an absolute faith in his future and the promise that one day he would receive a painting. He hoped for a racehorse, for this was his other passion, but eventually was given a small self-portrait which he hated and sold quickly for £17,000.

Walsh created a unique atmosphere, civilised yet carefree. 'Oh, the fun I've had at Wheeler's,' he exclaimed to me once as if the thought had suddenly struck him. His avuncular appearance was enhanced by a slight lisp which was so endearing in such an impressive man that he never made me feel intimidated, though I was always in awe of him. Francis, who shared his superior Edwardian mien, loved Wheeler's more than any eating place in London – even more than the beautiful dining room in the Ritz.

The advantage of a district like Soho is that everywhere is near. After lunch, we walked up Dean Street and climbed some shabby and disgraceful stairs into a smallish room with a faded air and a threadbare carpet which was known as the Colony Room. The pubs closed at two-thirty, so a crop of clubs had sprung up to accommodate those who liked to drink in the afternoon.

The Colony was owned by Muriel Belcher, so it was also known as Muriel's. Remembering her now, I realise that she was a truly remarkable woman. Paul Potts, known as 'the People's Poet', was a friend of George Orwell, T. S. Eliot and Sean O'Casey, all of whom praised his work though he remained an outcast until his death in 1990. His appearance, increasingly like that of a Soho wino, was tolerated with saintly forbearance by Muriel as he smouldered and stank in the corner, for he rarely washed. With her curious instinct she knew that he was all right, a man of some worth in spite of his failure. In turn he wrote me a letter in which he summed up her special quality of success:

54

I suppose what makes her so difficult to describe is her originality, a kind of non-ecclesiastical cardinal or perhaps a delinquent saint. She is a natural procurer whether it be the Bacon for the eggs or a date for a girlfriend. The relatively small room which is her domain and where she is an absolute sovereign must be one of the most unique rooms anywhere. It is not like other clubs at all, more like a cocktail party. It is the sort of place where you can't get much for ten bob but you can get an awful lot for nothing. Once you're in you're in; the poor and the private get treated just as well as the rich and famous. But if she does not like you – you've had it. She is as autocratic as the Dalai Lama and as kind as Sophie Tucker.

He concluded with the bull's-eye:

She could have run a great hospital if she had wanted to. She certainly could have been a successful impresario. But drink and conversation are her materials [he wrote this while she was alive] and she brought them together and has caused a huge amount of happiness to come people's way.

Discussing her recently with George Melly, I said the Colony was a place where you could take your grandmother and possibly your father, but not your mother.

'She rather liked *my* mother,' said George.

Her wit was scandalous and her language outspoken, yet she knew how far to go in rattling the skeletons in your cupboards, and I never lost my respect for her after that first afternoon. Years later I entered uneasily one Saturday at opening time, colliding with a little man in a bowler hat, clutching a well-worn leather tool kit, as he scuttled down the stairs. If I had worn a bowler myself I might have thrown it before me, for I had a haunting recollection of arguments and anger similar to the nights which haunted my father when 'meteor lights flamed through the sky of my mind and torn faces laughed at me'.

Muriel sat on her perch by the door like an imperial eagle and just as unsmiling. Otherwise, apart from the barman, the club was empty.

'You know who that was?' she asked me coldly.

I shook my head nervously, the images of those torn faces creeping back to me.

'That was the man who was kind enough to come here on a

weekend to repair the phone which you smashed yesterday.' I blinked at this, but she continued without a pause for breath: 'Not only did you break the phone when I was expecting some important calls but you upset one of my best-spending customers who may never come here again and in all my years in club business I doubt if I have ever witnessed such disgraceful behaviour and do you know I don't give a fuck cunty so what are you having to drink?' I felt I had come home.

On that first visit with Francis I asked him why he went there.

'Because it's a place where you can lose your inhibitions. It's different from anywhere else. After all, that's what we all want, isn't it? A place to go where one feels free and easy.'

I would soon discover that Francis had no inhibitions to lose, but it was evident that Muriel created an atmosphere where you could be yourself, and I had never been to such a place before.

Francis had been in at the birth of the Colony when he met Brian Howard (part model for Anthony Blanche and Ambrose Silk in the novels of Evelyn Waugh) in the street.

'I went there in 1949 with Brian Howard,' he told me. 'I met the old bastard across the road, and he said, "There's a new club opening. Come across with me." And for some reason I liked it so much that I went back the next day and Muriel came over and spoke to me. I don't know, perhaps she thought I knew a lot of rich people, which of course was untrue, but she knew I hadn't got much money and she said, "I'll give you ten pounds a week and you can drink absolutely free here and don't think of it as a salary but just bring people in." '

'So you were a tout?' I suggested.

'I wasn't even a tout. She said, "Bring in the people you like."''

It was intuitive of Muriel to sense that Francis would prove an asset to her club, and she possessed a radar instinct where money was concerned. She was correct in assuming that he knew rich people, and at that point she needed customers. The club was so empty the first afternoon that they played dice along the counter. It was smarter then, the stools covered with fake leopard skin and the bar backed by bamboo, and it was cleaned and redecorated once a year. Muriel's parents were rich Portuguese Jews who ran the Alexandra theatre in Birmingham. When her detested father died she had the freedom to come to London and run the Music

56

Box, a wartime club in Leicester Place, in partnership with Dolly Myers, before striking off on her own.

'I loved Muriel enormously,' Francis recalled years later, 'and for some reason we both got on very well, and so I went in there a lot. I could drink there for nothing, which was marvellous of course.' It was not long before he became her most famous and generous customer.

Muriel was one of the women Francis loved. They included his nanny and Isabel Lambert, who was married to the composer Alan Rawsthorne when I knew her; but though he admired Isabel he was closer to Muriel.

He painted several portraits of Muriel: one as a *Sphinx* (1979) with an echo of her face in *Oedipus and the Sphinx after Ingres* (1983), bought by Sylvester Stallone, apart from the more straightforward portrait of *Miss Muriel Belcher* (1959) – though even this verges on caricature. I asked him why he painted her so often.

'She's a very beautiful woman. It's as simple as that.' And I looked at her again.

Seated on her stool, her black hair combed back severely, chin tilted upwards, cigarette in raised hand, Muriel gave a deceptive impression of haughtiness as she surveyed the carrion of her membership, ready to rout strangers with her piercing cry of 'Members Only!' But though she was impressive it took Francis to let me see her beauty. Angus McBean took a photograph in the 1940s which shows her with a look of Hedy Lamarr, and when I knew her better I dared to ask about the rumour concerning a South American diplomat who had fallen in love with her: 'Perfectly true, deah. I did have a Colombian gentleman who was in love with me. I don't know how it started, or ended.' Trespassing further, I asked about her other lovers, men or women. She answered tersely, 'I'm glad to say plenty of both!' and shut the subject as firmly as a handbag. By the 1950s she had a West Indian lover called Carmel who frequently gambled with Francis though she possessed none of his luck. Once she separated from Muriel and returned to Jamaica to regret it bitterly, phoning London one night with the sing-song wail: 'I wanna come home.'

'You *are* home, cunty,' Muriel reminded her, putting the phone down. But Carmel came back and Muriel was pleased.

Where Muriel had genius as a club owner was in her ability to mix her members. The Kismet catered, as we have seen, for villains, cops and 'resting' actors. The club opposite the Comedy Theatre, run by an ample lady under an ampler hat who was known as a character but was lumpfish compared to Muriel's caviar, catered for 'queers'. Places off Curzon Street catered to former beauties and starched military men, others to the horse-racing fraternity. Muriel's, on the other hand, had a sprinkling of all of these with the odd Member of Parliament and a few 'titled folk' thrown in to give her club class. Members could bring their guests, and only those who were mean with money or boring were unwelcome – she was ruthless in disposing of them. 'And now, Ian,' she instructed the barman with lethal charm, 'we'll all have drinkettes with this lovely member,' followed by the firm command: 'Open your bead-bag, Lottie.' Such victims were rarely seen again.

Her habit of referring to her most respectable members as 'she', 'Clara' or 'Miss' never seemed affected. It was a compliment which even the most portly businessman rather enjoyed. Attention was being paid to him. Francis was known as 'daughter'.

Only rarely did anyone take offence, as John Braine did on the afternoon when I invited him to the Colony and signed him in. A few members sat at the bar and it was plain that everyone was in a vile mood, including Muriel who swept a look in Braine's direction and announced: 'She's not a pretty little lady, is she?'

A few moments later, hoping he had not heard this, I introduced him, explaining that he was the author of the best-selling *Room at the Top*. That will impress her, I thought, mistakenly.

'I can see there's plenty of room at *her* top!' she cried, suddenly animated, and like a pack which scents an alien musk the members chortled and guffawed while the wretched Braine quivered with indignation. When the braying died down, he protested: 'Madam, I've never been so insulted in my life.'

'On your way, Lottie,' she told him, opening the door, 'or you'll get a fourpenny one.'

To my lasting shame I did not leave with him, but joined in the callous laughter after the door closed. Years later I was phoned by his solicitor to confirm that I was present that afternoon. When I asked him why, he began to explain that Braine was suing Muriel Belcher for libel.

'But what was it she called him?' he enquired.

'She said, "There's plenty of room at her top" – and "She's not a pretty little lady, is she?" '

Until then the solicitor had sounded as dry as parchment; now he started to giggle. 'Yes, of course. I really think I'll have to advise my client not to proceed with this one.' He gave a screech of laughter. 'He'll look so *silly*! . . . Mind you,' he added, calming down, 'I'd have loved to meet Miss Belcher.'

If Muriel had a weakness, it was her confusion at being confronted by wealth, when her smile was almost a curtsey. Once I was surprised that she ignored a woman deep in conversation on the banquette, a woman whom I recognised immediately. After she had left with the member who had signed her in, I asked Muriel if she knew who she was.

'That drab little number in the raincoat, with the sallow skin?'

'That was Olga Deterding, probably the richest woman in the world.'

'Funny. Now you mention it, her complexion takes on a new radiance and her hair a new lustre. Yes, a *very* attractive number, that little Miss Deterding.'

Though she enjoyed her members' successes vicariously, Muriel had not the slightest interest in art. She once said to Francis: 'I don't give a fuck about art!' This was an added strength. Generally the last thing artists wish to talk about is art, and at Muriel's they gossiped about the things that really mattered – sex, drink, scandal and daydreams. Muriel's was anything but hallowed.

Though Francis was unknown to the public he was revered by his contemporaries, especially within the small coterie which met in the Colony Room and became known years later as the School of London. This was a label attached by the artist R. B. Kitaj and was just as misleading as such labels tend to be. In a Hayward Gallery catalogue in 1976, Kitaj made the following claim:

> There are artistic personalities in this small island more unique and strong and I think numerous than anywhere in the world outside America's jolting vigour. There are ten or more people in this town, and not far away, of world class, including my friends of abstract persuasion. In fact I think there is a substantial School of London.

59

Within eleven years, the label was sufficiently secure for *Art International* to run a series of articles on the 'School'.

Better labelled as 'Muriel's Boys' or 'The Colony Room Mob', this so-called School included Francis, Lucian Freud, Michael Andrews, Frank Auerbach and Tim Behrens. The bond they shared was drinking at Muriel's. Francis painted Muriel and Freud. In 1952 Freud painted his famous portrait of Bacon in oil on copper, a small portrait of extraordinary power measuring only $17.8 \times 12.8$ cm, of Francis full-face looking downwards. Acquired by the Tate Gallery, it was stolen while on loan in Berlin in 1988 and never seen again, despite the reward offered by the Director of the Tate, Nicholas Serota. Francis told me he was convinced it was stolen specifically because it was an outstanding portrait of himself: 'The thieves knew exactly what they were doing.' Lucian Freud also painted memorable portraits of Behrens, and of Michael Andrews and Frank Auerbach who became and remain his closest friends.

Michael Andrews, wide-eyed and popular with everyone, drank in the Colony with his wife June and painted a green hessian mural, in the style of Bonnard, for the wall behind the piano. Intended to cover up the stains, it was quickly stained as well. Admired for his painting of *The Deer Park*, based on the novel by Normal Mailer and bought by the Tate, he immortalised the club in his large painting *The Colony Room I* (1962) with Muriel at the bar, and Lucian Freud beside her next to Bruce Bernard; it is Virginia Law who is talking to Deakin, though she is often identified as Henrietta, who was married to Michael Law before her. There is doubt over the ample figure in the foreground leaning on the bar, glass in hand; it is either myself or Francis, but is usually identified as 'Bacon' because this gives the painting more class. Andrews prevaricates: 'It's either Daniel Bacon or Francis Farson', a compliment to me in either case. I am certain it is myself because I remember the red shirt, which was too gaudy for Francis; and his hair, though dyed, was never that yellow.

Kitaj served a purpose in drawing attention to the figurative artists in England who were neglected in favour of the trendier abstract artists in America such as Rothko and de Kooning, and it is true that they were virtually unknown at the time and isolated, even in their own country. The reason they came together was

Muriel, and when I asked her why they did so, she replied, 'I think it's my charm, deah.'

As for Kitaj, Francis started by praising his work and Kitaj met him frequently, by accident or design, as Francis came to suspect, in a café near South Kensington; but when he became famous Francis changed his mind, as he was apt to do. Having told Michael Wishart: 'There's one young painter I admire,' he veered in the other direction: 'I think they're just the worst thing ever painted,' he declared emphatically, adding: 'Don't mention my name.'

'Painters are very jealous,' said Wishart. When Francis met Michael's wife Anne, after his first successful show at the Redfern Gallery, she mentioned that his work had been described as that of 'an Expressionist'. He told her: 'I've always *loathed* Expressionism.' He detested such labels and scorned the alleged School of London. Yet in those early days in Muriel's, when they were fighting to succeed, they enjoyed a bond which was unsoured by jealousy. When they came together it was constant celebration, captured by John Deakin in his photograph of an epic lunch at Wheeler's. You can tell just by looking at it that they are enjoying a marvellous conversation.

They were formidable friends, ultimately, in one case at least, formidable foes. Perhaps it was because their work was so different that they activated each other to begin with. Though Francis was the acknowledged leader due to the sheer force of his personality, Lucian Freud was in the early years the more established.

Of all the Colony Room painters, Freud was closest to Bacon with their shared enthusiasm for gambling as well as art. Together they exhibited with Ben Nicholson when they represented Britain at the Venice Biennale in 1954. Francis painted countless studies of Lucian, whose affection for him was the main reason for his presence in the Colony Room – though he left in the early evening to work throughout the night, while Francis continued to carouse until the early hours of the following day. I remember Lucian sidling into the seedy room with a swift glance of recognition as he saw Muriel, followed by a furtive sidelong appraisal as his eyes raked the present company to see if there was anyone worth talking to. When the company pleased him, there were few sharper conversationalists. He would shatter my naivety as he turned accepted theories upside down, his wit enhanced by the slight, lingering German accent which gave an added emphasis to every word.

The odd man out was Minton. Johnny Minton was always the odd man out. A teacher at the Royal College of Art, he was popular with the students who admired his flouting of convention. Minton was homosexual and disliked it, trying to rid his guilt with a febrile gaiety, arriving in Soho from Chelsea in a taxi full of students and sailors. Always with this sort of entourage in tow, a Pied Piper of Soho, he was immensely generous. And this was another cause for guilt, that unlike the rest of us he had 'private means' inherited from a grandfather who had something to do with the London store D. H. Evans, and not Minton china, as we assumed.

'Let's spend the last of my inheritance!' he cried as he paid the bill.

As an artist Minton was a brilliant illustrator whose reputation is growing today; his distinct decorative style is instantly recognisable. His book covers, such as his design for Elizabeth David's classic on Mediterranean food, his film posters and advertising, enhanced the subjects so successfully that he was in constant demand as a commercial artist and well paid accordingly. That was another guilt.

Everyone took advantage of his generosity, as if the money had nothing to do with Johnny personally but was there for the taking. Bobby Hunt, at that time an aspiring painter, was staying at Minton's house in Shaftesbury Villas when 'Francis was always calling on Johnny, often to borrow money. One morning Johnny was in bed and Francis arrived, so we all went up and sat on the bed while Francis told us scandalously funny stories.'

Bobby Hunt remembers Minton with such affection that he wishes they *had* slept together. 'I mean, we slept in the same bed but we never had sex.' Minton bit his fingers so savagely that the sheets were stained with his blood. 'Now I think why on earth not, if it would have given him some pleasure?'

One day his father, a policeman, asked Bobby who this man was who gave him presents and took him to the ballet.

'He's my teacher,' said Bobby.

62

'Oh, I think I'd better meet him.'

'When I told Johnny that my dad was a huge copper he did not go for the idea at all, but of course when they did meet they got on like a house on fire! Finally my dad asked if I was a "nance" or "pansy", or whatever word was used then, for they were the only people I seemed to know. I told him I wasn't but I liked them – "They've been good to me, they're the only people who've really helped me." He thought this over and nodded: "Well, if they've helped you, you're quite right to be nice to them." Very English!'

In a varied career which included an unlikely spell as cloakroom attendant in the Colony Room, in the tiny back lavatory where he received more in tips than the irate barman's wages, Bobby started as an artist. 'In 1955 Francis saved my life. I was working in a factory, trying to paint at the same time, and was very, very depressed. I even thought of suicide. I decided to pull myself together and walked from Lewisham to Piccadilly with my illustrations, when I heard a cry of "*Chérie!*" from a passing taxi and there was Francis. "You look absolutely *awful*," he told me, and gave me a five-pound note to go to Wheeler's "for oysters, to cheer yourself up".'

In those days, five pounds went a long way and Bobby Hunt felt morally bound to spend part of it on half-a-dozen Colchesters in Wheeler's as he had been told. As he sat at the bar he found that Francis was there too, and then John Minton came in with five sailors.

'I thought you said that boy had talent,' Francis turned on Minton accusingly. 'Yet he's walking the streets.' Genuinely distressed, for he had not seen him for six months, Johnny told Bobby Hunt, 'I'm terribly sorry', and that evening he went to his digs and settled the rent. 'I owed her fifteen shillings and he gave her five pounds. She shook all over. He told me "Pack your bags" and gave me a room in Apollo Place [where he had moved]. He charged me ten shillings a week and paid me three pounds to be his assistant. But it was Francis who realised I was in a rocky position.'

I remember Johnny advancing, his long arms outstretched, crying: 'But what does it all *mean*!' He said it mockingly, but his dissatisfaction had much to do with his belief that he was not a major artist, and it was not enough to be a very good one. I am sure he watched Francis's ascendancy with despair.

Despite the fact that he was at ease in Johnny's company, as I sensed when the three of us had a long lunch in the staff dining room of the Royal College of Art, Francis did not really like him, even though he stayed for a short period at Apollo Place. Perhaps he resented Minton's generosity, especially towards himself.

Other artists also came to Muriel's even though they had no involvement with the 'School'. Edward Burra, one of the most interesting British artists this century and still woefully neglected, fitted the louche atmosphere perfectly, writing to William Chappel in 1972: 'I was reeling somewhat on Monday having fortified myself with one or 2 wee double drappies before lunch – a lot of white wayne and a double scotch & 2 vintage ports offered us by dear Francis who is a dear man and one at Miss Mews.'

One night Francis introduced me to Giacometti, declaring: 'This is the man who has influenced me more than anyone.'

And then, of course, there was Deakin.

Deakin was the court jester, and Francis was genuinely fond of him. 'John Deakin was a very interesting and amusing man,' said Francis. 'Very sarcastic. But he needed drink more than anything else. At about two or three o'clock, when he realised he'd had enough, he used to disappear. He used to have a flat in Berwick Street and he used to go to sleep, then come and join us at the beginning of the evening and start all over again.'

He worked as a fashion and portrait photographer for British *Vogue* and their studio was conveniently close, round the corner in Shaftesbury Avenue. Here he placed his sitters against a favourite backdrop and shot them in full face and profile, like mug shots of convicted prisoners. All they needed were the numbers and names. With a skilled darkroom to back him up and the support of the picture editor, Tom Hawkyard, Deakin produced gigantic prints with maximum grain, every blemish and pore exposed mercilessly. The impact was powerful, impressing Francis. Deakin traded on his background as 'a barefoot boy from Liverpool', and concealed his salary from *Vogue*. It was so unusual to see him buy a drink that once when he fumbled for coins in the Golden Lion (on the corner in Dean Street before the

French House) someone exclaimed: 'My God, it's so long since you handled money I thought they'd be sovereigns!'

Like others in Soho, Deakin played his threadbare role with such conviction that he convinced himself. He was brazen in demanding drinks, regarding them as a divine right. Muriel hated him, according to Francis, but she at least tolerated him. With her curious ability to see what was going on behind her, she noticed him bending down to stroke a handsome white husky dog that someone had brought into the club. Hardly interrupting the flow of conversation, she cried out the quick warning: 'Hold onto your sled, gal, or that one will bum a free ride to Alaska!' The dog happened to look up at that precise moment, and she turned to us triumphantly: 'I'm glad to see he's got the message!'

At Muriel's as at Wheeler's, Francis always signed the bill, or the round was simply added to the 'tab', and I assume that by the time of my arrival the days of his weekly ten-pound touting fee were over. Instead, Muriel seemed to allow him limitless credit. He waved his bottle of champagne, slopping it into the glasses of those around him, spilling much of it on the floor, with the Edwardian toast: 'Real pain for your sham friends, champagne for your real friends!', a habit he had acquired from his father. He would add his inimitable 'Cheerio!' with a radiant smile and a tug at his collar, an image that shines brightly in my mind today.

His declarations, particularly on the rare occasions he talked about art, were listened to attentively, and more especially when the glasses ran dry: 'I want very, *very* much to do the thing that Valéry said – "to give the sensation without the boredom of its conveyance' ", or 'What I *really* want to do is unlock the valves of feeling.'

When I first came to Soho he looked at least ten years younger than his age – thirty rather than forty-three. This was partly achieved by the carefully dishevelled hair of variable colour, and by his customary black leather jacket bought in the South of France. Such an outfit might not have worked with other men, but the masculinity of the jacket, and I think it preceded Brando's, enhanced his features so naturally that it was hard to imagine him wearing anything else.

But even on this, his home ground in the Colony, Francis was never wholly relaxed, observing people in the mirror as if he too

65

had eyes in the back of his head. It was some time before I realised that, when he wandered off to the lavatory with his glass in his hand as if he could not bear to part with it, he threw the contents away; he drank less while filling the glasses of those around him so they disintegrated sooner.

An artist – I think he came from Trinidad – came into the Colony one afternoon to present the Club with his latest painting, which was still wet. This well-meant and generous gesture was accepted politely until Francis made his entrance, when the pack turned against the man as the members were apt to do. Exploding with irreverent laughter, Francis shook his bottle of champagne, aiming it at the picture whose colours dissolved into an even more frightful mess than before. This calculated cruelty was accompanied by cheers, which drove the tearful artist out of the club.

Three years later, the artist was making a name for himself with a one-man show at the Chenil Gallery, who wrote to the Colony suggesting that it would be a nice gesture if the club, or Francis, sent a crate of champagne for the private view as a form of compensation. Ian Board replied that a crate of cold tea would be more suitable. On such occasions Francis could be pitiless to other artists, even if they were younger, poorer and offered no threat whatsoever.

Like a man whose threshold narrowed as he sensed the onslaught of boredom, Francis claimed his victims. Yet he could display his charm with the skill of a conjuror, as he did one afternoon to an art student who naively showed him a leaflet he had produced. Perhaps he was better-looking than the West Indian, but Francis asked if he could buy a copy, adding that he would be grateful if the young man would sign it for him. Francis made his day, as he had destroyed the other's.

Once a fashion editress made a spectacular, smiling entrance clad head to foot in the same baize green, including her bowler hat. As Francis studied her, we fell silent. 'Do you think it's just possible,' he informed us, 'that she's made the most terrible mistake?' Everyone laughed, including the unfortunate target, but she never wore that outfit again.

The barman, Michael Wojas, who missed nothing, realised that Francis enjoyed being 'mischievous' as long as someone noticed: 'He'd look to see if Ian was watching.'

'The wicked way he'd look in the mirror,' Ian confirmed, 'toss back his hair and say to Muriel, "Got yer comb, Mum?", and while she'd go through her handbag he was observing everyone in the room. Well, he *observed*!'

When people were precious they were fair game – an unfortunate poet who came up to Francis in the French one Sunday evening with an eager, confiding smile. Such occasions were painful to witness, for the victims stumbled in ignoring the warning signals of the slack mouth yet beady eye. The spectators were instantly alert.

'Francis,' said the poet, 'I think I've done some things which might interest you.'

'Oh, yaas . . .', a long pause, '. . . I rather doubt it.'

Nervously, the poet persisted: 'Yes, they have a lot of soul.'

'Ah,' mused Francis, momentarily defeated. 'Ah. Soul.' His face lit up – '*Arsehole!* Yes, they really do sound interesting.' The poet retired.

I cannot remember now where we went on to after champagne at Muriel's on that first occasion, but Francis's and Deakin's regular ports of call would become distinct over the next few days. I believe it was Deakin who introduced me to the Caves the following day. The Caves de France (always pronounced 'Calves') was two doors away from the Colony. It was more Deakin's haunt than Francis's. Here Deakin retreated if the Colony bored him, or if Muriel's aloofness indicated that his presence was unwelcome – and she could do this with devastating effect. Ultimately he was barred, after spreading a rumour that she embezzled money contributed by her members to a charity the Club had organised for handicapped children.

The Caves was a long ground-floor bar with a bouncer who bounced less often than my cheques, and a gentle giant of a barman called Secundo, the brother of boxer Primo Carnera whose mother had difficulty in choosing names and so settled for numbers instead. With a rich assortment of eccentrics and veteran drinkers, young and old and mostly poor, this was true bohemia. There is no place like it now, and I doubt if there was then. The closest to it in atmosphere was a traditional East End pub with music, with the crucial difference that the people who used the Caves were classless and nearly all were interested in the arts. On my first visit I saw the girl in white make-up who had walked barefoot past the French, as well as Gerald Hamilton whom Christopher Isherwood used as the endearing scoundrel in *Mr Norris Changes Trains*.

There were rejects of every kind, the drifters, the shabby genteel who had known better times. Their eyes were guilty with the recognition of impending defeat, ravaged faces barely crowned with thinning, silky hair, and musty clothes which needed changing. Elaine Dundy, the first wife of Ken Tynan, described it in her novel *The Old Man and Me* as 'a sort of coal-hole in the heart of Soho that is open every afternoon, a dead-ended subterranean tunnel . . . an atmosphere almost solid with failure'. Yet she failed in not seeing the joy. I preferred my father's comment, in another context, that he preferred 'hurt' people, meaning those who were not contaminated by the complacency of success. He would have found them in droves in the Caves.

Indeed he had an affair with Nina Hamnett, one of the painters whom Muriel had rejected. It was not that Nina was specifically barred, more that she had gone beyond the point where bad behaviour was acceptable. In fact Muriel had a particular fondness for Nina, who was photographed in her club, soon after its opening, seated on a stool by the bar and wearing a rakish beret. Even those few years ago she had looked smarter. She was still jaunty, rattling a tobacco tin for contributions when the drinks were unforthcoming, but she was a wreck of the woman she had been, once the 'proverbial' toast of the Left Bank in Paris, a talented artist herself, yet better known as the friend of artists. Once I was taken to an upstairs exhibition in the Café Royal by Francis and Lucian, who stopped at a painting which caught their attention. Lucian checked with the label on the back and reported: 'Sickert.' As we continued our circuit, this set me wondering, for if Sickert was capable of painting that, it meant that he was not a great painter. As we passed it again I rashly broke my disciple's silence, bending down to look at the back for myself.

'It's not by Sickert,' I announced triumphantly, 'it's *of* Sickert by Nina Hamnett!' If I had been more tactful I would have kept this information to myself. Neither artist was amused.

Is it better to hark back to the heyday of your life, or to exist on an uneventful plateau in which the present seems no better and no worse than the past? Inevitably, Nina recalled the wilder days when 'Modigliani said I had the best tits in Europe', one of which could be seen exposed in the Victoria and Albert Museum in *The Naked Torso* sculpted by Gaudier-Brzeska 'with my left tit knocked off'. She tried to maintain a façade and once, on the way from the French to the Caves, was daintily sick into her handbag (which she then clasped shut) in order not to embarrass her companions by doing this in the gutter. One reason why Muriel found her arrival in the Colony distressing was her tendency to wet herself on the stool or banquette. Yet Nina still took men home with her, especially sailors, 'because they have to leave in the morning'.

I seldom saw her in the Colony, for she was now a regular in the Caves, where she made a gallant if anxious entrance on a stick, her beret still cocked on the side of her head as she hoisted herself on a stool. 'Couldn't buy me a drink, could you, love,' she gasped, trading on her brief affair with my father, 'for old time's sake. A double whisky, *twice*, dear.' Boasting that she was 'the last of the Bohemians', she had more claim to that title than anyone else. 'I took my best dress to the cleaners, and it was so sodden with gin that all they gave me back was a spoonful of dust.' She was little more than that herself.

Invariably smouldering and shouting along the bar were the two formidable Scottish painters, Robert Colquhoun and Robert MacBryde, known as the Two Roberts. However difficult they became – and MacBryde told me he thought up new ways of insulting people every morning – they commanded respect from Francis.

MacBryde was born in 1913 in Ayrshire and Colquhoun a year later at Kilmarnock, twenty miles away. They met at the Glasgow School of Art in 1932 and stayed together for the rest of their lives. Like fallen boulders they obstructed the bar if you wanted to pass, and at first I was intimidated by their aggression. 'Get me a whisky, will yer?' Colquhoun demanded in his heavy Scottish accent, wild and windswept with a fall of cigarette ash on his well-worn tweed overcoat. He banged the counter so violently that the gentle Secundo winced.

'Why don't you fuck off?' MacBryde glared at me sourly.

69

The dandy writer with the silver-topped cane, Julian Maclaren Ross, described how women found Colquhoun irresistible because they knew they could not have him: 'Spinster girls nearly swooned at the sight of his aesthetic mouth, "so masterful and clamped determinedly tight", as one of them described it longingly to me. The girls of Soho were always subconsciously eager to break something up.'

At one of his lowest points in Soho, Colquhoun told me one afternoon of the promise of a retrospective at the Whitechapel Gallery on condition he contributed new work. With this incentive, he regained his confidence: 'This should mean a new lease of life. It may seem a bit early to have an exhibition like this, but the moment a painter has a retrospective there's a next move forward. I want to do something that looks like something.' In a rare moment of grandiloquence, he declared: 'The canvases are going to be even bigger than before.'

'Why is that? I asked him, infected by his enthusiasm.

He looked surprised. 'Because it's such a big gallery, that's why.'

They disappeared from Soho. Sober and industrious, they completed the new paintings and left for a well-earned holiday. While they were away, thieves broke into their studio and mutilated the pictures, probably in the rage of discovering there was nothing else to steal. Simultaneously the council evicted them from the studio, which was due to be demolished. So they returned to Soho and the doorsteps of pubs, waiting for opening time. Is it surprising that they smouldered?

When Bobby Hunt told Francis that Colquhoun admired his work ('My God, he can paint meat!') Francis replied angrily: 'Rubbish! I don't believe it.' Reluctant to praise, he disliked it when he was praised himself.

But back to my first visit to the Caves. By about six a curious transformation had taken place. The club assumed a suburban air as three middle-aged men stepped onto the tiny platform beside the wine barrels and started to tune their instruments with the solemnity of a string quartet. They wore evening dress with white shirts and ready-made bow ties. One sported a jet-black toupé which deceived nobody, while the drummer had a limp. The leader was a dignified personality with a grey, military moustache, who attached a cumbersome contraption to the piano which miraculously then became an electric organ. Once they were ready the organist, violinist and drummer launched into a sequence of genteel dance numbers which were preposterous in such surroundings, except that a new contingent of members arrived who looked more 'ordinary' until I realised they were just as drunk as the 'afternoon men'.

One couple sat on the platform, swaying in a blissful state of stupor. The man, who had a neat moustache like a bureaucrat in an Ealing comedy, moved his hands with serpentine gestures above his head as if he was a Javanese dancer, while the woman, an Amazonian with gigantic hands and feet and a flushed, fat face, danced alone, leaning backwards until she almost fell over, then suddenly recovering her balance with a plunge forward and a grimace that suggested pain – though I am sure it was intended to indicate pleasure.

Deakin appointed himself master of ceremonies. Twirling an imaginary moustache, he clambered onto the stage and introduced the daughter of the owner of the Caves, who was French – a plump, constantly smiling, middle-aged lady called Hortense. With a leer worthy of the compère in *Cabaret*, he resorted to a series of sarcasms which she accepted as graciously as if they were bouquets of flowers presented to a diva. 'And now,' he proclaimed, demanding silence from the crowd and a roll on the drum, 'let me present the girl!' – he eyed her up and down incredulously – 'the girl you have all been waiting for. She possesses the most incomparable voice – what you have done to deserve this I cannot imagine.' He bowed to the very few who were paying attention as she started to sing light opera with a fluttering of eyelashes. At first he watched, raising his spaniel eyes to heaven as she trilled archly up and down the scales. Then in a deafening whisper he told me: 'Come on, kiddo, let's get the hell out of here.'

'Why don't you two just fuck off!' cried Robert MacBryde as we left.

Like the smile on the face of a chorus girl as she reaches the wings, Deakin's face crumpled outside the Caves and he left me without a parting word.

One of the reasons why Francis went less often to the Caves

than did Deakin was that he was more vulnerable there, exposed to the idolatry of fans. Even very early on, before his international fame, the force of his personality had spread his reputation wide.

About five-thirty one day a young man came into the Caves and was introduced to Francis as an art critic. He was in his early twenties, dark but with an almost shaved head, a bit podgy, wearing dirty white baggy trousers and shirt, and a long cerise red overcoat (I had seen him coming out of the Golden Lion). Francis played up to me and gave the poor creature a terrible grilling.

'What makes you think you know anything about art?'

Embarrassed silence and shuffling. 'I prefer sculpture to painting.'

'Who's your favourite sculptor, then?'

More shuffling, utter confusion.

'Well, you must have some sculptor you like. What about. . . ?' Francis reeled off a list of names, and the victim latched onto Giacometti.

'Tell me *why* you like him.'

Silence and wriggling. It became obvious that the young man was not very clear what Giacometti's sculpture looked like. The Caves was packed, and like Romans at the Circus we were all enjoying the show. Francis then proceeded to take the young man to pieces and to demonstrate what folly it is to put such ignorant and inexperienced people into positions where they can make fools of themselves and mislead others.

When he had done that – which didn't take long – his tone suddenly changed, and he began to give a seminar on art criticism, of which unfortunately I can remember not a word – only that it was exceptionally perceptive and well expressed. Although it was personally addressed to his victim, everyone else shut up and for ten minutes you could have heard a pin drop as we all listened. He then clapped the young man on the shoulder, said, 'Now let's have some champagne,' and the two of them chatted on like old mates as we fell to drinking again.

Any antagonism had a noticeable physical effect on Francis. John McEwen, the critic, remembers 'standing close behind him when an artist he disliked entered the room. Immediately he stiffened, bristled, became alert as a dog. It was the only time I have witnessed the hairs stand up on the back of a human neck. No fight ensued, or hostile conversation. It was more menacing than that.'

The only criticism Francis would tolerate came from John Deakin. In fact he would beam with pleasure while Deakin poured scorn on his 'doodles'. Francis would protect Deakin too. There was a place called the Rockingham Club, pretentiously done up with flock-striped wallpaper and chandeliers and full of superior shop assistants on their evening off who behaved as if they were Dukes of Rockingham. The owner, a nice man with glasses called Toby, rather disliked his 'queeny' customers and welcomed the less predictable appearance of Francis, Deakin and myself. When Deakin passed out and had to be carried up the stairs like Hamlet, all the queens shrilled their horror, but Francis paused to shout down at them: 'Even unconscious, he's more fun than you lot!'

The last gasp of a typical Soho evening was drawn at the Gargoyle, in Meard Street. David Tennant had bought the building in 1925, when he was twenty-three, though it was two years before the ballroom was completed at a cost of £56,000. Though this was a staggering figure for the time, it became less so when you learned that the room had been designed by Matisse and executed by the architect Sir Edwin Lutyens. There were two Matisse murals, one subsequently sold to America for £1000, the other bought by Kenneth Clark for £600 and eventually bound for America too. Where Matisse had excelled was in his acquisition of numerous two-hundred-year-old mirrors, which he cut into twenty thousand squares.

When I arrived after meeting Francis, these mirrors remained surprisingly untarnished in view of the evenings they reflected. One night there had been two princes, three princesses and King Carol of Romania. The Duke of Windsor was a regular and in the membership book I spotted the names of Fred and Adele Astaire, Tallulah Bankhead, and Brenda Dean Paul – who brought her mother who smoked seven-inch cigars while she snorted cocaine. Skirts were worn above the knee, evening dress was compulsory, and people spoke in Mayfair French over the alfresco dinners on the roof which lasted until dawn.

With the Second World War, the party came to an end and a new, more raffish crowd brought their own brand of rowdiness. Anne Valery relates a stick-up by two gangsters, who were

73

outraged by the welcome they received from the members. 'Don't be silly, darlings!' cried Caryl Chance. 'You look absolutely lovely and I'm going to dance with you.' When the police arrived, the gangsters complained they had never seen such disgraceful behaviour. 'Oh yes,' the police agreed, 'it's not the place to come to.'

I just missed two members who signed the book in 1951: Guy Burgess and Donald Maclean, who added their names three days later. By now the Gargoyle had been bought by a man whose phlegmatic appearance was misleading, for he loved the club and enjoyed seeing the members fall apart. It remained exclusive, though he extended the membership to writers and artists and he did not mind what they wore or if they were penniless. Membership was three guineas, and people wandered about as if it were a private party.

The first time I went there I found an upper-class bedlam, where the difference between the drunks and the lunatics was imperceptible. You rose to the top of the building in a tiny white lift the size of a telephone box, so there was always an emotional queue at the bottom. Then you descended a staircase into the ballroom designed by Matisse, so you had the feeling of being on top of the world but with all the intimacy of a basement. Lady Diana Cooper's table was a pocket of decorum; while Johnny Minton's, a few feet away, was crowded with 'matelots' in uniform, his current favourite sitting on his right. Minton did not have the heart to sever relationships, so the former favourites lingered on at the far end where Johnny pointed to a couple of empty seats for myself and a new friend I had met in a pub at Piccadilly. As we'd left together, a policeman had come up to him and asked if his name was Arthur Lake. 'Of course not!' he laughed, with such a convincing smile that I thought there was some mistake, but as we entered Shaftesbury Avenue he confided, 'That is my name, but I call myself Mike Avery. I'm on the run from the navy.'

I felt as if I had crossed a border, and perhaps it was this element of danger that made me become infatuated. That he refused to have sex, though we shared a bed, gave him the absolute power which the inactive lover wields in such relationships. I was disconcerted when he told Minton's sailors that he was a naval deserter, but they were sympathetic and discussed his case intelligently.

74

The band was led by a tiny man called Alec Alexander, with a pencilled moustache and a pencilled smile to match; he conducted his few musicians with indefatigable zest, as if they were the Joe Loss orchestra at a grander 'venue'. Johnny Minton provided cabaret as he gyrated on the dance floor the size of a tablecloth, while the dapper Alexander played his perennial requests: 'My Very Good Friend the Milkman' and 'I'm Going to Sit Right Down and Write Myself a Letter', rewarded by trays of drinks sent over by Minton afterwards with his usual effusiveness.

When Minton danced there was little room for anyone else, but when he collapsed the relay was taken up by Rodrigo and Eleanor Moynihan, who jived with the sweat pouring down their faces, while a large woman spun a small man as if he were a top. An elderly man staggered about conducting an imaginary orchestra, and Lady Diana talked on regardless.

The painter Dennis Wirth-Miller, also Minton's guest, produced a pound note and stood on a chair. 'Look!' he cried, thrusting it into his mouth. When he followed this with a five-pound note, I was so shocked I called out 'Stop!' as he started to munch the beautiful white paper, but I was forestalled by Minton who snatched the fiver back and gave it to his favourite, Joe, a soft-voiced Scot, as a birthday present. 'Don't be such a bloody fool,' Minton yelled at Wirth-Miller, who belched and ran up the stairs to the lavatory, clutching his mouth in order to make himself vomit and retrieve the pound note so that he could wash it under the tap, or so I suspected.

'Have a glass of champagne!' Minton called to me from the far end of the table, 'to celebrate Joe's birthday and spend the last fifty pounds of my inheritance.' He fussed over Joe as if he were a chorus girl, which Joe did not object to, but soon the lugubrious shutters came down and Minton started muttering, 'I'm only liked because I'm rich. I can buy anyone I want.' The sailors continued to eat their steaks contentedly, and Joe's friend assured me: 'He's all right, but moody with it.'

Francis sat at a corner table having an angry though quiet argument with his friend Peter Lacy (often misspelt Lacey), a former Battle of Britain pilot. Tall, middle-aged, with thinning fair hair, blue eyes and a pleasant, nervous expression, there was little to suggest that he was one of the most important men in

Francis's life. I had seen them earlier in the Colony – this was now my second day in Soho – but it was obvious they wished to be alone. Before I could stop him, Mike Avery wandered over to join them and I could sense the irritation which tightened their faces. When the deserter staggered back, I made the mistake of going over to apologise.

'It's too bad', Bacon swung round indignantly, 'that we should have to pay for drinks for your friend and now have to submit to the boredom of your conversation.'

Bewildered by this change of attitude, I produced my last few shillings, all the money I had, and placed them primly on the table – 'I hope this covers my friend's drinks.' It was a gesture I could ill afford, and if it was bluff my bluff was called. Francis remembered the incident differently in 1989: 'The Gargoyle was open until four or five in the morning, so if you weren't working, life was a continuous party. It was also made for rows. You came across to me and said, "Are you Francis Bacon?" and I said, "Yes" and you threw a pint of beer in my face, and that was my first meeting with you.' He spluttered with laughter, tugging mischievously at his lapels, but I was less amused.

'Surprising how alcohol fogs the brain.'

'My memory is not fogged at all,' he insisted.

'I've never thrown a pint of beer in anyone's face . . .'

Francis interrupted joyfully: 'But it's part of your *charm*!'

In fact I remember the incident in every detail. I remember also that we met at the Colony the next afternoon, and though he was still with Peter Lacy he came straight over with a bottle and poured me a glass of champagne with his disarming laughter: 'You know, I can't remember a thing! But I think we had words in the Gargoyle last night. Anyhow, as I always say, if you can't be rude to your real friends, who can you be rude to?' I felt there was an answer to this, but was so pleased at being called a friend that I was delighted to accept this perverse apology. As rows tend to, this one confirmed our friendship.

Francis told Michael Luke, who wrote *David Tennant and the Gargoyle Years*, 'I've seen greater scenes than I've ever seen in my life in the Gargoyle – except for one's personal rows. They were nightly. They went on not only hours, they went on for days. It was like one of the instalments where it says tomorrow you'll get such and such – well, you certainly did in the Gargoyle. It was great fun, really, in spite of the rows. And there were marvellous evenings without rows. I remember once meeting Sartre who was there with his governess, Simone de Beauvoir, sitting with Sonia Orwell. Lucian and I were both invited to their table. Sartre got up and sat on it waggling his short legs and said, "Who is the good-looking one?" jabbing his Gauloise at Lucian. I do remember Sartre was very charming. He said, "When you come to Paris, ring me." But I never did.'

The artist Robert Buhler recalled an argument with James Pope-Hennessy, then literary editor of the *Spectator* and subsequently the victim of a particularly brutal murder by some 'pick-ups' who thought he had money concealed in his house. Hennessy was sitting at a table with Francis, Lucian, Minton and two paratroopers he had picked up earlier. Buhler admitted: 'With the drink I have an unfortunate tongue, like so many people. Evidently I said something about his brother John, a keeper at the Victoria and Albert Museum, which offended.'

Sensing trouble, Francis, Lucian and Buhler's girlfriend Prudence Branch wisely hurried Buhler into the lift, but when they reached the bottom they found Pope-Hennessy and his two paratroopers who had run down the fire escape. 'Lucian was very brave,' Buhler remembered. 'He jumped on the back of one of the bully boys while Francis kicked at his shins. Every time one of the paratroopers came near him, Francis just kicked – in a very lady-like way, I must say. In spite of their determined efforts, I got badly bashed up.' I remember countless black eyes myself, many to be inflicted by my deserter.

Even at the Gargoyle the gaiety ran out, like a gramophone winding down. Waiters bustled with bills and a hubbub of objections erupted.

'What's this?' a north-country voice demanded. 'I'm not paying any bloody ballroom fee. And what's this for sandwiches? We didn't have any bloody sandwiches.'

'Mr Deakin,' came an anguished plea from one of the staff. 'There's a small matter of eight shillings.'

Deakin swayed on the stairs, summoning a last vestige of dignity. 'You call yourself a head waiter and *dare* to bother me for a measly eight shillings! I'll sign for it when I come here again, *if* I come here again.' He continued to make his exit. A woman screamed as he lost his balance and almost fell down the stairs backwards, but he straightened up in time and tottered to the lift.

'That Mr Deakin,' sighed the waiter, addressing the couple at the next table. 'He causes more trouble than all the members put together. You recognise any of the staff? No, they all left because of Mr Deakin.' I thought of him with new admiration, wondering how he could run up a bill as little as eight shillings.

There was one last port of call, at Mrs Bill's coffee stall at the bottom of Dean Street on the bomb site by St Anne's church. I drank a cup of sweet coffee, eyed with hostility by the unsuccessful flotsam of the night. It was about two in the morning; Francis was wrong – the Gargoyle did not go on until four or five, not then.

The Soho night was nearly finished. The last lift decanted the last drunk from the Gargoyle. Minton's waving entourage swept past in a cheerful taxi. The air was cool, someone was being sick in the gutter, an indomitable chirrup in a doorway – 'Hullo, dearie!' and then with a final sigh, a degree of silence. Soho was a village once more.

Penniless after leaving my money on Francis's table, I walked back to Knightsbridge and my flat in Beauchamp Place with the naval deserter tottering behind me.

Though I was instantly entranced by Francis the painter, I was less interested in the painting. Perhaps this was just as well. It meant that I did not nose around the Millais studio looking for canvases, nor did I pester Francis with constant questions concerning art. Even Deakin, with his superior knowledge and intuitive taste, rarely raised the subject.

Instead, we complemented each other in different ways. Ours was an extraordinarily intimate friendship over the next decade. We met as if by appointment at midday in the French, where we laughed so spontaneously that strangers looked across wistfully as if they wanted to share in such happiness. We carried on, in every sense, until we flagged as the next day dawned. These were the happiest days of my life, and I am pleased that Francis said the same.

What did Francis gain from me? I suppose I was young. As Francis might have said, it was as simple as *that*. Straight from Cambridge, I had the freshness and enthusiasm of youth before life becomes muddied. Deakin referred to me as the *jeunesse dorée*, though I had little idea what this meant. I presented a good audience, and was not particularly venal then. I had a sense of humour. Francis had no need to be jealous of me in any way – though Deakin was consumed by envy and eventually tried in his Machiavellian way to turn Francis against me.

I have noticed that if you like someone very much there is usually a reciprocal feeling. Love is another matter altogether, but I was fond of Francis and knew he was special. He was a lovable man and few failed to respond. Later, when I met a couple of people who thoroughly disliked him, for specific reasons which I shall explain, it came as a shock.

# 7

# Bacon at Work

We nearly always live through screens . . . when people say my work
looks violent, perhaps I have been able to clear away one or two screens.
*Francis Bacon to David Sylvester*

When did we find the time to work? Maclaren Ross warned that
Soho was a dangerous place: 'If you get Sohoitis, you will stay
there always day and night and get no work done ever!'

I have known several writers and painters who drank their
talent away, describing the work they were going to do with such
eloquence that they convinced themselves they had done it. Their
daydreams became a substitute for the work itself. Some simply
found the pace of life too hard. In 1948 Nina Hamnett was given a
show by Rex Nan Kivell at the Redfern Gallery, where half the
pictures were sold to faithful supporters like Matthew Smith and J.
B. Priestley, and she exhibited with a local art society in 1951; but
by then most of her days were frittered in pubs and the Caves de
France. And after their disillusionment, the two Roberts lost
heart.

Deakin got the sack from *Vogue* after arriving several hours too
early to help with the decorations for a smart party the magazine
was giving. He helped himself to the drinks, and when the
distinguished guests arrived at midnight Deakin was too far gone
and had to be carried out like the corpse of Hamlet, yet again.

I tried to cheer him up: 'Who will they be talking about this
morning – Dame Edith, Dame Margot? No, John Deakin!'

'Hm, you may have a point.' But when he told me that Cecil
Beaton had just cut him dead in the *Vogue* lift, I knew the end had
come.

I was a casualty too, sacked from *Picture Post* because my job
had become too embroiled with the naval deserter who absorbed
both my time and money as I sold and pawned my few possessions.

I made the mistake of taking him with me on a 'silly-season' story about two girls and two donkeys on Brighton Downs. I had just passed my test, but knew already that cars were not for me nor I for them; even so, I allowed myself to make the shuddering, gear-screeching journey in a dilapidated van which at least convinced me that I should never drive again. Nor have I. The girls were jolly, Mike well behaved, but as we sunbathed I was startled to find strange little creatures among my hairs – my first experience of crabs.

Back in London I made the mistake of asking the *Picture Post* doctor for a cure; and this, coupled with reports from one of the girls, who happened to live with the assistant editor, proved the end of the job I loved. I received notice of my dismissal in the Saturday post, and in those days one accepted such a decision without any thought of running to a tribunal.

At his campest, Deakin came bustling into Beauchamp Place full of his visit to *Picture Post* the day before, when he had tried to sell them a story.

'After my few words with the editor,' he declared, 'I've certainly cooked your goose!' Without a comment I handed him the letter.

'Oh, my God!' He was so shocked he even bought the first round in the Bunch of Grapes at opening time. Ironically, my photos of the girls and the donkeys ran to several pages.

After struggling as a freelance, I decided to join the Merchant Navy – only to find myself in the usual predicament. I could not get a ticket unless I had experience; I could not join unless I had a ticket. Francis wrote a letter to Sir Colin Anderson, one of his patrons and the chairman of the Orient Line, which resulted in the offer of a job as postal clerk on one of the liners. Two deckhands off a ship warned me that this meant I would be neither crew nor passenger, so I opted for the post of utility steward instead. I spent the next year sailing round the world on the *Orcades* washing dishes, and have seldom been happier.

Like some exotic out of Tennessee Williams, I thought it might be dashing to have a tattoo designed by my friends. As far as I remember, Lucian took to the idea; Graham Sutherland suggested a rose; and Francis a Crucifixion to cover my back. At this point I lost my enthusiasm, returning from sea with a single shark on the back of my hand which four of us had had tattooed in Honolulu, having neither the time nor the money for anything more ambitious.

Francis examined it with exaggerated attention: 'What a very nice *sardine!*' I doubt if any tattooist in the world could have reproduced his Crucifixion, but how priceless I would be today if he had.

In contrast to my own aimlessness, Francis's discipline was extraordinary. He worked from six in the morning with the fierce concentration of a hangover, which had the advantage of excluding all distraction. He told me that drink and the after-effects forced him to concentrate on his painting, and that at times it gave him 'a sort of freedom'. Working at great speed, he attacked the canvas. It was hard to imagine him asleep, and such a concession must have been brief. His stamina was exceptional. I have observed him on mornings when he was grey and nearly sightless from fatigue after drinking and gambling through the night, only to see him reappear a few hours later totally refreshed. Deakin suffered miserably, but I cannot recall Francis complaining of a hangover – like a lady's name, it was not to be mentioned in the Mess.

Though he appeared to do no work, his output was consistent. The period between 1951 and 1962, during which Francis, Deakin and I raged around Soho, was also the period of his artistic ascendancy. If we compare his *Three Studies for the Base of a Crucifixion*, the painting with which he burst onto the scene in 1945, with the masterpieces of his Soho period (that is to say, the popes, the remarkable painting of a *Man with Dog*, his series on Van Gogh, the astonishing *Two Figures*, also called 'The Wrestlers' and 'The Buggers', *Miss Muriel Belcher*, the *Paralytic Child Walking on All Fours*, and the blood-bespattered *Three Studies for a Crucifixion* of 1962, completed while he was drunk, they confirm his formidable development in a comparatively short time. The first *Three Studies* stand apart from this company, for they are painted with deliberation. Indeed they are carefully drawn outlines filled in with paint. You feel that nothing has been left to chance. Although early on he told me how he liked to exploit the 'creative accident' – 'My ideal would really be just to pick up a handful of paint and throw it at the canvas and hope that the portrait was there' – I was never sure of the degree of flippancy in the phrase, and it was certainly never as simple as that, and earlier on it was hardly true at all.

Talking to David Sylvester, he instanced the *Painting* (now in the Museum of Modern Art in New York) which he did in 1946. Francis revealed that he started by trying to do a gorilla in a cornfield, then a bird alighting, 'and gradually all the marks I made suggested another image – a totally accidental image I'd never thought of doing'.

Here was the 'creative accident' in development. This historic picture was sold by Erica Brausen of the Hanover Gallery, who handled his work from the mid-forties to the end of the fifties; she was among the first to recognise his importance, though her financial backers disagreed. It seems incredible now, but his work was almost unsaleable and Bacon was delighted when she bought the *Painting* for £100.

With the confidence he gained, his approach became even more dangerous and as a result more vibrant. In the fifties he often talked about working as closely to instinct or as closely to his nervous system as he could. He was fascinated to see how the paint fell, turning this to his advantage, though there was something deliberate even in that. 'You find that the mark you make suggests another mark from which you can develop, and sometimes when I've been working I've been so sick of it that I just take the brush and put marks all over it, thinking it's not going to work at all, and then suddenly out of this chaos comes the possibility of making an image I hadn't thought of before.'

I spent so much time on the London School in the previous chapter because this is the art-historical context out of which Francis Bacon emerged. At the time it seemed almost a historical inevitability that painting should go further and further into abstraction. The little London School, headed by Francis, was very much swimming against the tide of artistic fashion.

Perhaps Francis's view of abstraction can best be gauged from Michael Andrew's account of the few weeks in 1950 when Francis taught at the Royal College of Art, substituting for John Minton. 'What modern man needs is a kind of shorthand,' said Francis. 'The bombardment of information to which we are constantly subjected should not overwhelm our capacity to receive it and render it down to a world-view.' Andrews remembered Francis's authority as he answered a student who asked why he was a figurative painter: 'Abstract art is so boring!'

At one point someone shouted out: 'Why does there have to be all this talk? Why can't we just go out and paint?'

'My dear,' said Francis despairingly, 'if only we could!'

His constant assertion about abstraction was not shared by Victor Pasmore, his fellow artist at Agnew's in 1937, who wrote to him fifty years later:

I am naturally interested in your objections to abstract painting particularly as Picasso is reported to have said the same thing for the same reasons! Certainly his *Guernica* could not have been so emotionally effective in terms of abstract espressionism. But on the other hand, it would not have been so free and modern without the imitation cubist collage slapped independently right across the central figures! Does this mean that the future of modern painting, if it is to achieve great art, must be hotch-potch? Well, maybe: after all, Nature itself is hotch-potch!

Francis replied tersely: 'Thank you very much for your letter. For me abstract art can be nothing but decoration because there is nothing to anchor it by except its artistic allure. All best wishes, Francis.'

In the early days Francis's choice of materials was limited by his resources. To start with he used an absorbent wood-fibre board called Sundlea, recommended by Roy De Maistre and Graham Sutherland. Apart from its being economical, Francis found that it 'held' the pastel, though he turned to canvas as soon as he could afford to. Surprisingly, this held the pastel less well, lacking the 'tooth' to receive it. When he was broke in Monte Carlo in 1947, unable to buy more canvas, he painted on the reverse side of pictures he disliked and discovered that the unprimed surface held his paint exactly as he wanted. This became his method until he was able to pay for canvases stretched back to front, already primed but not sized.

John Richardson, the author of the definitive life of Picasso, described how Francis used to let his stubble grow for three or four days and then rehearse the brushstrokes on his face in front of the mirror: '. . . those strange revolving brushstrokes, that are so familiar from his pictures, would be rehearsed with Max Factor pancake make-up. He had a series of these Max Factor pots and he would take one and do a sort of smear across his face, and these are the smears that you see on so many of the faces of many of those early paintings.' Richardson even compared the reverse 'woolly' side of the canvas to the stubble on Francis's face!

'Drawing' directly onto the canvas, then, with a brush but no preliminary sketch, he began with the central image, his furious brushstrokes contrasting with the careful background area. As Andrew Durham explained in a Tate Gallery booklet, the sedate background would be adapted as the image progressed: 'He may not always work fast and furiously, but the paintings he regards as the more successful are in general the ones he paints quickly.' The brushstrokes varied

> from calligraphic arabesques, through sharp stabbing strokes to the almost watercolourist's delicacy of the treatment of the hair in the right-hand figure of *Triptych 1972*, to voluptuous impasto with a heavily laden brush, and the dragging of dry paint across the surface to leave encrustations rather than brushstrokes. Elsewhere he picks the brush off the surface to leave sharp peaks and serrated ridges of paint.

Francis told me once that he never had the studio in Reece Mews cleaned because it helped him to lift up dust from the floor and apply it to the canvas when painting his sand dunes; he also rubbed his fingers along the dust and then onto the wet paint. He used traditional artist's oils without the addition of varnish, and squeezed them directly in thick dollops from the tube onto the canvas – in Andrew Durham's words 'high impasto and dry scumbles where the medium seems to have been soaked out, to very thin washes where a good deal of turpentine has been added to modify the tube paints. He seems to delight in the subtlety and malleability of this medium.'

Like many artists, Francis used his fingers and small sponges to smear effects, and even a piece of corduroy to impose a cross-hatching impression by pressing it against a face on the canvas. Though he obeyed no rules, he took advantage of practical methods to create his straight lines, and Letraset for his lettering – the closest he came to collage, though he used it haphazardly to enhance the central image. I once mentioned that I had seen Michael Andrews's studies of Ayers Rock and was not entirely happy with his obvious use of acrylic and spray gun. Francis looked at me knowingly and chose his words carefully, as he replied slowly: 'As a matter of fact I use a spray gun and acrylic myself.'

'You do?' I exclaimed.

'Yes,' he smiled, 'but I use them less obviously!'

He explained that acrylic was quick-drying and useful, especially for the large expanse of flat colour in the background, unless he exploited the bare texture of the canvas itself. Against this, Francis would use the canvas like a dartboard, flicking paint to let it drip. A ploy which came dangerously close to gimmickry consisted of the red arrows pointing at the severed torsos in *Studies for the Human Body*. Remembering that I had seen a similar use in an early picture by Richard Hamilton, it occurred to me that Francis had 'borrowed' the technique from Hamilton, who was one of the few contemporary artists whom he admired. Hamilton replied: 'I doubt very much that Francis would have borrowed my arrow from *Transition IIII*. I probably borrowed it from Paul Klee, so he could have had it from the same source. I don't know if he could have seen my painting, which was not exhibited until a show at the Hanover Gallery in 1956.' Of course it is perfectly probable that Francis saw it there and remembered it, albeit subconsciously, years later, but I discovered recently that Francis said he really got the idea from a golfing manual which used arrows to indicate which way the ball should go after it was hit. This sounds unlikely, but no more so than throwing sand at the canvas.

Francis was blessed with his friends and mentors: Roy De Maistre; Patrick White; Graham Sutherland; his first patrons, Eric Hall, Robert and Lisa Sainsbury, and Colin Anderson; and, particularly, his first dealer, Erica Brausen, who ran the Hanover Gallery with Arthur Jeffress, the rich American expatriate. Robert Sainsbury thought that Jeffress was too effeminate for Francis's taste, and I agree. He fluttered too far. Jeffress was closer to Graham Sutherland, who may have introduced them in the first place in his determination to see Francis succeed.

Consequently, Francis dealt directly with Erica Brausen. I remember her as intense, possessive of Francis, and speaking with a slight accent which I took to be German. Unwilling to join the Soho revelry which Francis rejoiced in, she was known to mutter: 'These artists, why to they haf to drink all the time? They drink so much, what can you do with them?' But she did a lot for Francis. Her loyalty was absolute and selfless and her faith in his future supported him through difficult years when only a discerning few shared her belief. After his death a letter appeared in the *Independent* signed by Sir Robert and Lisa Sainsbury, Stephen Spender and David Sylvester, pointing out that there had been little acknowledgement of the

> key role played in his career by his first dealer, Erica Brausen of the Hanover Gallery, who handled his work from the mid-40s to the end of the 1950s. She was among the first to recognise the magnitude of his importance as an artist and, at a time when his work was almost unsaleable, whether to public bodies or private collectors, was passionately committed to supporting it. This created great problems for her, since both her successive financial backers disagreed with her judgement of the work. Nevertheless, for all the unsold canvases by him in the basement of her gallery, she somehow managed to provide for his constant need of money to survive.

From 1949 to 1957 there were yearly exhibitions at the Hanover except for 1956; he also showed at Durlacher Bros in New York in 1953; at the British Pavilion in the Venice Biennale in 1954; at the Galerie Rive Droite in Paris in 1957; and at the Galleria Galatea in Turin in 1958, a show which continued to the Galleria d'Ariete in Milan and L'Obelisco in Rome.

Because he had no permanent home in London, Francis was constantly on the move. Travel was never a problem except financially and, as far as she could, Erica Brausen supplied him with money – though it cannot have been easy to keep pace with his extravagance and gambling debts. Considering their different temperaments, she was remarkably tolerant. Any agent or dealer will find Francis's requests for money painfully familiar – after all, it is part of their function to be a private bank; Oscar Wilde was a master at the game, cajoling, prevaricating, pleading in his exile. Erica Brausen never let him down. Arriving at his studio, she saw and bought the *Painting* (1946) which Francis regarded as a major work. Francis left for Monte Carlo a fortnight afterwards to live on the proceeds.

From then on she supplied him with constant sums of money; as little as £15 to Wivenhoe, when he stayed with Dennis Wirth-Miller and Dickie Chopping; £200 to Monte Carlo; regular payments to Tangier, including £100 when he wrote that he had finished four paintings – 'the best things I have done . . . two scenes of the Pope with Owls quite different from the others and a special portrait of a person in a room. I am very excited about it and hope to come back with 20 or 25 pictures. . . .' In the event, only the *Owls* survived.

As Francis rarely dated his letters until the end of his life, it is hard to know what year he was writing in. I assume it was 1948 when he wrote from Monte Carlo to Arthur Jeffress, thanking him for advancing £200. 'The pictures seem to be going well I am at the moment working on some heads which I like better than any have done before I hope you and Erica will like them I shall come back in November or December and bring some of the stuff and leave with you I am rather disturbed about frames . . .'

A subsequent letter to Erica Brausen announced the good news that he was moving to a villa on the hills above Monte Carlo with a 'wonderful room to work in. . . . There are plenty of rooms and bathrooms so do come and stay if you feel like it *any* time . . . I saw Graham and Kathy and Eardley last night. Do hope the show sold better by now love to you and will you tell Arthur I have not been able to track down movements of the fleet yet.' (This referred to the role performed by Graham Sutherland and other friends in alerting Jeffress when the American fleet sailed into Villefranche. Obsessed by uniforms, Jeffress pursued the British fleet during the Royal Tournament at Earl's Court, which he described as the 'Royal Torment', and left a substantial sum in his will to the welfare of British sailors provided that not one penny should go to officers or Wrens.) Francis concluded his letter to Erica Brausen: 'I do hope you are feeling better it is wonderful here terribly expensive and the days hot and trembling like the middle of summer all my love Francis.'

His first show at the Hanover – at 32A St George Street, off Hanover Square, from 8 November to 10 December 1949 – was shared with Robin Ironside; his fellow artist took second place with pictures like *The Gondolas of Delos*, which sold for twenty-five guineas, while the scribbled figures on the side of Bacon's work in the gallery catalogue were considerably higher. The typically enigmatically titled *Studies I, II* and *III* were not for sale; *Figure in Landscape 1946* was priced at £400 – the most expensive of the twelve paintings, and rightly so. Tony Hubbard bought *Head IV 1949* and *Head II* was earmarked for the Contemporary Arts Society. *Head VI 1949* was priced at £125.

Such figures seem negligible today, but they were substantial then. Even so, Erica Brausen may well have sold them privately for less. It shows how difficult it was to sell them that eight years later the prices had scarcely moved: the *Owls*, painted in Tangier and bought by Tony Hubbard, was priced at £250; *Study for Figure I* and *Study for Figure II* at £450 each, and *Study for Portrait X 1957* at £600.

One morning in 1955 he phoned me urgently to ask if I knew of anyone who might buy one of his latest paintings, of a pope based on Velasquez's portrait of Pope Innocent X. The snag was that he needed the money, £150, that same day. I never asked and do not know the reason for the urgency. I contacted John Knight, with whom I shared the flat in Beauchamp Place after we went down from Cambridge, and persuaded him to buy it. It almost wrecked his marriage when he agreed, for his wife, Wendy, grew to dread the purple figure which loomed in violent silence at the top of the stairs in their mews cottage. When I handed Francis the £150 in pound notes I was taken aback when he gave me £15 as my 'dealer's commission', something I had not expected. The Knights, tired of the Pope's presence, sold the Bacon a few years later, the first to go to auction. It fetched £7,000 in 1964 and was re-sold by Christies in New York for a record $5,720,000.

This 1957 exhibition included four studies for *Portraits of Van Gogh*, painted during 1956 and 1957. The first had been bought by Robert and Lisa Sainsbury and was lent to the show. Based on Van Gogh's *The Painter on the Road to Tarascon* of 1888, which was destroyed during the war, this became one of Francis's most successful themes and confirmed his brilliance as a colourist. Sir Robert Sainsbury stressed that his version is unlike those that followed, showing Van Gogh half obscured in the high grass in contrast to the later full-length figures. The face is a blur, though the easel strapped to his back is unmistakable.

The Sainsburys are among the greatest patrons of the arts this century, worthy to be described as modern Medicis, and the English equivalent of the American millionaire philanthropists Guggenheim, Getty, Mellon and Frick. Their discerning eye spotted Bacon long before he was fashionable. Robert Sainsbury came back from work one evening in 1953 to be greeted by his wife, Lisa: 'You'd better see what's in the other room.' She had gone into the Hanover that morning and borrowed the *Study of a Nude* which Francis had just completed. 'I took one look,' he told me, 'and rushed back to her. When she told me it cost £125, I said: "We've got to have it!"' '

From then on they bought everything through Erica Brausen except for a small triptych of Isabel Rawsthorne from the Marlborough in 1965. By then the first excitement was less and the pictures cost more. Sir Robert adhered to his limited art account – 'When the prices went up, it meant sacrificing other things if I bought a Francis Bacon at a fancy price.' One picture which they regretted not purchasing was that of two men writhing around on grass – a version of *The Wrestlers*. Alfred Hecht, who framed all of Bacon's pictures, claimed he was the man underneath – 'Didn't you recognise me, Bob?' Sir Robert told me he could not imagine Francis painting it if they hadn't slept together but in this he might have been naive. For just as Jeffress was too effeminate, so was Hecht, and I should have thought such a coupling was unlikely. As Sainsbury's children were very young he felt that he and his wife had enough problems without having to explain what the two men were up to in the long grass.

He avoided meeting an artist before seeing his work – 'If I like the work, *then* I wish to meet the artist.' Though he believes that Francis was closer to his wife because of his homosexuality, the three became close friends. When Sainsbury's father committed suicide: 'Francis wrote me a most understanding letter. You could go to him for advice for he was fundamentally a nice man. He showed terrific sympathy.'

Francis's affection for Lisa and Robert Sainsbury was genuine, and of course he was grateful for their patronage at a time when it was needed, and to Robert also for guaranteeing his bank overdraft. For once, Francis encouraged them to sit for him: Lisa for several pictures, and 'Bob' when she commissioned his portrait for £400. This involved nine sittings in 1955 in the studio lent to him by the Hon. Michael Astor at 28 Mallord Street, SW3. It was so cold that Sir Robert sat huddled in his overcoat with a thermos of hot coffee and a sandwich lunch because he had to hurry back to Sainsbury's where he was joint general manager.

Francis had such exacting standards that he was impatient with paintings which just failed to satisfy, turning against them impetuously as if they were strangers who displeased. Consequently the Sainsburys were dismayed when his friend Paul Danquah warned them that the best of the eight portraits had been destroyed, and dreaded the early phone call: 'There's no need to come for the sitting today – it's *gone*.' They were so anxious when he referred enthusiastically at a party to a new painting of a pope as 'a wonderful picture' that they offered him a lift home in the hope of seeing it and possibly buying it. On the way he decided it was no good after all; by the time they arrived, he declared that it had to be destroyed.

'You can't,' they pleaded.

'You'd better come in and see if you like it,' he relented. But once inside he took a razor blade and slashed it. 'He gave us what was left of the canvas,' they said, 'which we rolled up and put on the roof of our car before he could change his mind. The next morning we went to Alfred Hecht, who trimmed and framed it.'

When I remarked that the picture looked successful despite the slashing, Sir Robert suggested that 'If a picture is really great, each square would be all right'; this reminded me of Rembrandt's *The Anatomy Lesson of Dr Joan Deyman*, which survives as a fragment after it was damaged by fire and may now benefit from not having too many distracting figures in the background. One of the hardest lessons for an artist is to know when to leave well alone. Usually Francis drew back in time, but when he realised he had gone too far he was ruthless. *The Times* claimed he destroyed seven hundred paintings in this early period, and if only half that number was correct there is reason to fear it included many paintings which should have been saved.

Altogether, the Sainsburys acquired thirteen Bacons, three of which were presents. He painted nine portraits, of which three survive – two of Lisa Sainsbury and one of Sir Robert. Nine Bacons were given to the University of East Anglia at Norwich.

One evening in the fifties Francis took me to the Sainsburys' elegant home in Westminster, with their first *Nude* hanging in the wood-panelled hall. They received me courteously even though I had not been invited, and showed me their prize possession – the bronze of the *Petite danseuse de quatorze ans* sculpted by Degas in 1880. Unaware that Degas had done such work, I gazed with awe at the little figure complete with bodice and feminine tutu, which was dusty and slightly frayed. I was over-awed as we climbed the staircase, myself following with their son. Recognising a Bacon, I exclaimed brightly: 'I say, that's an awfully good likeness of your father.'

'Yes,' agreed David Sainsbury coldly, 'except it's my mother.'

Francis sailed to South Africa in 1951 to see his mother who had settled there, though she was not mentioned in his letter to Erica Brausen from Salisbury in Southern Rhodesia. For once there was a date: 22 February. This was the occasion when he was taken out by Robert Heber-Percy, the close friend of Lord Berners. Diana Mosley told me that she met Francis at Berners's country home, Faringdon House in Berkshire, where the doves were dyed in different colours; Francis remembered her as 'very beautiful'. On the ship to South Africa, while Heber-Percy travelled first-class, Francis was put in steerage.

'More fun?' I enquired.

'*Much* more fun,' he said.

A tantalising scrap of letter remains which suggests that Francis enjoyed himself regardless of the class. Written to Paul Danquah on ship's notepaper, with a Union Jack crest below 'Union Castle Line' and the heading S. S. *Kenya Castle*, it is undated because there is no first page:

. . . are absolutely charming and helpful and terribly good looking and sweet they think we are a honeymoon couple isn't it camp – at our table there is an old boy queer who has a physical culture school in Nairobi, and a very nice woman who is the wife of a gold mining technician. Also a young man and his wife going to a bank in Uganda. I have got off *with* him isn't it strange – especially as he says he can't stand homos. I don't know what he thinks I am – the fish-nets are a terrific success I've never enjoyed a journey so much only wish you were here all my fondest love to you and Peter . . .

92

Despite their acceptance by the other passengers on board, it was an odd ménage even for the fringes of the dissolute British aristocracy and soon after their arrival there came a falling-out. This explains Francis's urgency.

I got here about a week ago I stayed at Zimbabwe [presumably to see his sister] and the country from there to here is too marvellous it is like a Renoir landscape and Zimbabwe itself is incredible. Robert Heber-Percy has left. I met someone who has a farm near Zimbabwe and am going back there now that I have got shot of Robert the work has started terribly well. . . .

Then he got to the point: 'Could the gallery possibly advance me £50 as now that I have left Robert I have practically no money.' He explained that he hoped to catch a cargo boat at Beira and continue up the East Coast to Port Sudan on the Red Sea, travel inland to Thebes and rejoin the boat at Alexandria, leaving at Marseilles. I believe this journey was accomplished, though I got the impression that he had taken several cargo boats.

He ended the letter: 'I would be terribly grateful if you could do this for me everyone is so terribly nice here I don't like sponging on them all the time and paints are very expensive.' The money could be sent from Cook's in Berkeley Street to their office in Salisbury where he would be, in and out, for the next three weeks. A message to Arthur Jeffress extolled the toughness of the Salisbury police.

On the 27th he wrote that he had secured his passage. 'I am sorry to ask again but could you send me the £50 immediately. I've done three small paintings which I am excited about . . . it is so difficult having to ask all the time for little sums of money. As I did not come on with Robert I am without anything but my fare. I am enjoying being here terribly.'

In the spring of 1952 he made a second visit to South Africa, returning first to 6 Beaufort Gardens in London, then renting a cottage in the late summer of 1953 at Hurst near Henley-on-Thames to be next door to his friend Peter Lacy, a fascinating figure, about whom more later. In March 1954 he moved to the Imperial Hotel at Henley and afterwards to 9 Market Place. Though the upper-class ambience of Henley appealed to him, his sporadic stays must have been due to the proximity of Lacy, who

93

still had money at that time, before he wasted it on the promotion of a pop group. Then Lacy even possessed a house in Barbados, the subject of a picture which Francis painted from a photograph which Lacy asked him to copy as closely as possible. This was in 1952 and the picture, which I have never seen, was given to Lacy, subsequently joining the collections of Erica Brausen at the Hanover, and then the Galerie Claude Bernard in Paris. Francis's portrait of Peter Lacy, titled *P.L.*, was bought by the Sainsburys.

Francis rarely referred to his visits to Henley, though he had a favourite restaurant there, coincidentally called Chez Peter. A letter from the Imperial Hotel to Erica Brausen reveals that at one point (undated) he was far from happy:

> I am not able to finish any paintings at the moment so will you please put off the exhibition – I am terribly sorry about this but as you know these things happen with work I will let you have the paintings as soon as I possibly can but please do not have a show of the things you have got in the gallery of mine I think it would be a great mistake to show them both for you and for me As you know I want to replace most of them when I can also there have been too many shows of mine – I am desperate and completely broke and am going to try and get a job for a time – I am terribly sorry about this. . . .

Plainly he was in a disgruntled mood, probably agitated by more than work. Such setbacks must have been vexing.

Francis's requests were modest and justified by his work. For him, these were years of exhilaration despite the occasional malaise, as at Henley. He enjoyed the excitement of shows in America and Italy; though he disliked the social life of Rome – 'so expensive due to the American invasion' – he found Naples 'wonderful and would love to work there for a time'. There was constant optimism, rarely shown in later years, with the assurance that the 'new' work was 'much better and more concentrated than before'. Admittedly this could have been an inducement, followed immediately by a request for £300 – 'I have to buy a lot of paint' – to be sent c/o Auto Gears and Spare Parts Co., 51 Main Street, Gibraltar.

In June 1957, Erica Brausen sent £100 with her friend Toto who was going to Tangier, mentioning that a show had been discussed – 'As you have had so much success lately it would be a good idea to

94

have your American exhibition in the not too distant future.' In July she warned him that she would be away on holiday until 1 September, but assured him: 'Should you need any money urgently in the meantime, provided it is not a very large sum, please get in touch with Margot at the Gallery and she will arrange it.' The following March she wrote excitedly:

> We are in a terrible stew here as we have almost completely sold out your paintings in Italy (of all places!) even mine which I didn't want to sell, but which they insisted on having. I know you don't think like painting but I do wish you would, as Germany, the United States and Mexico, all want shows and I think it is not a good thing to have to refuse them. I too would love another show next year. . . .

She confirmed this in June in answer to a telegram which complained that he had not received the money sent him via her bank.

Perhaps I am reading too much into it, but the phrase 'I know you don't think like painting' strikes me as odd, raising the possibility that Francis did not want her to know the extent of his work. Also, he needed to settle down in London – 'I am so sick of never having a permanent place.' There had been another faint warning signal that their relationship would not last in the summer of 1953 when Erica Brausen closed the gallery for August and Francis was so short of money that David Sylvester brought him into the Beaux Arts Gallery off Bruton Street to introduce him to Helen Lessore: 'He thought I might be interested to buy some pictures.'

Helen Lessore's gallery was the most sympathetic in London. You were happy to enter it, and this was due largely to Helen, who showed the work of such young artists as Frank Auerbach, Michael Andrews, Tim Behrens, Craigie Aitchison and Leon Kossoff at a time when they needed exhibitions and encouragement.

Francis made an extraordinary impression when he came through the door – something she has never forgotten. 'He was not the same shape as any other human being, especially not his face. There was the sense of an aura about him. Of course the pictures were amazing too. During the next months I bought several, including the Pope with the bloodstains shown in the last Tate retrospective.'

95

Ronald Alley's definitive book, *The Collections,* lists the Beaux Arts in reference to: *Man Eating a Leg of Chicken 1952*: David Sylvester; Beaux Arts; Hanover; *Man in a Chair 1952*; Beaux Arts: Junior Common Room, Pembroke College, Oxford; *Study After Velasquez's Portrait of Pope Innocent X 1953*: Beaux Arts. During November and December these pictures were exhibited at the Beaux Arts without a catalogue as *New Paintings by Francis Bacon.*

Then Erica came back. 'I had bought enough for an exhibition in November,' Helen Lessore confirmed to me in 1992, 'but she came round and made a scene, sitting on the balcony crying: "Francis is my baby. Would you let me buy the pictures back?" ' She refused. Afterwards, Francis introduced her meticulously as his 'dealer'; but that was the extent of his business partnership with Helen Lessore, though they remained the closest of friends up to his death. Francis respected her; she loved him. In 1992 she spoke with special warmth of Craigie Aitchison and Leon Kossof, but remembered Francis as

> most extraordinary. You must convey his stature and his *radiance*! There was not a day when he did not think about death, but by temperament he was an optimist. He used to come into the Beaux Arts every few days and though he talked in a light way he was always serious with me.
>
> I've met two geniuses: Walter Sickert [her brother-in-law] and Francis Bacon.

So on 17 October 1958, Francis called at the Hanover obviously upset 'and in some trepidation'. Erica Brausen was on holiday and he told her colleague Michael Greenwood that he had not wanted to tell her the true state of his financial affairs, which was now so desperate that he had decided to make an arrangement with the Marlborough Gallery. Though Francis said he would never have taken such a step without consulting her, he had brought a cheque to clear his account at the Hanover, explaining that he was up to his neck in personal debt through gambling – about £5000. Michael Greenwood wrote to Erica Brausen at once to break the bad news: 'He felt that you would never be able to take over such a liability and therefore had not spoken to you about it.' Even so, Greenwood asked if he was still in the middle of negotiations and whether there was any possibility of delaying a final decision until her return; but Francis said it was irrevocable. He hoped that the Hanover and the Marlborough might come to an arrangement to allow her to buy some pictures in the future.

In fact, as Michael Greenwood suspected, he had signed the contract the day before. 'Obviously he has already signed up and received money. He knows that you will be distressed, as he is himself, but he says that his position was desperate and that he had no alternative.' Greenwood concluded: 'I'm terribly sorry about Francis after all you have done for him all these years.'

It was hardly the cleanest of cuts, but it is the regrettable yet inevitable fate of the first champion of an artist's work to be replaced by someone more high-powered as soon as the artist becomes commercially successful. The Marlborough was able to lift Francis Bacon onto a higher level. It was a crucial turning-point.

Henrietta Moraes claims that the first exhibition at the Hanover Gallery was done in such a rush that, when David Sylvester leaned against one of them, he 'got half a naked man on his back'. (Presumably the pictures were so wet that they were not encased in the usual glass.) Francis did not bother to repair the damage.

I was there when in 1957 the gallery in George Street was so crowded with friends and their hangers-on that numerous people might have emerged with Bacons on their backs. Many of Bacon's friends brought their friends, thirstier for wine than for art, so it was more of a party than a private view – though Deakin went around informing everyone: 'No, this one is really good', rolling his eyes as if he alone could understand them. In the middle of the mêlée, Francis stood there smiling, perfectly composed as he always was on these fraught occasions.

Because I was in at the birth, these are my favourite pictures. I may not have understood them fully, but I recognised the excitement. He was painting with the assurance of an Old Master. *Figure in a Landscape* of 1945 hints at assassination. Francis gave me a postcard of it when the Tate bought the picture and I have had it on a wall ever since, beautifully faded now. He signed a photograph of the astonishing, circling dog painted in 1952, which is now in New York's Museum of Modern Art, but this is in black and white and it needs the colour.

*Figure Study 2* of 1945–6, donated to the Batley Art Gallery by the Contemporary Art Society in 1952. In this northern town noted for its night club rather than its interest in art, a motion was put forward to the Council to sell it; but the painting was saved due to the perseverance of the Director and it hangs today to greater advantage in Huddersfield. An apparently naked figure, loosely draped in this herringbone coat, leans over a palm, his mouth open in a scream, topped by an umbrella. The background is the colour of blood. What does it mean? There is no telling, but something terrible has happened.

Then came the five Heads admired by Lawrence Gowing, and the popes based on Velasquez; the *Two Figures* based on Muybridge's wrestlers (1953); the *Study for Portrait After the Life Mask of William Blake* (1955); *Van Gogh Going to Work* (1957); and *Miss Muriel Belcher* (1959). A total of just over forty paintings may not seem much in the span of a decade, but for this period alone Bacon would have secured his supremacy in twentieth-century British art.

If Francis was impeccable at his own private views, he could be vicious at those of others. I feel a twinge of shame as I remember how ungenerously we behaved at the private views in Cork Street. Francis knew that you are vulnerable when you praise but cannot go wrong if you criticise, for who can deny you? It was one of his few weaknesses that he was grudging in his support for other artists. We emerged from galleries spluttering with ill-concealed mirth. 'Well!' Francis exclaimed on one occasion as he leaned against a lamp-post because he was laughing so uncontrollably. 'I really *am* better, aren't I!'

The danger was that with his exact emphasis everyone found his commentary hilarious. Again signs his victims ignored the warning as they dared enlist his attention or curry favour. Lady Caroline Blackwood remembers one instance: 'Francis was being pestered by an irritating artist to come to his studio to look at his paintings, and the man concluded that Bacon refused because they threatened him. Francis replied that he did not feel in the least threatened: "I don't want to come to your studio," he explained with devastating accuracy, "because I've seen your *tie*!" '

98

Throughout this period Francis saw less of Graham Sutherland, whose influence diminished because Francis needed him less. Yet I believe it was crucial to begin with. Francis once wrote Graham a rare letter of thanks doubting if he would have sold anything if it had not been for Sutherland's promotion. Tired of London, he was thinking of renting a studio in Paris which they could share. His trust is revealed by his request that Sutherland should spray a fixative over the painting of a grinning man underneath an umbrella surrounded by carcasses of meat against a pinkish mauve background. Subsequently titled *Painting*, this was the important picture bought by Erica Brausen in 1946 and which she sold two years later to Alfred Barr for the Museum of Modern Art in New York for £150 – the first museum purchase of a Bacon.

It is beyond doubt that Graham helped Francis in numerous ways, while conceding to Roger Berthoud's claim that 'If any one influence seems to have predominated at this stage [1951] it was Bacon's, though the traffic in ideas was not wholly one way. One possible deduction is that in some cases Sutherland seemed to be painting Bacon-like works on a given theme *before* Bacon himself tackled it.' Berthoud pointed out that Sutherland saw key paintings in Francis's studio, even if they were subsequently destroyed. Indeed, how could you spray fixative over the *Painting* and *not* be influenced by such originality? Inevitably the Bacon touch began to show.

Seeing a splendid new painting in Tony Hubbard's house in Regent's Park Terrace, I exclaimed: 'That's a very odd Bacon! I haven't seen one like that before.'

'Hardly surprising,' said Hubbard. 'It's a Sutherland.' The origin was obvious on closer inspection. The subject was Sutherland's – foliage and tree trunks in his inimitable vivid green – but he had used a number of Baconian tricks such as the reverse of a massive canvas, the horizontal line near the edges suggesting a cage, the same heavy glass and frame by Alfred Hecht. For a moment the presentation had fooled me. A critic wrote that Sutherland was beginning to owe 'too heavy a debt to Francis Bacon', while *The Times* thought he had been inspired 'uncommonly near in style and sentiment to Francis Bacon in one or two recent moments'. Such comparison must have been devastating to the older man, for Graham was no less ambitious.

Berthoud writes: 'As a friend, Bacon was now fading from Sutherland's life. Sutherland continued to admire his work, though later he thought it had become a shade too "autobiographical". He came to find Bacon's drinking bouts tiresome, and also Bacon's denigration of those Sutherland admired like Picasso, Braque and Matisse,' for after the early praise Picasso was dismissed by Francis, who compared him to Walt Disney.

Francis told me of the extreme poverty Graham and Kathy suffered when Graham was struggling as an artist and engraver, claiming that Kathy was jealous of women who were smarter and richer than herself. At the same time, with a confidential smile, he added that it was really Graham who had a snobbish liking for grand parties and the perquisites of moving in high society.

Berthoud explains there was another reason for this falling out: 'Bacon was far from enthusiastic about Sutherland's growing friendship with Douglas Cooper, who had turned against him.' Conversely, Graham came to believe that Cooper's seal of approval on his work as the greatest contemporary British artist was vital to his future. In this respect he may well have welcomed Cooper's disassociation from Francis, whom he had known in the days of Roy De Maistre.

Bryan Robertson gives a curious assessment of Francis during this time. 'He was really quite a private person, despite all the conviviality, and tended to put on a gramophone record in the late fifties – set speeches, distancing ploys.' There is truth in this: there was more guile than appeared on the surface. Francis was ambitious. The disconcerting thought occurs that he was kinder to lesser artists like De Maistre who presented no threat, but recognised in Sutherland an adversary who had to be overtaken – even destroyed. After all, in the mid-fifties Sutherland was considered the finest British artist.

As Francis overtook Graham Sutherland as Britain's most highly regarded painter, I too reached a turning point. I joined Associated-Rediffusion in the exciting early days of TV when no boundaries were set and we were able to explore, startled to find that viewers liked documentaries as much as the showbiz fodder which was their main diet. The 'live' interviews for *This Week* were terrifying. I rose to fame when I had to cut off Caitlin

Thomas, who had been force-drunk by Deakin throughout the afternoon in the Caves de France. Afterwards I was soon given series of my own and the managing director asked me to make a programme on a friend of his called Cowan Dobson, a society painter with bow tie and smock who called his wife 'the most painted woman in London'. He was a nice old boy, though odiously self-satisfied because he was a successful artist. That his work was terrible had occurred to no one.

The delightful director I worked with, Rollo Gamble, and I decided to take the curse off Dobson by making a feature on art with Francis Bacon as the antidote. This proved fraught with problems. Francis dismissed the idea, but I persevered until in a moment of weakness he said he might consider it if we paid off his bill at Wheeler's. When Rollo and I went to see Bernard Walsh we were aghast to learn that the bill was close to £1500, while our top fee was £15. Even Rollo's natural exuberance was deflated until Walsh came up with a gleeful solution: 'I'll tell you what,' he said with a grin, 'I'll charge Francis's bill here against tax, as publicity, on one condition – that you do the filming here.' This was what we had hoped to do anyhow, and Rollo agreed enthusiastically. In the face of such joy, Francis had to submit.

We filmed *The Art Game* on the afternoon of 27 August 1958. This was Francis's first appearance on television and, though the historic film was destroyed when Associated-Rediffusion lost their franchise, at least the continuity sheets remain to record the dialogue – though not the laughter, nor the way we seemed to get drunk at astonishing speed. In those days film magazines ran out after four minutes, and during the long delay while they were reloaded Francis and I consumed quantities of oysters and bottles of champagne. When the three hours of filming were edited down to fifteen minutes, the startling effect was an instant transformation, from two sober Jekylls into two alcoholic Hydes.

'Do you paint for money?'

'No, I paint entirely to amuse myself.'

'Then why do you exhibit?'

'Because afterwards I need the money to go on.'

'Do you mean to say that if you had enough money of your own you would not exhibit?'

'No, certainly not. There's no pleasure in exhibiting at all. The only pleasure is to work for yourself and hope that sometime you'll do something that you really want.'

'Wouldn't you mind that your pictures would never be seen by someone else?'

'Not at all, no.'

'Isn't that unusual among artists?'

'I don't know. Most artists are exhibitionists and I may be – but to myself rather than to the public. I would much rather have money and leisure and not have to have exhibitions.'

'But you would continue to paint?'

'Certainly, it's a way of life – to me.'

I suggested that most people feel they are hoaxed when they go to art galleries because the whole thing is so remote from anything that they know.

'Well, most people are hoaxed all their lives, so I don't see why they should go to an exhibition of paintings and expect to have a moment of revelation.'

'Surely that's one of the things that art is supposed to do – to reveal things to people?'

'It might reveal to people *after* they have knowledge, but why would it suddenly to someone who is completely unlearned and knows nothing about it? Why should he expect suddenly to know what is going on? Because, actually, modern art is a very simple thing. It's not more complex than art has been in the past.'

'But surely in the past,' I persisted, 'the ordinary person could recognise the subject and could bring standards by which he could tell whether they were good or bad? But how can he possibly tell what is good or bad among all the stuff that's done today?'

'Well, he couldn't actually tell what was good or bad – superficially, he could tell if the painting was *like* somebody if it was a portrait, or if it was a bowl of fruit or something. On that level he could think about the representation, and now the representation has been cut to a great extent and he does feel himself a bit hoaxed by the whole thing.'

I mentioned the 'action painters' who had dispensed with the brush.

'The means don't matter,' he explained. 'It's only the end that matters. It doesn't really matter if you bicycle all over your picture, or what you do to it.'

102

'And that is not new in painting?'

'Not at all. If you take the late Rembrandt paintings – he was perhaps the greatest, in a sense, action painter. Because if you take the very late Rembrandt self-portraits you'll find, if you look carefully at them, that there's no mouth, there's no nose, there's no eye-socket, but the thing is that he made a very great image. . . . The only difference with action painting is really, unfortunately and unlike the Rembrandts, it's a form of decorative art. He tried to make a head or portrait of somebody, whereas action painters are nearly always trying to make a decorative pattern.

'Is that good?'

'No, that's a very bad thing. But action painting is only a very recent thing and probably a passing thing. The only interesting thing about it is that if you splash a spot of paint down on the canvas, it is more interesting – because it has more vitality – than the inanities of academic art.'

Asked if it was possible for a bad painter to paint a good picture, Francis replied that it was unlikely. 'After all, painting is not cricket. The rules are there to be broken if you can break them to your advantage, and it's quite possible that you will find that the greatest luck goes to the greatest painters because they're the people with the sensibility to make use of the luck which is given them from time to time.'

I referred to his contemptuous way of saying that he simply 'sloshed' the paint onto the canvas, and asked if this was meant as a joke.

'I often say anything, you know, to pass the time.'

'It isn't as simple as that?'

'It isn't simple at all. But sometimes, naturally, every painter hopes that the paints are going to work for him and that he will be given all the things he was trying to do. That one day there'll be a coagulation when everything will come together, and for a moment he will have fulfilled what he wants to do.'

'How many painters alive have done that?'

'I couldn't tell you how many painters have done it, but it happens I suppose in most good artists' lives, or a great artist's life, from time to time, and that is the reason why nine-tenths of even the greatest artist's work is very boring . . . if one could cut out all the boring stuff and just leave the best things, you'd have something that was really very interesting. But of course it's an uneconomical thing because you have to be able to buy the materials and carry on.'

'Is that why you destroy such a lot of your paintings, which I believe you do?'

'Well, certainly, Dan, I destroy nine-tenths of them. Unfortunately I have to let some of them out because I have to live.'

'If you didn't have to exhibit, would you destroy them all?'

'I don't know. From time to time a few things come up that one likes.'

'Do you think that art matters at all?'

'I think art matters a great deal, because all the greatest aspirations of the human race have been left in art. We would know nothing about the civilisations of the past if it had not been for the traces they've left through art.'

I pointed out that he had just contradicted his earlier statement that he would not exhibit if he did not have to make a living.

'I don't think the cavemen were exhibiting anything. I think they were drawing out objects that they liked, either because they wanted to see them again or drew them from the point of view of magic – that if you drew the object it brought it to you.'

'How can the ordinary person judge what is good and bad – can tell if a cave painting is any better or worse than a Rembrandt or a Bernard Buffet?'

'I think it's a very, very difficult thing, because this whole question of what is an ordinary person is difficult. But I suppose that people who have thought about it most of their lives are perhaps more likely to come to a conclusion of what they like, and what's got some value, and what in fact has got some reality about it, than somebody who has never thought about the subject at all.'

'Does it matter that most people don't understand modern art?'

'Certainly there's not very much to understand. Art's no different, it never changes. The only thing is that when there is a strong element of representation, people *think* they understand it. But all through the ages only a few people have really had the abilities or qualities to appreciate art.'

104

Because I was a photographer myself I wanted to raise the whole question of photography as an influence.

'Would you say that photography has driven art in a completely different direction?'

'It's not driven it in a completely different direction, but the representational side of it, to a great extent, has been taken over by photography, and of course the logical conclusion to that is that you go to something like abstract art. But the trouble with abstract art is that it appears that man needs to struggle with the object before he can . . . because great art has always returned people to life more violently. And they appreciate life in a more intense way – abstract art is a form of pattern making.'

'Isn't it also painters painting for other painters, more than ever before?'

'No, I don't think so. Because, after all, what are most painters interested in? In life. All artists are lovers, they're lovers of life, they want to see how they can set the trap so that life will come over more vividly and more violently. And how do they do that? Let us reason, why would one paint for oneself? Not to say how clever I am, but how can I trap this transient thing.'

'Is it necessary to be able to draw a perfect likeness of someone, to be able to paint a great picture?'

'Well, that's a very interesting thing. Because perhaps two of the very finest artists of our time – Picasso and Soutine – are two diametrically opposed types. Picasso is a man with enormous gifts who can do almost anything he wants. Soutine was a man with an enormous love of painting, who never drew, who painted his pictures directly and had deliberately never developed his technique. And he didn't develop his technique because he thought he would keep the thing cleaner and rawer by that method.'

This could have applied to Francis as well as to Soutine, and it is significant that Francis echoed Soutine's *Side of Beef* (1925) in his own *Painting* (1946) and *Figure with Meat* (1954). Asked again whether it was necessary to do a good likeness, Francis recoiled. 'There's no necessity at all to be able to do that, because, after all, you might well use a camera that gets the better likeness . . . actually when artists paint a portrait they're generally painting something which is very much more revealing of themselves than the sitter . . . I don't think it matters that a portrait should be

105

almost unrecognisable, but when you go to the great portraits of the past how are you ever to know that they looked vaguely like the people? How are we ever to know whether the pharaohs looked like that? In fact I believe it was quite a well-known thing at the time of the great Egyptian art that when one of the kings died, they took out his name and put the name of the next one on to the same portrait.'

'Do you think there's any point in talking about art at all?'

'It's always a fascinating subject because people reveal themselves talking about art – not about art, but about their attitude to life. And you know, it's almost an impossible thing to talk about . . . because I think Pavlova was right when somebody asked her what she meant when she was dancing *The Dying Swan* and she said: "Well, if I could tell you, I wouldn't dance it." '

'If you could tell all about art, would you paint?'

'Certainly not, because it's something that lies long and far below what is called coherence and consciousness, and one hopes the greatest art is a kind of valve in which very many hidden things of human feeling and destiny are trapped – something that can't be definitely and directly said.'

'Your art is often referred to as being sensational. Can you explain that?'

'What do you mean by the word "sensational"?'

'They're shocked by it. They find it evil, horrifying, un-pleasant. . . .'

'I think it is that sometimes I have used subject matter which people think is sensational because one of the things I have wanted to do was to record the human cry, and that in itself is something sensational. And if I could really do it – and it's one of the most difficult things to do in art, and I wouldn't say that I've ever been able to do it, or perhaps anybody has yet been able to do it – it would be of course sensational.'

'When you say "the human cry", what do you mean?'

'The whole coagulation of pain, despair. . . .'

'What about the reverse side of life, Francis – happiness and love? Why paint only despair and pain?'

'*Well*. Happiness and love is a wonderful thing to paint also – I always hope I will be able to do that too. After all, it's only the reverse side of the shadow, isn't it?'

'Does it matter that a lot of people are not able to understand your paintings?'

'Well, I don't think you can be interested in whether people understand your paintings or not. It's only due to your own nervous system that you can paint at all. And you know – this is perhaps an aside, but there was a very interesting thing that Valéry said about modern art, and it's very true. He said that modern artists want the grin without the cat, and by that he meant that they want the sensation of life without the boredom of conveyance. One of the things that is very interesting is that in the last fifty years people – all the movements – have been abstract . . . so the thing is, how can I draw one more veil away from life and present what is called the living sensation more nearly on the nervous system and more violently?'

By this time we were merry and Francis made his point about the veils with great emphasis and gesture. Joining in, I suggested: 'And you're the Salome of the modern art world, taking off the veils?'

With a huge, expanding smile, he replied: 'I am sad to say I would hardly say that. But of course it would be a very nice thing to be.'

'Have another glass of champagne.' This was a rare opportunity to play the host.

'Thank you very much, Dan.'

When *The Art Game* was transmitted, Cowan Dobson complained to the managing director that we had insulted him by including him in such despicable company. Plainly Mr Dobson expected the entire programme to be devoted to his art, and was told that this would be the case. The controller of programmes sent Rollo and myself a pained note of rebuke.

# 8

# The Gilded Gutter Life

*'Seduire c'est tout!'*

*Francis Bacon to the author*

Monte Carlo with its lush life and casino was where Francis had been on gambling trips paid for by Eric Hall. In the fifties, when the friendship was going well, the Sutherlands witnessed a historic win, though the amount seems negligible now – £1,600. It was so considerable at the time that they urged him to return to England or entrust the money to someone to take it back for him: 'You've made enough never to worry again.' But that is not the way of the gambler. Instead, he invited them to the Hotel de Paris for one of the most memorable dinners of their lives, taking the precaution of renting a villa for the rest of the year with a large deposit at a nearby delicatessen. Then he went back to the casino and lost the rest.

Bryan Robertson met Francis in 1951 when he was looking for somewhere to stay with friends on holiday: 'Francis told me how to rent his favourite villa on the heights above Monaco, which he had taken for many winters as a place for himself and his old Nan. Francis painted all day, gambled all night, and the nurse knitted in the sun. Francis's kindness touched me, and the villa turned out to be delightful, secluded and spacious. It was amusing to find that the furnishings included the most comprehensive library of literature on sexual perversions imaginable, which added a certain zing to hot afternoon siestas, as well as a cupboard off my own bedroom filled with intensely alarming images on canvas left by Francis in various stages of abandonment.' Francis could be careless in this way.

Similarly failing to learn from experience, Francis frequently left behind canvases which were sold by those who came after him. In the sixties, the playwright Frank Norman witnessed a scene in

Bond Street when Francis passed a gallery and spotted a picture of his which he had discarded in Tangier. Going inside, he asked how much it cost and was told £50,000. Writing out a cheque without a moment's pause, he carried the picture outside where he stamped it to death on the pavement.

By then he could afford to do so. When he went on one of his visits to the casino in the early fifties with Muriel Belcher and Ian Board he needed to win. Ian was driven to Monte Carlo by a delightfully aristocratic lesbian, with a sugar daddy apparently waiting for him at the other end. The car broke down and the journey took ten days, by which time 'daddy' had departed, as daddies do. 'I took a taxi,' recalled Ian, 'and joined Francis at the Hotel Victoria in Nice, I think it was – he preferred ordinary little places. To start with everything went wrong. Francis loathed the sun, and all of us lost everything we had at the casino – *everything*!

'We were so broke we had nothing to eat. That American lover [Norman Fowler] of . . . who was it? [Peter Watson, a wealthy American who subsidised *Horizon* and helped Francis financially] was staying there too, in another little hotel. He lived on baked beans but was stinking rich, so someone suggested a little burglary while he was out. Francis shinned up the drainpipe – he had tremendous strength and vitality. He copped £300, worth a lot in those days, and went straight back to the casino while we sat in the bar drinking champagne. Francis had a real winning streak, going from one table to another, which was the way he liked to play.

' "She's got her roller skates on," said Muriel. When he came back she said, "Your hair has gone a funny colour – it must be the sun."

'He looked in one of the casino's mirrors and cried: "Oh, my God, it's gone honey-coloured! What if I can't find a chemist's for some dye?"

'The next evening his hair looked as usual. But then obviously he was having another fucking good win and it was hot and he was sweating, rubbing his face to wipe it away.

' "Look at yourself in the mirror, gal," said Muriel.

' "Oh, my God!" he cried again.

'He was almost in black-face,' Ian explained. 'He hadn't been able to find the dye so he used his usual boot polish instead, which had melted.

109

'Anyhow, Francis won so much that the first thing he did was climb up the drainpipe again and put the money back. We had enough left to settle our hotel bills and paid up everybody.

'Morally,' Ian declared, 'we were absolutely *marvellous*!'

But what if Francis had lost?

Michael Wishart remembers when they played the casino together at Nice in 1952, for there were three at Nice compared to the one at Monte Carlo. Everything was fine until Francis received a telegram or phone call telling him that Nan was dead.

'Francis looked as if he wanted to die,' said Michael. 'He adored her instead of his parents, and treated her with extreme tenderness. Anne and I took the same train back to England without realising that Francis was on it too, and we got out at Lyons to find him on the platform in a terrible state. More than you'd expect . . . I did wonder,' Michael confided, 'if Nan was his mother.'

During the first half of the fifties Francis was nomadic, without a home of his own, reflecting his restlessness as a painter trying to establish himself. These days of drifting ended in 1955 with his move to Battersea, instigated by Alfred Hecht, the picture framer who by now was becoming as famous as the artists whose work he framed. Though particularly fond of the Sutherlands, Hecht was one of the first to recognise Francis's genius. Always a helpful go-between, he asked Peter Pollock and Paul Danquah if they would consider having a friend as a lodger – 'His name is Francis Bacon.' Francis stayed at 9 Overstrand Mansions in Prince of Wales Drive, Battersea, for the next six years – a tribute to the patience of Peter and Paul and their lively companionship. They provided sympathy without friction and proved immensely tolerant, becoming two of his closest friends.

'Alfred thought he was doing a young painter a favour,' said Peter Pollock in 1991.

'I can't imagine why,' added Paul, 'but for some reason Francis had nowhere else to go.'

'That's simple!' Peter gave a sardonic laugh. 'He had no money!'

'You must remember,' Paul explained, 'that throughout this time Peter was paying the rent.' This meant that Peter Pollock paid for them all, though I suspect that Francis's innate generosity and the meals at Wheeler's surpassed the normal contribution from a conventional lodger.

110

Because of their closeness to Francis, Peter and Paul became friends of mine in the fifties. They were and still are a striking couple.

Peter's family were part owners of the steel firm Accles and Pollock, and he was able to afford a farm in the country as well as the flat in Battersea. His looks were romantically English – deceptively boyish and blond in the Rupert Brooke tradition. He had been interned as a prisoner of war, which seemed to have left him in a state of shock, explaining his reticence. He was shy by comparison with Paul, and suffered the annoyance of being fancied by men in whom he had no physical interest – including Guy Burgess, who at least became a friend. When Burgess defected, Scotland Yard descended on the farmhouse and subjected Peter to interrogation while the farm was searched for clues, which proved unforthcoming.

He retained an aloofness that I admired, especially as it was redeemed by a sardonic brand of humour. Paul was black, although his mother was white; she was separated from her husband, a West African politician. Always good company, good-humoured and deservedly popular, Paul possessed an exuberance that complemented Peter's reserve. With a relish for camp, Paul offered tips on the latest male fashions and make-up and briefly attended ballet classes. He attempted to unravel the intricacies of English etiquette such as 'M.I.F.' – milk in first when pouring tea, which was rejected by cries of 'No!' from Francis and Peter – and 'M.I.L', or milk in last. These social points interested him more than the points of law which he studied at the Bar.

It is not surprising that Francis became devoted to these two, and he could hardly have found a more suitable place to live. Paul enhanced every occasion with his instinctive sense of fun, so it did not seem illogical when Tony Richardson asked him to play the part of the butch merchant seaman in his film of Shelagh Delaney's *A Taste of Honey*. To become a film star was the height of Paul's daydreams, and he played the part charmingly. It was the beginning and end of his film career, though forty years later, his letter-head bears the inscription: 'PAUL DANQUAH: BARRISTER, ACTOR, WORLD BANK CONSULTANT'. When I asked him of his strongest memories of the time that Francis stayed with them, Paul remembered the morning when he received a letter from

Tony Richardson telling him that his voice had been dubbed throughout because his north country accent was wrong. 'I was really upset – it was the worst moment of my life, and Francis was really kind, really marvellous. He told me, "Don't be a cunt, dear." '

Whenever the English describe a block of flats as 'Mansions', I fear something dank; Prince of Wales Drive was an unsmiling row of Edwardian buildings, fronted by a dismal park and hedged by laurel. But the three occupants were evidently so high-spirited that it hardly mattered. Peter told me how before Francis set off for Soho, he and Paul would spend the morning 'chatting', relishing the exchange of the latest gossip: 'Paul knew him better than anyone.'

Paul experienced Francis's need to be accompanied by a friend when he was invited to some occasion: 'I was a bit of a snob and Francis always took me along. Towards the end of his time with us, the whole world began to realise his importance.' Francis was being lionised, taken up by Sonia Orwell and Anne Fleming. Anne, formerly Lady Rothermere and now married to Ian Fleming, the creator of James Bond, was famous for her dinner parties. 'I'd tell him to go, little snob that I was,' said Paul, 'and he'd say: "I don't really want to." He had a real contempt for things you and I might enjoy, like social things. But if he did go, he'd ask me to go with him, almost as if, he were shy.'

Francis, Deakin and myself all hated the formality of dinners and small talk. On the rare occasions when we accepted, the hostess had cause for regret. Restaurants were another matter, regarded as treats. Peter Pollock remembered that the happiest times with Francis were the evenings at Wheeler's – 'Just the three of us, long dinners with Francis talking endlessly. Half the meals were put down on the slate. One of the other happy moments was when I got him out of Savile Row police station. He must have been held for drunkenness and probably they asked him where he lived, wanting to get rid of him. We were young enough not to mind being woken by calls at three o'clock in the morning. It is just a lovely memory – I scooped him up and took him back to Battersea by taxi.'

Paul recalled one of the worst moments. 'It's my most horrific memory of Francis. Once at Wheeler's – and I should have known

112

better – I was showing off and Francis took my drink and poured it over me, and I was mortified because it was so deserved.' Though Francis had accused me of pouring a glass of beer over him in the Gargoyle, he seems to have poured numerous glasses himself.

'Did his homosexuality make a crucial difference to his life?' I wondered.

'If he'd been straight he would not have been so daring.' Francis indulged in rampant promiscuity. According to Paul, 'Francis had a regular lover, very much into whiplashing, who later married a top model of the sixties. Of course there was Peter [Peter Lacy, the former Battle of Britain pilot who was with Francis that first night in the Gargoyle]. Then there was Ron – very good-looking.'

I remembered Ron. I met him in Soho and we spent the night together. My memory is hardly photographic from this distance, but he certainly was 'good-looking' in a dark, aggressive way, and well-built though not tall. He was an exceptionally active man, not at all 'gay' in any conventional sense, except that I assume he was bisexual. He was everything I liked. It was taken for granted that we should stay together, though nothing was discussed. It might appear unseemly to make such confessions, but as I am being candid about Francis it is only decent that I should be equally candid about myself.

Francis liked him too – few people are so attractive as the lovers of your friends. I was foolish enough to confide to Francis that I had 'fallen in love'. There were no warning signals, and one evening after the pubs had closed the three of us ended up together at a boring café near the corner of Dean Street and Shaftesbury Avenue. The food was filthy and so was Francis's temper. At first I assumed that the one was the cause of the other, but suddenly he started to attack me verbally with bewildering venom. Then he railed against my father and his 'second-rate books'. I made the mistake of laughing, pointing out that Francis had never read one. 'I don't have to. I *know* they're second-rate.'

It did not occur to me that this was a sort of courtship of the young man he was determined to steal. In retrospect I am sure that Ron was aware of it, but I was lulled by happiness. When the three of us left, Francis walked across to the other side of Shaftesbury Avenue while we waited for a taxi, and waited. All the time Francis stood there looking straight at Ron as if he were trying to mesmerise him away, and at last the penny dropped. Masochistic-ally, hoping he might say no, I told Ron that if he wanted to go with Francis that would be all right with me. And he went. That was the last I saw of him. I could have held him, but I knew I had lost the game. I was not really in a position to look after him or supply him with unlimited money as Francis was.

And I was no match for Francis's decisiveness. He never spoke to me of Ron, and I doubt if he had a twinge of guilt as far as I was concerned – nor should he have done. But when I learned that Ron had been involved in a robbery in the Kings Road, and the police had been called in, causing Francis considerable embarrass-ment, I was delighted.

'Wasn't there some trouble?' I asked Paul Danquah.

'He stole some pictures. Don't forget Ron was a sort of petty crook – Francis rather liked that sort of thing, and the Kray Twin lot.'

Most of us had known the Krays.

Francis told me of the conversation he had with one of Ronnie Kray's boyfriends, for Ronnie did not conceal his preference for boys – 'Little angel faces, less evil-minded than girls.'

The boy explained why the Krays were so beloved in the East End: 'They're good to their muvver.'

'Yaas?'

'At Christmas they send more than three hundred cards to their mates inside.'

'Do they really?'

'And when a member of the Firm is nicked, the Colonel sees they get flowers sent to their wives . . .'

The catalogue of virtues continued until Francis could stand it no longer.

'Fair touches the heart!' he interrupted.

'Oh, it does, doesn't it!' agreed the wide-eyed boy.

After Francis's death I wrote to Ronnie Kray, who was kind enough to reply from Broadmoor Hospital on 12 May 1992. The letter had been opened, under the Mental Health Act 1983.

Dear Daniel, Thank you for your letter, I hope you are well. Yes Daniel they where good times in the East End in the few year past, Daniel, Frances Bacon was good Freind of mine it was my privilege to be his Freind, and I am proud that he had me as on of his Freinds.

114

It was Stanley Baker that inturded me to Frances. I always found Frances a kind and nice man. I only know good about Frances there is not much more I can say about my Freindship with him. I hope that your Book goes well and I wish you all the Happyness for the future. May God Bless You, from your Freind Ronald Kray

I heard, also, from his twin brother Reggie, currently in HM Prison at Colchester: 'I never met Francis Bacon . . . [unintelligible] Have you read my Books', ending with 'God Bless, Reg Kray'.

But back to Paul Danquah, who continued: 'When you come to think of it, three of Francis's most important boyfriends came out of the East End. He seemed to like people who were bad news. Excessive manhood. Not sailors – though he had a deep-sea diver once. Masculine in suits, that's what he liked. Also, Ron was very big in that particular department and Francis liked that.' Curiously, I had forgotten that.

Another sidelight on Francis's sexuality comes from Keith Vaughan's journals, from an entry dated 22 January 1955:

Interesting account this morning from Dennis Williams of the time he lived and worked in a small room adjoining Francis Bacon's studio; idolising Francis at the time, longing to be of service to him and ending by becoming so wholly enslaved to his personality that he was incapable of any independent action.

'There was nothing I could do. He would lie in bed in the morning, purple in the face, looking ill – terrible – unable to move until he had taken enough pills, but talking all the time about the paintings he had dreamed of. If I offered him a cup of tea he wouldn't drink it. He just didn't see me. I could have been anyone else and he wouldn't have noticed. I was in his studio one day and he came in with a suit which had just come from the cleaners. He laid it down on a large table in the middle of the room which was thick with paint, cotton wool, bits of dirty paper. As the suit had just come from the cleaners I picked it up and put it on a hanger and hung it out of the way by the wall. My only reason for doing this was that I thought it would be helpful – a small thing – but something he was incapable of doing himself. Directly he came back into the room, without saying a word, he went over to the wall, took the suit down and laid it again on the paint on the table. I felt absolutely shattered, as though my personality had been wiped out.'

115

One can sympathise with Mr Williams and his good intentions, yet understand how he grated on Francis's nerves. I can hear his impatience: 'Oh, her, the arch-depressor.'

Keith Vaughan took the incident to heart, suffering vicariously with Mr W. in his rejection:

It was moving to see how affected D was by the recollection of this incident. I felt how easily I could occupy the same role to him. His impressive dignity [Vaughan was referring to Bacon], his ardour and natural grace, his extraordinary physical beauty – supple – gentle – sensuous. 'He sees people as mountains of flesh,' complained the devoted Dennis. 'He is obsessed by this extraordinary capacity for flesh to breathe, walk, talk.'

It did not occur to Vaughan that the last thing a masochist wants is another masochist hanging around him.

Though Francis was a masochist physically, he was sadistic mentally and had no time for the weak. Neither was he enamoured of Johnny Minton's sailors. 'All they want in the morning,' he told Frank Norman, 'is love and eggs and bacon for breakfast, and I don't eat breakfast, nor do I have bacon and eggs.' He told this to Frank, when he was attempting to write about him but abandoned the contest after trailing Francis around the pubs and clubs of Soho. Frank wrote to me afterwards:

I felt like a spy. He spoke marvellously about Berlin in the 1920s but things deteriorated and I was reduced to keeping my ears open, nipping into the lavatory to scribble notes on bits of toilet paper! In the morning I'd find all these screwed-up pieces in my pocket scrawled in a barely legible hand with such choice remarks as: 'I have never had any love in the whole of my life – and what's more I don't want any. All I do is cast my rod into the sewers of despair and see what I come up with this time.'

An episode followed which is so little known that even Peter Pollock and Paul Danquah were unaware of it: Bacon's arrival at St Ives in Cornwall with Ron.

The concept of Francis in such an 'artists' colony', smacking of smocks and dirndls, is so incongruous that people laugh when I tell them that Francis stayed there, unless they have been there themselves. Too easily derided, St Ives has attracted more distinguished artists than any other provincial centre. I discovered

116

why as soon as I arrived there myself in the early spring of 1992 – it's the light. The sea is translucent and the white surf sweeps into the town, which is bordered by five white sandy beaches and remains unmarred by the usual concrete ugliness of today. The effect is luminous, reminiscent of northern France.

Continuing to Zennor, with its famous mermaid carved on a church pew, I met Patrick Heron, by now in his early seventies. His house, aptly named the Eagle's Nest, overlooks a pattern of Bronze Age fields; beyond is the sea, and below the house is the cottage where D. H. Lawrence stayed with his wife Frieda during the First World War.

Heron told me of his amazement when he saw Francis walking along a street in St Ives in 1958.

'Good God! Francis!' he exclaimed. 'What on earth are you doing here?'

'We've just come from Penzance, which we simply *loathed*, so we thought we'd come here.'

Heron told me that Francis nodded towards a tall chap (obviously my memory is faulty) whom he knew later as Ron.

'To stay *here*?' he asked Francis, incredulously.

'Well, you see, I had to get away.' (Away from me – or do I flatter myself? Probably.)

Heron told me with some acerbity: 'He certainly didn't come here to hob-nob with *us*. In fact he told me: "I had no idea *you* were all here, *dear*!" He stayed for seven months and the light improved his colours, even though he complained about those "terrible abstract artists living next door" – which was mainly directed at myself. You know . . .' Heron paused, trying to be as fair as possible, 'his colours have never been better. He never used such large areas of green and purple.' Heron also took pleasure in quoting Roger Hilton's damning verdict that 'Bacon needs a good lesson in painting.' He added, quietly, 'I rather agree.'

Perhaps sensing the antagonism, Francis once turned on Heron in an art gallery in London where he was with the painter Louis le Brocqy. 'Look!' he exclaimed in a shrill voice. 'Here comes the Prince of Colours, and he absolutely *loathes* me!' In this characteristic way, he reversed a compliment to Heron while making himself out to be the injured party. Yet they had been close enough in St Ives for Heron to invite Francis and Ron to Christmas lunch at the Eagle's Nest, which Francis nearly set fire to when he poured most of a bottle of vintage brandy over the Christmas pudding and then set it alight.

Giles Auty, later the *Spectator*'s art critic, was visiting St Ives then and recalled that time. 'Ron, believed to come from Battersea, was dark-haired, fresh-faced, blue-eyed (I think) and expensively dressed (by Francis). He became a particular buddy of Françoise Spencer-Chapman. On the occasion when I had a long afternoon talk with Francis, mostly about Bonnard, and drinking whisky sent by the Marlborough for Christmas, the discussion was interrupted by the return of Ron, who fingered his belt and enquired: "Are you ready for a thrashin' yet, Francis?" I made polite excuses to leave.'

Francis never referred to their time in St Ives, though he did tell me that Ron had become friendly with April Ashley in Jersey and wanted him to have a sex change too. 'It was quite an interesting idea,' Francis said, 'but can you imagine the tedium of being a woman?' He paused and gave a savage tug at his collar: 'Or an *old* woman – think of the horror of *that*!' He burst out laughing.

Though it goes against the grain to admit it, Ron was good for Francis at the time. Anyone who encourages an artist to work and is not a hindrance deserves credit, and such people are surprisingly few. 'A very nice boy,' said Peter Pollock. 'He really adored Francis and they stayed friends afterwards after living together for two years.' It gave Francis the chance to prepare for his first exhibition at the Marlborough Gallery.

As I say, I never heard Francis's version of the St Ives trip, but I do know he professed to loathe the countryside. When an accountant suggested he should become a tax exile in Switzerland, he said: 'All those fucking views.' Nevertheless, there were a few occasions when I had a chance to observe him outside his natural Soho habitats. Our weekend in Devon took place on a Spring Bank Holiday when the weather was glowing. With my parents safely out of the way in Portugal, I invited several people to stay at their house at Putsborough Sands which overlooked the Atlantic and Lundy Island on the horizon. Francis was driven down with a crate of champagne in the sports car of a mutual friend, Michael May, a dashing young milord whose fortune came from the match manufacturers Bryant and May. Deakin came with Tony

Hubbard, the Woolworth heir, and his new girlfriend. John and Wendy Knight, whom I persuaded to buy the *Study for a Pope 1955*, drove down on their own, while I took the train from Waterloo accompanied by a cheerful guardsman called Rumble, who suited such a Dickensian name as much as did Sam Weller.

The Grey House, built from local stone, was too small for so many guests. Francis had my father's bedroom, Deakin my mother's, and Lord May went in the spare room. The Knights stayed in the primitive hotel at the top of the hill, while Tony Hubbard booked into the grander Saunton Sands Hotel a few miles away, with his girlfriend pencilled in as his wife. I stayed with Rumble in the annexe next to our empty garage.

The guests were a mixed bag and promised to complement each other. Hubbard was referred to by Deakin as the 'poor little rich boy'. He was devoted to Deakin, who was one of the few people who dared to tease him – for Hubbard's temper and generosity were variable. In fact this spring weekend was so consistently perfect that Hubbard, who was a keen aviator, hired a small plane from the nearby aerodrome at Chivenor, enthralling Rumble as they zoomed across the estuary of the Taw and Torridge rivers which joined at Appledore, pouring majestically into the Atlantic Ocean.

Inevitably, it was drink which turned it into a lost weekend.

Lord May, who cut a romantic figure, fell headlong for Hubbard's girlfriend with a passion that she reciprocated, doubtless with daydreams of becoming 'her Ladyship'. Cross-eyed with frustration, they whispered plans for their future. Their immediate dilemma was resolved when she caught Deakin trying to put his aubergine tongue down Hubbard's throat as he embraced the barely conscious millionaire in the dining room. She saw this as her excuse to leave, protesting that if her fiancé preferred Deakin she would break off the engagement. This had the beginnings of a French farce. But Hubbard, who had no such interest in Deakin, was furious at this interpretation, however absurd, turning on Deakin, as so many had before, crying: 'It's all *your* fault!'

While Deakin wandered around with a glass in his hand, blissful to be the centre of such commotion, Lord May seized his chance and the girl after shaking me emotionally by the hand, his eyes brimming with remorse as he confessed: 'This is by far the worst thing that I have ever done, but I am not strong enough to help myself. . . .' And they drove off into the night. When the girl arrived at the Saunton Sands Hotel to collect her luggage, the manager refused to give her the room key because she had arrived with her husband and was now departing with another man. And after she protested that Hubbard was not her husband he became adamant – this was not the sort of behaviour tolerated in North Devon in the fifties. He relented the moment he realised that her new companion was a lord of the realm, and handed over the key obsequiously.

The girl's departure confirmed her in Hubbard's eyes as the only woman he wanted to marry. When I returned to the drawing room it was empty, until Francis made a dramatic appearance from the garden. 'I'm afraid something *really* terrible is about to happen,' he announced. 'Tony's gone completely off his fucking nut and is going to throw himself off the cliff.'

I laughed. 'Oh, that's all right. They're only sand-dunes. If he does throw himself off, he'll just fall a few feet and have a nice, sandy landing at the bottom.'

The next morning the Knights returned to London, giving Rumble a lift, while Francis, Deakin and I did our best to console the grief-stricken Tony Hubbard as he wandered around in love-torn agony. The usual reassurances – 'If she went off like that, it shows she didn't think much of you. You're better off without' – did not help at all.

'It's all your fault,' he repeated to Deakin, who assumed an air of injured innocence. Because he regarded Tony Hubbard as a useful 'meal ticket' he tried to cheer him up by suggesting that we went into Barnstaple to visit the pubs. Francis took an inordinate time to get himself ready, the reason becoming apparent when he emerged at last from my father's bedroom.

'Good God!' Deakin exclaimed. 'You didn't need to go to all that trouble making yourself up just for *us*. I doubt if the Devonians will notice your *maquillage*.'

But they did, with many a stare and scowl in the Three Tuns. In the evening we were invited to drinks at Vention Cottage by one of our neighbours. William Henderson, known as Billy, was a gentleman-artist who painted flower-pieces framed at great expense by Alfred Hecht – so at least Francis and he had something in common. I thought he would be honoured to meet Francis, but he retained the erect formality of a former ADC to Wavell when he was Viceroy of India and was unimpressed. Little escaped him, certainly not Francis's *maquillage*, and on my parents' return he told them treacherously how astounded he had been by Bacon's appearance: 'After the violence of his work, I did not expect someone so effeminate.' I cringed when my parents told me this, for though Henderson's homosexuality and that of his manservant were an open secret, mine was still tightly closed from them.

The next afternoon, in a fit of boredom, Francis took my box of paints and a tiny canvas onto the slope outside the Grey House and made a few strokes while I watched with delight from a discreet distance until he tired of this effort and threw the thing away. Deakin persuaded Hubbard to drive us back to Barnstaple, where we sat despondently in a pub. Hubbard told us how good he had been to the girl – 'Why, only last week I gave her several yards of expensive material for a dress, and do you know she didn't even say thank you?' There was silence while we absorbed this ingratitude, broken by Deakin who exclaimed sympathetically: 'She really was La Belle Dame sans Merci, wasn't she?' At this, Francis and I laughed so much that Tony flounced back to Saunton Sands where they refused to let him into his room, accusing him of immoral behaviour. He drove straight back to London. Francis, Deakin and myself took the London train the next morning, thankful to return to the sanity of Soho after the rigours of the country.

As for the 'girl', whose name is long since forgotten, she exchanged the beckoning millions for the sake of a title, but in the end she lost them both.

Following his success with *Lucky Jim* the author Kingsley Amis was the subject of an article of mine, published in May 1956 under the title 'Look! There Are Llamas on the Mountain' after I had interviewed him at his home in Swansea. When they saw the page proofs, the libel lawyers were so alarmed by our drinking that they insisted Amis initial the pages before they were passed. Highly amused, the jovial Amis, as he was then, suggested we meet halfway in Cardiff where there was a superb French restaurant in the docks at Tiger Bay. I was surprised the night before when Lucian and Francis announced they would like to go with me. Lucian changed his mind, but Francis was waiting at Paddington Station. I doubt if he had read *Lucky Jim*. I am not sure he knew who Kingsley Amis was, apart from a currently fashionable name, but in this I might be naive.

I was unprepared for the wooden hotel on the edge of Tiger Bay. Once notorious for its fist-fights, it was now a quieter place of exotic beauty with the peeling façades of former dignity and low-lying streets named after women: Sophia, Maria and Alice. The dock quarter was full of different nationalities with their respective religions – Muslims, West Indians, Somalis and Arabs in colourful costumes, even a Spanish population in an area known as Little Madrid. Few names could have been so inappropriate as the Windsor Hotel, with a few well-scrubbed bedrooms where sea captains stayed, and a rough bar known as the Snake Pit through which we reached the restaurant where Amis sat smiling behind a red-and-white checked tablecloth.

Amicably, if not excitedly, we talked the afternoon away. The dining room emptied, and the ancient regulars who fell about from 'scrumpy' were expelled from the Snake Pit. We were the only customers left, allowed to linger with our bottles of wine in opposition to the English law; the bill was left on our table with the trust that we would pay it. Cooked by a French family, this was the best French food that I have eaten in Britain, and I returned several times in the next few years.

Sated, we emerged in the glow of the late afternoon and leaned on a parapet which overlooked the cracked mud of low tide. I went off with my camera, photographing the row-boats tilted on their sides which proved to be filled with weeds. On my return Amis produced a 'girlie' magazine he had bought at Swansea station, and to my consternation Francis matched this with a physique magazine of body-builders. It had proved an amusing day, though I was alarmed by the size of the bill which covered a third person identified as 'Mrs Amis'. Luckily the editor of the *Standard*, Charles Wintour, knew of Amis's taste for good wine and signed the feature which Amis had initialled.

There is a curious footnote to this innocuous episode. At the end of February 1991, I received a phone call from Adam Edwards for whom I worked as the arts correspondent for the *Mail on Sunday*: 'Did you know there's a chapter attacking you in the Kingsley Amis autobiography? Would you like to reply?' I would, I said. This gave me the chance to put the record straight, for in spite of his claim that the *Memoirs* depended 'on good memory', Amis remembered the incident differently: 'Farson then said he thought Swansea was rather a long way to come (to see an unknown youngish shag teaching at a Welsh college). What about Cardiff? Any tolerable restaurants there? I thought then and still think this suggestion of venue a bit off. . . .' *Venue? Youngish shag*? What an odd phrase to use about himself; no wonder he protected it in brackets.

Apart from making me sound intolerably pompous, it implied that I had never gone to Swansea in the first place. I still possess the photographs I took in the morning after spending the night between flannel sheets in the Amis nursery: pictures of Kingsley, his wife 'Hilly' and eight-year-old Martin.

The chapter was headed 'Francis Bacon', which enabled Amis to cash in on the name while writing about him with contempt.

> When Farson arrived he was dressed, I thought, more appropriately for some hiking or rock-climbing expedition than lunch in a provincial town, and he had someone else with him as informally dressed, smallish, middle forties, nondescript.
>
> 'Do you know Francis Bacon?' asked Farson.
>
> Well, I had come across that name in the papers as that of a man just beginning to make a reputation with paintings of cardinals, or perhaps popes, screaming inside transparent boxes. 'I've heard of him,' I said.
>
> 'I thought you wouldn't mind if I brought him along,' said Farson. 'Not a bit,' I said, reasoning that, though this was not as far as I knew a Welsh name, he might perfectly well have had an auntie in the area, or some similar reason for making the (in those days) three-hour journey down from Paddington.

Sir Kingsley, as he had become, added that Francis said 'almost nothing . . . though he looked at me a fair amount. Perhaps sizing me up for a drawing of me screaming inside a transparent box to accompany Farson's article.' Though highly flattering, the idea that Francis Bacon might illustrate something of mine was hilarious. Amis revealed his real suspicion a few paragraphs later when he disclosed that I disappeared dramatically over the mudflats of Tiger Bay for my own purposes, 'whatever they may have been' – a strangely sinister comment.

On their own, Bacon

reached inside his jacket or blouse and brought out some sort of magazine which he handed me.

'Are you interested in this sort of thing?' he asked.

It was a not very expensively produced piece of homosexual soft porn, featuring black-and-white photographs of young men in inviting or provocative poses, done in quite a refined way except for the taste in clothes shown, with nothing vital exposed or even prominent in close outline. Although needless to say unprepared for this turn of events, I was able to work out what would be the best time to spend on this vile object, not so short as to imply disgust, since I had no wish to offend or provoke Bacon, and certainly not so long as to imply any sort of affirmative to his question. After perhaps eight seconds, then, I gave him the magazine back.

'No,' I said.

As far as I remember he said nothing to that, just nodded philosophically. Perhaps unseen by me, he sent some signal to Farson, who at almost that very moment turned about and began making his way back to us.

The inference is clear – that Francis accompanied me in case he fancied Amis, and 'made a pass' (as one critic concluded) while I made myself scarce. Plainly, with our prearranged 'signal', my role was that of a pimp. In this way Amis distorted the incident into something faintly squalid, deliberately using such words as 'blouse', 'homosexual soft porn' and 'vile'.

Unaware that the *Memoirs* were being serialised, I was disconcerted to open the *Sunday Times* on 10 March 1991 and see the headline on the front of the Review section, 'Amis on SEX', with a picture of Francis and the caption: 'An odd proposition in Cardiff docks'. On the Monday morning Francis rang me in the best of spirits to say he had gone to his chemist, which was run by Arabs – 'They're all run by Arabs round here nowadays' – who showed him the paper.

'Were they impressed?'

'I think so.'

'Good for credit, as Muriel might have said.'

'Oh yes!' Much laughter. 'You know, I've never read anything Amis has written. Is he any good?'

I replied that I thought his reputation inflated though his books made excellent television, and recommended *Money* by Martin Amis, which he had not heard of. Returning to Sir Kingsley, he asked in his sly voice: 'Did he have any looks to speak of in those days?'

'Not for you, he didn't.'

'That's what I thought. It's all so ridiculous, such a pack of lies. Perhaps he thinks it's going to help to sell his book?'

'Exactly.'

By chance Lucian telephoned me and mentioned the *Memoirs* too. 'Amis is playing about with his assumed philistinism – even his homophobia is phoney. You know that it is said that Francis tried to grope Melvyn Bragg under the table when they did that interview? Well, Francis never, *never* did that to anyone. Nor would he have thought of making a pass at Kingsley Amis. It's so silly.'

As for my unaccustomed role as pimp, I was thrilled to be libelled in such company.

# 9

# Bacon and the Age of Violence

The truth comes in a strange door.

*Francis Bacon to David Sylvester*

Few painters have been so unwilling to discuss the 'meaning' of their work. I can hear Francis's voice ringing with scepticism at some, for example, Freudian explanation: 'Is that what they say? How very interesting. I wish I'd thought of it myself.' However, he did show some signs of interest in many of the areas of ideas with which his work has been associated, and his complete and utter denial of any connection at all undoubtedly held an element of teasing.

The cinematic and theatrical nature of his art is undeniable. He was so enthusiastic one lunchtime about Roger Vadim's *Les Liaisons Dangereuses* that Deakin and I went the same afternoon and were surprised to see Francis a couple of rows in front, having returned a second time. We were shocked by the indifference of the London critics and composed a telegram to Vadim of congratulations, but did not know where to send it. Otherwise, Francis told me to read and see Genet, and Tod Browning's film, *The Freaks* and spoke of Andy Warhol's films with interest, though he could not be bothered to waste time looking at the motionless Empire State Building.

I remember the occasion when he took his sister from South Africa to see *Cats*. 'Do you know,' he told me afterwards, 'it was rather good!' *Cats* was not the unlikely choice it seemed at the time, for it is based on T. S. Eliot's poem *Old Possum's Book of Practical Cats*. I have already mentioned Francis lending Mollie Craven a copy of his poems. I also talked earlier about the famous triptych, produced in 1967, which was named by the gallery after Eliot's *Sweeney Agonistes*, as I said, after Francis happened to mention that he was reading *The Waste Land*.

126

A Tate Gallery booklet suggests that his use of newsprint with dry transfer lettering creates 'a version of the newspaper sheets that flutter through empty streets as in Eliot's lines:

> And now a gusty shower wraps
> The grimy scraps of withered leaves about your feet
> And newspapers from vacant lots.'

Few artists have suffered more from wilful interpretations, even from such an eminent authority on modern art as Sam Hunter, who recognised Francis's use of the umbrella as an echo of Neville Chamberlain's on his way to see Hitler at Munich; while others seize on the umbrella as the Freudian symbol for an erection, presumably when it opens.

Lawrence Gowing suggests that certain panels could have been evoked by Eliot's verse:

> That's all the facts when you come to brass tacks:
> Birth, and copulation, and death . . .

And Grey Gowrie, in his introduction to Bacon's Moscow catalogue, refers to the artist's grace under pressure as 'the same feeling of a civilisation undergoing nervous breakdown that we find in T. S. Eliot's poem *The Waste Land*'.

Rimbaud, Baudelaire, Proust, Racine and Aeschylus were other names that come up in conversation with Francis. In 1959 he wrote to John Rothenstein that the *Three Studies* were sketches for the Greek Furies – the goddesses of vengeance euphemistically called the Eumenides from the *Oresteia* by Aeschylus.

The *Oresteia* tells how Agamemnon returned from Troy to Argos, where he was murdered by his wife Clytemnestra in revenge for his sacrifice of their daughter, Iphigenia. When their son Orestes returns he kills his mother in revenge for his father's death; this provokes the revenging Furies, the Eumenides who dwell in the bowels of the earth, who are determined to drive Orestes mad:

> Gorgons I'd call them; but then with Gorgons
> You'd see the grim, inhuman . . .
> . . . I saw a picture

Years ago, the creatures tearing the feast
Away from Phineus –
*These* have no wings,
I looked. But black they are, and so repulsive.
Their heavy, rasping breathing makes me cringe.
And their eyes ooze a discharge, sickening,
And what they wear – to flaunt that at the gods,
The idols, sacrilege! Even in the homes of men.
The tribe that produced that brood I never saw,
Or a plot of ground to boast it nursed their kind
Without some pain and tears for all its labour.

It would be rash not to accept that such images and the very theme of nemesis haunted Francis. 'The reek of human blood smiles out at me', also translated as 'the reek of human blood is laughter to my heart', was a favourite quotation of his from the *Oresteia*.

But, as with the photographic sources, he used such literary references to jolt or excite him, with no thought of illustration. As late as 1981 he painted the stupendous triptych *Inspired by the Oresteia of Aeschylus*, though you would not know this unless you were told. He always preferred to avoid explanatory titles, choosing instead *Study* – 'because I do not believe paintings are ever finished' – or *Head I*, *Head II* and so on; or simply, and confusingly, *Triptych* with the date.

Much has been written on Bacon and the Age of Violence. Most of it is nonsense. 'You can't be more horrific than life itself,' he said with a shrug. 'You only have to watch the news on television.' Once, when I asked him for his definition of horror, he answered sensibly and instantly: 'People bashing someone's brains in for no particular reason – just to pass the time. *Pour passer le temps.*' He ridiculed the phrase in his sing-song French.

Francis was fascinated by the handsome murderer Neville Heath, who was sentenced to death for the murder of one of his victims, Mrs Margery Aimée Gardner, 'with a tearing instrument [said to be a chair leg] being thrust into the vagina and rotated'. This information came from the forensic pathologist Professor Keith Simpson, who helped me with my research into Heath and showed me a lump of Mrs Gardner's flesh, still bearing Heath's toothmarks, preserved in a bottle. 'Her breasts were almost bitten off, there were seventeen lash marks on face and body. . . .' I was with Francis when he spoke for an hour on the subject of Neville Heath. It particularly piqued his interest that the murderer had said in court: 'I got excited and I went too far.' Francis's own art was the art of going too far.

Francis liked the colour of blood; this was his own justification for his morbid subject matter. 'You've only got to go into a butcher's shop like Harrods Food Hall,' he said. It was typically Baconian that he saw it in the context of Harrods. He continued: 'It's nothing to do with mortality but it's to do with the great beauty of the colour of the meat.' Rembrandt and Soutine shared his attraction to the raw flesh of hanging carcasses. When Deakin photographed him for *Vogue*, he flanked him with carcasses suspended on hooks. Francis commented: 'Yes, that was rather amusing.'

Similarly it was not the anguish of the nurse in *Battleship Potemkin* which moved him but the 'beauty of the shot, the mouth, and I was excited by the idea of it being done in colour, the colour of the lips and the flesh and the tongue'.

Francis told Peter Beard during the course of an interview:

> I did the whole series of the Popes for a curious reason. I bought a book on diseases of the mouth when I was quite young – it had always fascinated me, and I'd also been hypnotized by the portrait of Innocent X at that time. I thought that with the colour of the portrait and the mouth, the saliva and the glitter of the mouth, I would be able to make a marvellous image – but I never succeeded in doing it. When the Pope was screaming, it wasn't screaming. I wanted to make the scream into something which would have the intensity and beauty of a Monet sunset.

Cecil Beaton thought that he took distortion too far, recoiling from his own portrait by Bacon:

> 'In front of me was an enormous, coloured strip cartoon of a completely bald, dreadfully aged – nay senile – businessman,' he wrote in his Diaries. 'The face was hardly recognisable as a face for it was disintegrating before your eyes, suffering from a severe case of elephantiasis . . . the hands were clasped and consisted of emerald green scratches that resembled claws.'

Realising Beaton's horror when he saw the finished work Bacon deystroyed it. As early as 1959, in the catalogue for the Museo de Arte at São Paulo in Brazil, Robert Melville wrote that Bacon was 'highly gifted and satanically influential; he discovers in the art of painting the felicities of the death warrant'. He continued: 'To put it somewhat gruesomely, Bacon might be said to have covered the lampshades of his immediate predecessors with human skin, for although he has been far from unreceptive of the symbols of the human condition which inform the invented personages of surrealism, he presents this symbolic material as studies of human appearance.'

Giacometti's biographer, James Land, expressed the common view:

His favourite images were of men screaming, naked male bodies, interlocked in throes that looked more like agony than bliss, figures sitting on toilets or vomiting in washbasins, crucifixions wrought out of slaughterhouse refuse, and multitudes of portraits, including profusions of his own, in which both limbs and physiognomies had undergone gruesome metamorphoses.

Even Picasso's distinguished biographer, John Richardson, wrote with the recklessness of youth a year after the first Tate retrospective:

His blood-chilling pictures of alcoholics and madmen, sadists and perverts, epitomise all the sickness of our sick period. In the present show Bacon exploits his kinky themes in a characteristically kinky way. Each of the figures in his pictures inhabits a private hell. A naked man has a hypodermic in his arm [in fact it was a woman]; another looks as if he is in the throes of shock treatment; yet another is a victim of alcoholism.

Recognising that the squeamish would ask: 'Why paint such subjects?', he replied: 'Why not? By holding a mirror up to our degenerate times Bacon proves himself to be one of the most moral artists of the day. Far from titillating us, he castigates us.'

I think he is right. To appreciate his work, it helps to see Bacon as a deeply moral artist. As the art historian Michael Peppiatt wrote in the *Connoisseur* in September 1984:

Even his detractors would agree that there is nothing of the easy chair about the work of Francis Bacon. Far from ease, it offers extreme disquiet. Its vision of man is of an animal trapped and tortured in the awareness of his mortality. Human appearance is attacked accordingly – violated and brutalized with what might seem a sadistic fluency of invention. But out of that unremitting onslaught have come images of a potency rarely equalled since the early and most disturbing transformations of Picasso. That potency is by its mysterious, quicksilver nature impossible to define. If it could be explained, it would not exist.

Francis told me how much he disliked the 'willed brutalism' of Kiefer. Photographs of Himmler and Goebbels were, he told me, tacked on his studio wall because the *images* were astounding; alongside them were Christ carrying a Cross, a man with a monkey, the Velasquez Pope and a hippopotamus – there is no thematic link there. On another occasion he confided that Himmler and Goebbels represented the apotheosis of the hard men he admired. Why then did he include a swastika armband in a triptych of the Crucifixion? Francis admitted to David Sylvester that it was 'a stupid thing to do', explaining that he wanted to break the continuity of the arm and add the colour of red around it: '. . . it was done entirely as part of trying to make the figure work – not work on the level of interpretation of its being a Nazi, but on the level of its working formally'.

'Then why the swastika?' Sylvester persisted.

'Because I was looking at that time at some coloured photographs that I had of Hitler standing with his entourage, and all of them had these bands round their arms with a swastika.'

'You must have known that people would see a narrative thing there, or didn't this occur to you?'

'I think it occurred to me, but I don't think I cared much about it.'

When I told him about a brief television documentary in which, interspersed with newsreel clips of Hitler, Belsen and Hiroshima, the critic stood in front of a Bacon painting and explained to the viewer that it represented the artist's condemnation of man's inhumanity to man, Francis expressed surprise: 'Well, he would say that, wouldn't he? That's the last thing I think of.'

He *was* interested in enclosure, the isolation of a prison cell, the courtroom cubicle of Eichmann, the centre stage of a set for Kafka, Genet, Eliot, Sartre or Beckett – Bacon's Room.

Few have written so shrewdly on his work as Helen Lessore. She explains that, notwithstanding his innate originality, he spent fifteen years developing the skills of the Venetian tradition – 'mostly by way of Velasquez, Degas and Monet' – and that this imposed a discipline: 'This discipline to some extent curbed the natural dramatic force of his imagination and his instinctive way of designing his pictures.'

131

Her use of the word 'dramatic' is deliberate. Even referring to Bacon's lack of academic training, Helen Lessore compares him to somebody

> coming into a theatre in the middle of a play without knowing the language, but so immediately and intuitively sensing what the drama is about that, quickly picking up a few words and phrases in the current idiom – which happened to be Surrealism – he at once, as if sleepwalking, steps on to the stage and begins to take part – even an important part – in the performance; and in hardly any time, swept on by genius and destiny, he is playing the lead, and becomes the great tragedian of the age.

This is a splendid concept of Bacon as the strolling player of art, performing the great tragic roles. Even on my visit to the first Tate retrospective, I could see that he was in the tradition of the Old Masters, his images as tragic as Grünewald's altarpiece at Colmar with its central panel of the Crucifixion; as simple as Cimabue's *Crucifixion*, which he thought of as 'a worm crawling down the cross'. Bacon told David Sylvester that he tried to convey 'the feeling which I've sometimes had from that picture of this image just moving, undulating down the cross'. Also, he shares the poignancy of Rembrandt's last self-portraits with his unflinching acceptance of the trespass of age. That Bacon never tried to emulate such deterioration in his own later self-portraits is simply explained: he remained as ageless as Dorian Gray.

Jane Alison Hale has made a comparison with Samuel Beckett in

> the way their human figures tend to spill over into their environment; even as the beings are stripped down, laid bare, exposed, they seem to melt into the decor around them. Bacon's figures are often seated on furniture with which they seem to be organically connected so that it is impossible to tell where the body ends and the inanimate object begins.

She cites the *Sphinx – Portrait of Muriel Belcher 1979*, adding that 'Beckett's theatrical images are often characterised by a similar contamination between character and decor. In *Play*, for example, the three heads are made up to resemble the granular texture and colour of the urns from which they protrude.' She adds: ' . . . both artists have chosen an isolated room as the most persistent setting for their human figures', and to compare some of Bacon's rooms to a stage-set is irresistible. Helen Lessore confirms that 'Whether or not his personages are exalted, there is always the feeling of a theatrical presentation. They are isolated and as if elevated on a stage. Often a curved floor-line contributes to this effect, and so does the stark prominence of chairs, beds, and platforms – the minimum that will serve.'

In contrast to Giacometti's greater objectivity, she writes, 'Bacon's art . . . is always a dream, and almost always a cry of despair. The preponderance of this note in his work is probably unique in great painting.'

Writing of the second, 1988 version of the *Triptych 1944*, Richard Dorment concluded in the *Daily Telegraph* on 3 February 1989:

> It is a cliché to say that Francis Bacon's lifelong theme has been despair. But in the light of this latest painting I think we should begin to look back on his work and ask whether the cliché is really true. There is something here more deliberate, more chosen and more willed than despair. Something vicious, and purely evil.

When I mentioned this to Francis on the telephone, emphasising the word 'evil', he laughed and said: 'I thought they were rather *nice* myself.'

Obviously extrovert as a personality, Francis was introverted as an artist and I believe his despair was a distillation of his sense of oppression. The enclosures of his paintings enabled him to concentrate on the essence of his despair, that of an atheist unable to break free from his lack of belief. In his perverse way, Francis Bacon is one of the deeply religious painters of the century. Richard Cork was spot on when he wrote: 'The forcefulness with which these three Greek Furies . . . hurl their misery and rage at us proves the extent of his own loss of faith.' In *Francis Bacon*, Michel Leiris claimed that the paintings 'express the human condition as it truly and peculiarly is today: man dispossessed of any durable paradise'.

This is the nature of the atheist: that he is constantly enquiring and dissatisfied, without the certainty, solace and security of belief. Yet this is not at variance with the claim that Bacon was a religious painter. 'For the truth is that Bacon's works are great religious paintings,' wrote Helen Lessore in her *Partial Testament*. 'The very agony of his unbelief becomes so acute that, by the intensity of its involvement with final questions, the negative becomes as religious as the positive.'

When I interviewed him for Kenneth Tynan's *Tempo* on architecture, Sir Basil Spence confided to me privately that he wished he had asked Francis Bacon, instead of Graham Sutherland, to design the altar tapestry for the new Coventry Cathedral in 1951. Francis was a devout atheist and the result could have provided an extraordinary and historic moment in the great tradition of religious art, whose images, particularly those of Cimabue and Grünewald, moved him so much.

Francis told me over and over again that he believed in *nothing*: 'Man now realises he is an accident, a completely futile being.' But, of course, such ringing statements were not the whole truth. At times Francis described himself as a profound pessimist, at others as a natural optimist. 'I've always been an optimist,' he once said, 'even if I don't believe in anything.' If he painted the Crucifixion it was 'just an act of man's behaviour, a way of behaviour to another'. He had no belief in an afterlife: 'When we're dead we're no good. When I'm dead, put me in a plastic bag and throw me in the gutter.' He also said: 'Faith is a fantasy', and believed that 'religion is a way of disciplining people. Governments use religion to control the people.'

If people talked religion in front of him, he could lose his temper. Robert Medley remembers a dinner party in the early fifties at which Francis, W. H. Auden and Stephen Spender met. Everything seemed to be going well when, in the middle of the main course, 'Francis suddenly turned on Wystan: "Never before have I had to submit to such a disgusting display of hypocritical *Christian* morality!" Declaring that he could no longer sit at the same table with such a *monster* who considered himself an *artist*, he leaped to his feet and stormed out of the front door into the street.' Medley hurried out after him, trying to pacify him, but returned alone; Wystan was talking much as usual.

To an extent, then, Francis Bacon's interest in the Crucifixion reflected a personal obsession – himself. 'You're working then about your own feelings and sensations, really,' he said. 'You might say it's almost nearer a self-portrait.' It seems a wild claim, but it is conceivable that Francis regarded himself as crucified. It is the cross the atheist has to bear that he yearns to believe. Just as a kindly man can turn nasty in drink, Francis, the most gregarious of men, purged his atheistic angst and self-doubt in paint.

He had the highest ambitions for his art. When he wasn't being flippant he would say that art can unlock 'the greatest and deepest things a man can feel'. He wanted, as we have seen, to get near on canvas to 'the actual fact of being a human being', as he saw it, with no hope of resurrection. In his introduction to the Catalogue, John Rothenstein wrote: 'There is a sense in which to look at a painting by Bacon is to look into a mirror, and to see there our own afflictions and our fears of solitude, failure, humiliation, old age, death and of nameless threatened catastrophe.' I believe this is very close to the truth. Grey Gowrie wrote: 'Bacon is unique in this century in his ability to render the indoor, overfed, alcohol-and-tobacco-lined flesh of the average urban male. His painting is how most of us look.' Francis portrays how we look to ourselves and the 'radical unloveliness of those we love'. 'All I want to do', he told me, 'is distort the reality of the human figure into reality.' Something he never ceased to say was: 'We are meat', and then he would raise his champagne glass with that inimitable: 'Cheerio!'

# 10

## The Fates Have Their Revenge

What is love? There is only sexual obsession.
*Francis Bacon in conversation with the author*

What of love? Was it true that Francis didn't believe in it? Was there nothing more than the rough and the rich trade? In his interviews with David Sylvester he said he believed that love and artistic aspiration were incompatible.

Francis made the first of several visits to Tangier to see Peter Lacy, the man I had first seen with him in the Gargoyle in the mid-fifties. Later he said: 'Oh, I loved that period. Tangier was a free zone, international. I remember Tennessee Williams, very depressed. He spent his time with young Moroccans and couldn't understand why they weren't in love with him. They were prostitutes: one had to accept that they're unfaithful to us.'

'*Masculine in suits*.' Paul Danquah hit the bulls-eye. The man in the suit, a constant figure both in his portraits and in his life, was personified in his friendship with Peter Lacy. My early impression was of an exceptionally nice man, innately shy, with a slight, endearing stammer which caused him to blink. He was attentively polite in a pleasant, old-fashioned way, and because of his reticence I felt gratified when he included me in his company. I was impressed to learn that he had been a fighter pilot in the Battle of Britain, an exploit that belied his diffidence.

Lacy did not give the appearance of being homosexual. I assume that because he belonged to a period when it was important to be accepted as 'normal' he played the part accordingly. His nephew, a Royal Navy padre, wrote to me: 'It would figure in my mind that he was happier in male company and that he mixed in "art" circles. What a fascinating man Francis Bacon must have been.' Ian Board remembers that Lacy loved his drink, and also that he was very fond of Leonard, the man who

136

introduced him to Francis – a diminutive stockbroker with the tortoise-like face of Leslie Henson, a well-known comedian of the time. 'Francis was very jealous,' he recalled. 'He *loathed* Leonard.'

Lacy's looks were interesting: too desiccated to be described as handsome, with the bleached appearance of someone left out in the tropical sun. In those early days, he gave the sense of a man who did not belong in England, a remittance man on leave feeling his way after an absence of several years in a city he scarcely recognised. There was a touch of vulnerability, though no effeminacy, a characteristic that Francis deplored. I regret that I failed to buy the portrait of *P.L.* painted in 1962, one of Francis's simplest, of Peter sitting on a banquette facing the artist. The Marlborough were asking £1,000 at the time, and offered to let me pay in instalments. But I was daunted by such a sum – which was particularly foolish as I liked the picture, without any thought of investment. My life is strewn with 'if onlys', especially as far as Francis's paintings are concerned.

Did any relationship mean as much to Francis as that with Peter Lacy? Years later he told me how lucky he had been to meet Lacy when he was nearly sixty, though in fact he was in his late forties: 'This made it all the more extraordinary that Peter should have fallen for me at any age. We got on really well. He was a remarkable man.'

There has always been a band of 'Brits' who do not fit their country and seek solace in the sun. Today it is commonplace to settle on the Costa del Sol; then they basked on the Côte d'Azur or in Tangier. The youngest of three brothers, a homosexual with a stammer, a thorough gentleman, Peter Lacy was a born expatriate.

Francis was first driven to Tangier in 1955 by Peter Pollock in his white Rolls Royce. After that he went annually for the next six years, and rented a flat there. It is one of my regrets that I did not join them on any of these jaunts. 'Francis was marvellous to travel with,' said Peter. 'When the Rolls broke down and we were stranded in Spain for four days he turned it into fun. We stayed at a lovely hotel in Algeciras, two hours away by ferry, called the Reina Christina.'

Tangier, when they eventually arrived, was exotic. It offered the temptations of an international zone, sporting eighty-four banks and more than five hundred brothels, and a louche atmosphere that attracted smugglers, spies, speculators and paedophiles. Many of the brothels offered boys. The knowledge that the Djebella tribesmen in the Rif mountains were known to favour homosexuality tantalised travellers from America, where it was still a greater shame to be gay than in Britain.

The raffish way of life was an inducement to those who relished an element of danger: Truman Capote, Gore Vidal and Christopher Isherwood arrived with high expectations, not always to be realised, and Paul Bowles settled there. Tennessee Williams stayed at the posh Minzah Hotel; William Burroughs wrote *The Naked Lunch* at the seedier, aptly named Manuria. Hollywood stars, too, were drawn by the city's bad reputation: they included Marlene Dietrich, Errol Flynn and Humphrey Bogart, who came with Lauren Bacall. The film he immortalised should have been called *Tangier* instead of *Casablanca*, for Casablanca was as tame as Cheltenham by comparison; and of all the bars in all the world it was only a question of time before Peter Lacy ended up playing the piano in Dean's.

What Harry was to Venice, Bricktops to Rome and Muriel to London, Joseph Dean was to Tangier. He was a coloured man with a mysterious past, though no one was sure what it was.

Conflicting rumours suggested that he was Jamaican or half-Egyptian, and Robin Maugham claimed he had been a gigolo in London involved in a famous pre-war scandal after the death of a Gaiety Girl at Brilliant Chang's opium den in Limehouse. Others alleged he was the illegitimate son of 'titled folk' who had sent him to Westminster School and, presumably, washed their hands of him afterwards.

The writer Rupert Croft-Cooke's feelings towards him were ambivalent: he wrote that Dean had never done a kind act for anyone and that 'few who frequented his bar during their holidays in Tangier failed to receive a letter from Dean on their return to Europe explaining that he had to go into hospital immediately, and had no one else to turn to for the few pounds he needed in order to save his life'. Cooke admitted that, though Dean was a malicious name-dropper and scoundrel whom he would have avoided in his more fastidious days, 'in the atmosphere of that city

138

in that time I was quite fond of him'. He was a natural bar-owner, attracting the elite as well as the riff-raff: Ava Gardner, Ian Fleming and, of course, Francis, who told me how he saw Tallulah Bankhead's sister, Eugenia, take out a pocket mirror, study it disdainfully and smash it on the floor with the disclaimer: 'They don't make mirrors like they used to!'

Robin Cook, who uses the pseudonym Derek Raymond for his brilliant studies of evil such as *My Name Is Dora Suarez*, remembers Dean as a tyrannical employer to Peter Lacy. He evokes a scene when he was twenty-six years old, on a hot afternoon in Tangier in July 1956:

> Three o'clock. Terribly hot. Woke parched, so got downstairs from my room in the Minzah somehow (no lift again) and crawled across the courtyard past the potted palms, keeping well clear of the sunlight. I did what I knew I was going to do anyway and steered for the eternal twilight of Dean's Bar, partly to watch him trafficking in small purple birds whose bottoms he stuffed with cannabis and sold for export, but mostly for the music which forever poured from an upright piano whose top was four ranks deep in empty glasses. This cigarette-scarred instrument produced an inspired stream of music which I had never known to end before seven in the morning, at which hour the performer would sway and his face collapse gravely into the keys with a faint but haunting discord.

This was Peter Lacy.

> At half-past three, the bar was quiescent and the clientele as unremarkable as one could wish . . . although my glance did linger on a large man in rolled-up shirt-sleeves. He was broad-shouldered, rubicund and definitely looked like an Englishman, except that I thought his eyes probed a little too far, further, in fact, than was good for them. He had a bottle of champagne beside him and was covered in splashes of paint; he leaned carelessly on the counter with his back to the bottles, his crossed legs adorned with a pair of green wellington boots. I had a feeling I ought to know who he was and that I had seen him in Soho – but that didn't surprise me at all, since Dean's Bar was 'twinned' with Muriel's. 'Have a glass of champagne,' he said lazily.

This was Francis. Robin refused the champagne, for he was drinking gin and tonic. He ordered two more, one of which he carried over to the piano.

139

'Thanks,' said Lacy, relinquishing the bass with his left hand to take the glass; his right was already rippling into the opening of 'I Get a Kick Out of You'. He took a profound swallow of gin. He was a man who could do several things at once.

'Cigarette?'

'No, mustn't stop. Dean's watching.'

I never thought about it but I suppose Peter Lacy was about forty when I got to know him at Dean's. I never met him anywhere else, and I don't think many other people did either. He was rumoured to have a flat out at Mirimar, along the beach, but nobody I knew had been there. Perhaps he didn't live anywhere. As far as I was concerned he lived in Dean's.

To look at him, he ought never to have been just a pianist, not even an enthralling pianist, not even a pianist in a place which attracted as many eccentric people as Dean's. He had the face of a poet who has dropped in to remark that life after death is tolerable – a calm, ageless face impossible to classify as either drunk or sober until the last gin went into reverse, usually at about sunrise: his long hair was brushed smoothly back to show the whole of his well-shaped face. This day – I suppose the one I remember him best – he was, as always, wearing a pristine lightweight suit and bow tie. His white shirt was spotless, and he had the pale, elegant fingers of people whose admirers say 'You should have been a pianist', with the difference that he was one. People chatted to him as he played; he loved that, particularly when they brought him drinks. He exchanged gossip best, he said, in minor keys, for he believed that all gossip had black undertones, so that for the latest news from London he would slip into B flat minor or a diminished seventh, nodding thoughtfully at whatever the person standing beside him had to say.

'You look absolutely exhausted.'

'I'm all right.'

I disagreed. I went over to Dean. There were still only about a dozen people in the bar; Dean was sitting in his corner alone, staring into space like a tranquil old prophet. I said: 'It's Peter. Look Dean, this round-the-clock piano-playing you're making him do has got to stop, it's insane.'

'But everybody adores his playing.' He lapsed into the barely accented public school English that he did so well: 'You adore it. He adores it. And you are so good for Peter. Your youthful admiration inspires him.'

'That's not what I mean,' I said. 'He's going to drop dead with a heart-attack if he goes on like this.'

Dean said: 'I look how much he owes me every day – he'll soon be off the hook.'

I turned pale. 'Are you trying to tell me that you charge him for all the drinks he has while he's playing, as well as the hundred thousand dinars he owed you when he started?' I thought uneasily of Evelyn Waugh's *A Handful of Dust*. 'But he'll never pay you off! Don't you understand. If you don't show Peter some mercy he'll never be even. He'll be playing the piano here till the end of time.'

'He's never happy except when he's playing the piano,' said Dean, 'unless he's playing baccarat in the casino when I give him money.' He gestured at Peter's elegant back. 'Very bad. But now he is working, enjoying himself, not throwing my money away.'

'*His* money, Dean.'

'His money, my money – who knows whose money it is in the end?'

'But this is appalling. When does he sleep and eat? Doesn't he get to bed even when the place closes?'

'He lives on music. Besides, you know, I never close. It's true he misses London sometimes,' he added. 'He talks about Soho until I almost feel I have been there. I shall go there one day and see your famous Miss Belcher. When I retire. For my ninetieth birthday I shall walk in and buy your Miss Belcher some good champagne.'

By chance, I was there years later on the night that Dean came to the Colony, though it was not his ninetieth birthday and nor did he buy Muriel champagne. He was so intimidated that he tried to impress her by remarking that they had many friends in common.

'Yes,' Muriel replied with unusual animosity, 'all *dead*!'

Dean paled and left.

Francis – whose image, in green wellington boots on a hot day in Tangier, still unnerves me – stayed at the Hotel Cecil with Peter Lacy before he moved into the Rembrandt and then the small Manuria, the favourite of William Burroughs.

In his biography of Burroughs, Ted Morgan describes Francis Bacon as forty-seven, looking thirty-five,

with a spoiled tragic face. He [Francis] said his reputation was a lot of chic shit and that his real love was gambling – he had once won four thousand dollars at Monte Carlo. He told Allen [Ginsberg] that he had also once been offered a gambling stake for allowing himself to be whipped, with a bonus for every stroke that drew blood. Bacon's painting technique was what he called psychic representation, the face formed as if by accident in a whirl of feathery brush strokes. Bacon said De Kooning was the great man in the United States, for bursting through the abstract and planting an image on the canvas.

Allen thought that Bacon painted the way Burroughs wrote. It was a sort of dangerous bullfight of the mind, where he placed himself in acute psychic danger of uncovering some secret that would destroy him.

Burroughs had these unpublishable mad routines about talking assholes, with the recurring image of the spurting hard-on as the hanged man's neck snaps, and vast paranoic theories of agents and psychic senders taking over the world in bureaucratic conspiracies. But Burroughs, although fond of Bacon, denied that there was any connection, and said: 'Bacon and I are at opposite ends of the spectrum. He likes middle-aged truck drivers and I like young boys. He sneers at immortality and I think it's the one thing of importance. Of course we're associated because of our morbid subject matter.'

Ginsberg's suggestion that Francis painted the way that Burroughs wrote has some validity, and Francis was certainly impressed by his haphazard method of working as if his sentences were thrown in the air and reassembled with little thought as to their meaning. He advised me to read *The Naked Lunch* as well as *The Sheltering Sky* by Paul Bowles, who had introduced Francis to Burroughs in the first place.

Usually so swift to denigrate, Francis was respectful when he spoke to me of Burroughs – though he measured his words carefully – 'His work is *really* interesting' – as if everyone else said it was rubbish. After I interviewed Burroughs and Alexander Trocchi on television, when they admitted they had just had a 'fix' in the lavatory, sensational for the time, Francis took them to the Waterman's Arms, the public house I had taken over on the Isle of Dogs. The visitors' book has a page of unlikely signatures: Emlyn Williams, Alexander Trocchi, Michael Portman, Francis Bacon, William Burroughs, George Melly, John Fraser and even Harry Carpenter.

Years later, in 1986, Francis and Burroughs came together for the last time when they filmed an interview for BBC's *Arena* which was never transmitted, though it was recalled by Rupert Haselden and quoted in the *Guardian* on 2 May 1992:

*Bacon:*   I don't know if critics of literature are the idiots that critics of painting are in this country, because they're the biggest idiots that exist. They know absolutely fuck all about it to begin with. They've got no instinct about it, they've just got theories.

*Burroughs:* In Tangier, I remember, we had several discussions about painting.

*Bacon:* Did we? [I can hear the faint sceptical query in his voice.]

*Burroughs:* Yes, much of the time. I remember you saying most of what is going on in painting isn't painting at all.

*Bacon:* Did I? Maybe we were talking about abstract painting. Once it was the height of fashion – I don't know why, it's never meant anything to me. To me, even the best of it is just decoration. Jackson Pollock's paintings might be very pretty but they're just decoration. I always think they look like old lace. But that's a terrible thing to say to an American, of an American hero. [Again, I can hear his spluttering laughter as he said this with deliberate provocation.]

*Burroughs:* No, not mine.

*Bacon:* I always think marvellous painting will come out of America, because it should, a country with an enormous mixed race. But it doesn't, it's so dreary, those super-realists, the abstract expressionists, all so very dreary.

*Burroughs:* But there must be some modern painters you admire?

*Bacon:* Not many, not now. They're all dead. There's Mark Boyle, Richard Hamilton; I'm interested some-times in what they do. But I'm afraid this isn't really a country of painters – just Turner; at least we had Turner.

*Burroughs:* And what about the Americans, say Jasper Johns?

*Bacon:* I try never to think about Jasper Johns, I hate the stuff and don't like him either. I met him in Paris. It was mutual, he didn't like me. It does happen.

Discussing Hollywood's attempts to film *The Naked Lunch*, since fulfilled, Burroughs described how the studio sent a Daimler to fetch him, shrinking to a two-seater when they did not like the script: 'Really learnt about Hollywood.'

*Bacon:* It's always those bastards with the money behind every-thing, but what do they know? Nothing, nothing but money. I read somewhere that you write to make people aware of what they know themselves. I don't think I paint for that

143

reason at all. I paint to try and excite myself, which doesn't often happen.

*Burroughs:* There was an exhibition of Monet in Chicago recently; I was excited by that, really beautiful.

*Bacon:* The Impressionists, Cézanne, Picasso; you're right, that's wonderful painting. Look at Cézanne, really look, and you realise that Cubism, as good as it is, is perhaps only a kind of decoration on Cézanne's work and ideas.

Suddenly they switched to memories of Paul and Jane Bowles, whom Francis always told me was the better writer. She drank; he preferred drugs like *majoun*. She called herself, with self-lacerating cruelty, 'Crippie the Kike Dyke'; he preferred artistic young Moroccans.

*Burroughs:* Do you remember the alligator that Paul and Janie Bowles had in Tangier? Such a delicate little thing.

*Bacon:* She died here, you know, Janie.

*Burroughs:* Didn't she die in Malaga?

*Bacon:* Died in a madhouse in Malaga, it must have been the worst thing in the world. Looked after by nuns, can you imagine anything more horrible?

My personal knowledge of Francis's visits to Tangier came in letters. This one, written to me in the mid-fifties, was dated 6 September. I am uncertain of the year, though the reference to Colin Wilson suggests it was 1956:

I have been meaning to answer your last letter. In the last month anyway I hope I shall see you soon as I think I shall get back to London about the 23rd or 24th of this month but don't mention it if you can help as I shall have all the people I owe money to down on me at once.

I have not been able to finish anything here but have *done* a lot of preparatory work and feel I shall be able to paint a series I want to do quickly when I get back – I love it here but not for too long. All the Arabs here are so wonderful looking and more especially the Berbers I think they are. The answer to almost everything you like. I am so glad you have made such a friend of Colin Wilson it is exciting to meet someone one is really in sympathy with – Peter is playing the piano in a bar here and staying on – I will probably come back when I have finished the work – but I find it very hard to paint here – it is a terribly limited life unless one

144

speaks Arabic but exciting never the less. I long to see you again, all my love to you and your grandmother please give her my kindest regards Hope to see you soon best love and wishes Francis.

Encouraged by his enthusiasm for Tangier, I flew there with Deakin and Lady Rose MacLaren in the summer of 1960. Unfortunately Francis was not there himself, nor was Peter Lacy playing in Dean's Bar. Presumably, both were in England.

For some reason I rented a villa on a hill and, when it dawned on me that I would be bored on my own, I asked Deakin to stay in one of the numerous empty bedrooms. He gave me a pitying smile, preferring to stay in the hotel which Lady Rose was paying for: 'You've made your bed, so lie in it! I like to be in the thick of things, kiddo.' So I slept each night in a different room, as if to make it more lived in.

Rose was staying with her cousin, the Hon. David Herbert, sometimes called the King of Tangier. He invited us to dinner on our first night before continuing to a small party of Barbara Hutton's, and the first alarm was sounded as he handed us our personal invitations for her ball at the end of the week: 'Mrs Barbara Woolworth Hutton requests the pleasure of your company for a ball on the roof of her house in the Kasbah.' This was followed by a warning: 'In case of wind, your hostess requests you to indulge her by coming another night.'

'I see the poor old thing suffers from flatulence,' said Deakin, who had been drinking in Dean's in the afternoon. Herbert, who was acting as her social secretary, winced. After we had finished dinner, we drove up the hill to the Kasbah. From the distance came the echo of drums and trumpets as soldiers practised for the Sultan's visit in two days' time. As we drove around twisting alleys, Deakin pondered aloud – 'Barbara Woolworth Hutton, it's a name to conjure with.'

We stopped outside a nondescript exterior and were led to the Throne Room, where one of the richest women in the world was waiting for us. She wore a bright red sari; her hair was soft and yellow, swept neatly upwards; her figure was lithe, almost fragile; and her dark eyes moved restlessly like an actress listening to a distant prompt which none of us could hear, for she was surrounded by a claque of fawning admirers. They expressed

145

murmurs of delight when she announced brightly that she would give us a tour of her palace.

'Do we have to?' asked Deakin. 'I'd much rather stay here.' His eyes raked the room for a drinks cabinet or a Moroccan servant with a tray. Finding neither, he joined the cortège.

'Ever since I was a little girl I wanted a Moorish palace,' she told me, speaking in a little girl's voice. 'This was built by the correspondent of the London *Times* in the early thirties and was taken over by our Consul, who was going to sell it to Franco when he retired – but I topped Franco's bid.'

'It must have been satisfying to beat *him*,' I smiled sycophantically.

'Not at all,' she reprimanded me. 'I consider Franco a truly great man.' After that I kept silent; Deakin did not.

As we entered a room lined with mirrors, she declared: 'Venetian.'

'I am perfectly aware of that,' he said with a crocodilean smile. 'Unfortunately of the wrong period.' He put a finger to his lips as he scrutinised the room: 'Now if this room had been mine . . .' The Americans stared at him appalled, and moved on to show they were not in his company. Rose said 'Shush', Herbert glared, and Barbara Hutton gave him a warning glance as she continued on her tour with Deakin's running commentary: 'No one likes chinoiserie more than I,' he announced, 'but it's a shame that . . .'

Finally we entered a room with little furniture except for a large bed draped by a delicate mosquito net; this she revealed, surprisingly, as her bedroom. There was not much to say, but Deakin said it: 'The sort of bed movie actresses are strangled in.' The next room was even emptier, with nothing but a pile of mattresses upon a bed.

Unnerved, the Woolworth heiress abandoned the tour, leaving the Americans to stare at the mattresses, bemused.

'Ah!' Deakin exclaimed with heavy significance. 'Now I understand. The Princess and the Pea.' I understood at once, though I had the suspicion that the Americans had never heard of the fairy story and thought instead in terms of . . . another kind of pea. After all, she had been the Princess Midvani. By now there was no stopping Deakin. We returned to the Throne Room, where she sat on the dais pointing out the jewels which encrusted the scarlet tapestry. When he declared that they would supply him with forty thousand cufflinks, she ignored him. To everyone's relief Deakin then disappeared and the conversation flowed, though the drinks did not – presumably the reason for his disappearance.

When she confided: 'If I love, I love, but I've never flirted,' I assumed she was referring to the dark young man of twenty-three who watched her with a stillness which suggested he was Spanish – though in fact Lloyd Franklin was a former trumpeter in the Life Guards who had wandered south with his guitar after finishing his national service, ending up in Dean's Bar where David Herbert asked him to play at a private party. Barbara Hutton was one of the guests and offered Lloyd Franklin a lift home, with a nightcap in the Kasbah on the way. He had not been seen outside the Kasbah since, and the newspapers were hinting at yet another romance. The Americans made a point of being supportive, even when he produced his guitar and began to perform. It was not the flash of flamenco, which might have been bearable in such a setting, but a song called 'The Hole in the Elephant's Bottom', which the Americans greeted with squeals of shocked delight.

When he finished there was loud applause, followed by one of those disconcerting lulls which fall on any party inexplicably. It was shattered by a deafening cry from behind the arras which ran down the far side of the room: 'When that second-rate strummer has finished,' came an infuriated yell, *I'd like a drink!*'

'Cousin David's taking it awfully well,' said Rose the next morning as she broke the news that Barbara Hutton was cancelling the ball.

'But it's the social event of the Tangerine year!' I exclaimed.

'I know,' said Rose with a sad sigh, looking at Deakin tragically. 'You see, she refuses to hold it while Deakin is still in Tangier.'

'I have my invitation,' he pointed out defiantly in spite of his hangover.

'That's the trouble. She won't be so discourteous as to ask for it back, so she's cancelling the whole thing. Oh dear, I am so sorry.'

I suspected that Cousin David had told her where her duty lay, and this was confirmed when she added: 'If it will make it any better, I'll fly back with you. David's booked us seats on the day of the ball.' The Tangerines sighed with relief when Deakin was duly decanted back to London.

147

With a twinge of guilt I stayed for the ball. The Kasbah blazed 'like a palace ready to receive a Sultan in *The Thousand and One Nights*', as Paul Bowles, another guest, described it. Later I drove into the mountains with Peter Pollock and Paul Danquah before my own return to London.

Deakin had written to me: 'The reason I drank so much was from fear. I hated having to return to England and face all my debts, I was good and scared and with reason,' but by the time I saw him his ebullience was restored. 'The news reached Soho,' he bragged, 'and far from being shunned for my bad behaviour I have been wined and dined for my blow-by-blow report.'

I shared his new fame at a crowded lunch in Wheeler's where I contributed my eye-witness account of the ball. At one point he looked forlorn: 'Did Barbara Hutton really dislike me that much?' he asked.

'Do you want to know what she said?' I asked unkindly. '*Really* want to know?'

'Oh, come on,' said Francis impatiently. 'What did she say?'

'She told David Herbert that you were the second-nastiest little man she has met in forty years.'

The others hooted with laughter, while Francis leaned forward intently and enquired: 'But who was the *first*?'

When Francis returned to Tangier in the early sixties after the separation from Ron, he wrote to me from the Hotel Djenina. There is no record that he stayed there, but he might have been using the restaurant:

Dearest Dan

Thank you so much for your card. I hoped I would see you before I left but think I will be back early in August it is too difficult to work here. There seems to be lots of new and wonderful looking people in from the country – am going to Marrakesh today – although it's terribly hot. I long to hear about your time in Australia – Barbara Hutton and Lloyd Franklin are back again – I am pleased to hear Deakin has got such a helpful friend it is marvellous for him [I am not sure if this is sarcasm] will see you soon I hope – I've got the new place in London it is supposed to be being done now. Love and all best wishes Francis

The 'new place' that Francis referred to was a cottage in a mews where he was to stay for the rest of his life. A couple of minutes' walk from South Kensington Tube Station, it was right for him. South Ken was known as a final resting place for generals and their lady wives, governors and top civil servants after their service in India or the Far East. Significantly, he told me, South Ken was the place where he found it easiest to paint.

Several years later he bought an additional, grander house round the corner in Roland Gardens; it had the advantage of a beautiful studio with perfect light, but 'I did it up so well,' he said, 'with carpets and curtains and everything, that I absolutely couldn't work in it. I was absolutely castrated in the place. That was because I had done it up so well and I had not got the chaos.'

The mews cottage preserved the chaos he loved. 'I like to live among the memories and the damage,' he said. With his utter contempt for possessions, the cottage looked as if it was waiting for furniture and decorators to arrive, and still did so twenty years later. The immediate impression was one of spartan panache. Naked light bulbs hung mournfully from the ceilings, unprotected by shades; there were blankets over the windows instead of curtains, and no carpets on the floorboards. He added a large studio with a skylight: a magical cave of old paintbrushes, easels and canvases, newspapers and copies of *Paris Match*, all bespattered with paint. Apart from a small and somewhat primitive kitchen and bathroom, there was an ample bedroom which served also as a sitting room. The double bed in the far corner was strewn with an exotic green silk tapestry he had brought back from Morocco – the only touch of luxury in the place. There were no pictures apart from postcard reproductions of his own work tacked to the wall, with more of these in the studio among the Muybridge photographs and *Potemkin* still. Once I gave him a lithograph of a warrior by Robert Colquhoun which I bought for £100, and he tore it in half in the Colony. This was my fault for failing to realise that the work of a contemporary painter was the last object to infiltrate the mews.

One loose-end Sunday afternoon I took two East Enders to visit Lionel Bart, the author and composer of *Oliver*, who lived next door to Francis in a house so dense with chic that it was either an interior decorator's dream or nightmare. The East Enders thought it was fabulous and were slightly shocked when we went

149

on to see Francis in his monastic splendour – or squalor as it appeared to them.

'Poor old Francis,' said one sympathetically as we left. 'He's not doing very well, is he?'

In fact Francis was doing extremely well, at last. This was due to the professionalism of his new minders at the Marlborough, who regarded his work as potential big business and swiftly made it so. Francis K. Lloyd, known as Frank Lloyd, and Henry Robert Fischer, referred to by Francis as 'the Uncles', had the acumen to realise that Francis was unique – a British artist with the promise of international appeal. This was not the obvious revelation that it seems today.

It was the Uncles who gave him the exhibition in March 1960 at the Marlborough Fine Art, then at 17 Old Bond Street, of paintings done in 1959–60. These were a limbering up for the first Tate retrospective, in 1962, which they helped to organise. Harry Fischer was responsible for Bacon's promotion abroad until 1912. In 1964 this job was taken over by Valerie Beston.

Referred to by Francis as 'Miss B', she started to look after Francis Bacon and the pictures. He needed to concentrate on his work to the exclusion of all distraction, including other people. To have someone he was able to trust as he could Valerie Beston, to know that she put his interests first and possessed the rare quality of absolute loyalty, provided him with an anchor he could rely on. Miss Beston was to prove indispensable in guiding him through the storms ahead, the triumphs and disasters, and she still looks after his work. She does not wish to discuss their relationship, and I respect this and understand it.

So with the Marlborough behind him, Francis was ready to be tested. I saw a lot of him at this time and shared in his excitement. He knew that the retrospective was the turning point of his life, and assisted in arranging it without argument – a tantrum would have been self-destructive. It meant postponing a visit to Tangier, where Peter Lacy was ill – due to alcoholism, as Francis confided to me later. Unfortunately, Lacy would have to wait until Francis could snatch a day or two before the opening. But there never was a free day, and flight bookings had to be cancelled due to the demands on his time in London.

On 21 May 1962, the evening before the private view, Francis took me around the Tate, which was closed to the public. The two of us walked slowly through the empty rooms – empty except for the dominance of those awesome pictures – and we lapsed into silence. For once there was nothing to say. Francis knew he had achieved something different.

The exhibition contained nearly half of his surviving work – the *Three Studies for Figures at the Base of a Crucifixion* inspired by Grimald; the *Figure in a Landscape* based on the snapshot of the dozing Eric Hall in Hyde Park; the extraordinary *Head* of which he said, 'one of the problems is to paint like Velasquez but with the texture of a hippopotamus' skin'; the early *Pope with Fan Canopy*; the dog trapped in a circle . . . so many. Paintings had been lent by Sir Colin Anderson, Chairman of the Tate's Board of Trustees; David Sylvester; Roy De Maistre; Diana Watson, Bacon's cousin; and Mr R. J. Sainsbury, as he was then, who provided a painting of himself, Bacon's first commissioned portrait, three of Lisa Sainsbury, and *Study for Portrait of P. L. No. 2. 1957*, a portrait of Peter Lacy.

As we made this amazing tour, I sensed that for once Francis was deeply content, possibly as satisfied with his work as he had ever been – yet overwhelmed, too, and possibly frightened. I was overwhelmed with pride and admiration and did not attempt to express my feelings apart from muttered praise. I was virtually speechless from the impact, and had the tact to remain so. When we left the Tate, I was different from when I went in.

Early the next morning I received a phone call from a bossy researcher on the TV programme I was employed on, *This Week*.

'You couldn't go to Paris right away, could you?' I had the impression she was hoping I would say no.

'Yes.'

'But we need you there this afternoon.'

'Fine.'

'Well. . . ,' she explained reluctantly, 'someone's let us down at the last moment and Jeremy Isaacs has asked if you'll interview James Baldwin.'

'Delighted.'

Grudgingly, she told me what flight to take and where to meet the director. I was tempted to stay for the razzmatazz of the private view, but felt that my experience the previous evening was

151

unique and should remain that way. So I needed no persuasion to go to Paris.

On the morning after, enjoying the luxury of strong French coffee outside the Deux Magots, I opened the London papers to read the reviews for the Bacon retrospective. Rarely does an artist receive such recognition in his lifetime. For years there had been rumblings of his impending greatness in London's introverted art scene. Now the whole world was aware of the arrival of a painter of unparalleled excitement, a painter who could be counted among the most important of twentieth-century art.

Returning to London that afternoon, I headed for the Colony Room to find it awash with emotional drunks, evidently celebrating Francis's triumph. My God, I thought in my pristine sobriety, how silly everyone is – I had better catch up quickly. I was seized by Eleanor Bellingham-Smith who asked me tearfully if I had heard the news. As she cried at the ring of the telephone I was not surprised by her emotional state and smilingly replied: 'Isn't it wonderful? Francis must be delighted.' She slapped me hard in the face. Have they all gone mad? I wondered. At this moment Francis pushed his way through the mob and steered me towards the lavatory at the back, where he explained that he had received a sheaf of telegrams that morning, congratulating him on the show. But the last informed him that Peter Lacy had died the night before.

In spite of having known him, in spite of all I learned, Peter Lacy remained a shadow, almost too saintly to be true – the shy Dooley Wilson of Dean's. In 1991 I returned in the hope that I could find out more.

Tangier takes one by surprise with its beauty: on the corner of the Mediterranean and the Atlantic, it has the advantage of these two contrasting seas. That spring the surrounding fields were lush with wild flowers in contrast to the arid deserts in the south. It is a city of contradiction: highly sophisticated on one side, tough and treacherous on the other. Friends had told me that the place to go to was the Tangerinn (as in Tangier Inn), run by an eccentric Englishman called John Sutcliffe – another character – described in the *Daily Telegraph* as 'a former Lifeguard whose Adonis-like portrait adorns the wall of his cosy bar. He still holds court here, to a mixture of gays and backpackers, recounting stories of the old

Francis Bacon's mother – Christine Winifred Firth, courtesy of Paul Danquah and Peter Pollock

Canny Court – one of his father's houses outside Dublin (© Daniel Farson)

Portrait of Francis Bacon, probably aged 25, by Roy De Maistre

Francis Bacon in the garden of his cousin, Diana Watson (© Marlborough)

Portrait of Francis Bacon, by John Deakin

Timothy Berens, Lucian Freud, Francis Bacon, Frank Auerbach and Michael Andrews at Wheeler's, by John Deakin

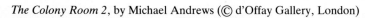

*The Colony Room 2*, by Michael Andrews (© d'Offay Gallery, London)

Francis Bacon (unusually smoking a cigarette) and the author at the first Soho Fair, photographer unknown

Daniel Farson, John Deakin and Francis Bacon with customers at Charlie Brown's pub in Limehouse (© Marlborough)

Lucian Freud and Francis Bacon in Bacon's studio, by Daniel Farson
(© Marlborough)
Francis Bacon and John Minton lunching in the staff dining room of the
Royal College of Art, by Daniel Farson (© Marlborough)

Muriel Belcher and Francis Bacon in Wheeler's, by Peter Stark (© Marlborough)

(Below left) Ian Board, Muriel's successor at the Colony Room, (© Daniel Farson)

(Below right) John Deakin in the French Pub (© Daniel Farson)

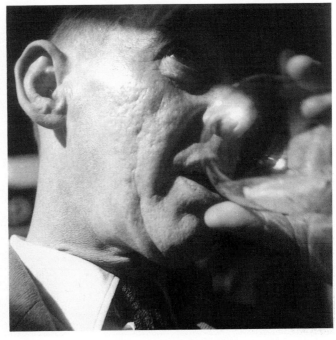

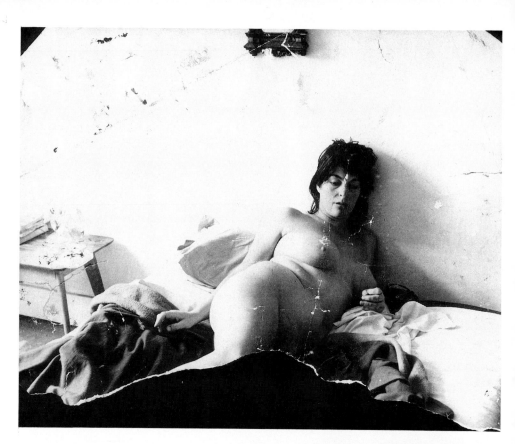

Henrietta Moraes
posing for photographs
by Deakin
commissioned by Bacon
(© Francis Bacon
Estate)

Isabel Rawsthorne, one
of Bacon's favourite
models and closest
friends, by John Deakin
(© Francis Bacon
Estate)

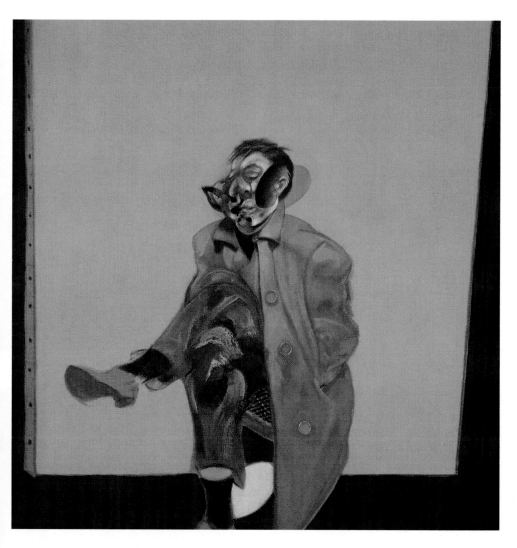

*Self Portrait*, 1970, by Francis Bacon. Oil on canvas, 152 x 147.5 cm. Private collection.

*Three Studies for Figures at the Base of a Crucifixion*, 1944, by Francis Bacon. Oil and pastel on hardboard. Triptych, each panel 97 x 74 cm. Tate Gallery, London.

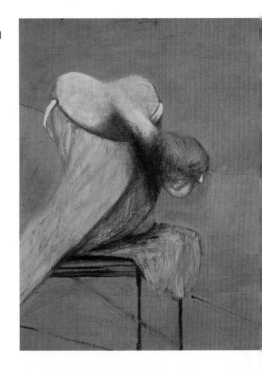

*Triptych May-June*, 1973, by Francis Bacon.
Oil on canvas, 198 x 147.5 cm. Private
collection, Switzerland.

*Portrait of John Edwards*, 1988, by Francis Bacon. Oil on canvas, 198 x 147.5 cm. Private collection.

Francis Bacon
(© Daniel Farson)

Peter Lacy in Ostia
(© Marlborough)

Francis Bacon and
Peter Pollock in
Tangier, courtesy Paul
Danquah and Peter
Pollock

Francis Bacon and Paul
Danquah at the Second
Tate Retrospective
(© Tate Gallery,
London)

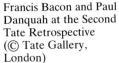

(Below left) Francis
Bacon and the
Moroccan painter
Yacoubi in Tangier
(© Francis Bacon
Estate)

Francis Bacon and
Dean outside Dean's
Bar, by Fred G.
Mossman
(© Marlborough)

Graham and Kathy Sutherland at Cap Ferrat (© Daniel Farson)

(Left) David Sylvester, responsible for the Interviews, with a figure by Giacometti, (© Daniel Farson)

Peter Bradshaw: 'Dear Peter, I love the painting. I think it is beautifully done. . .', by Dan Farson

George Dyer –
Bacon's friend and
model, by John
Deakin (© Francis
Bacon Estate)

George and Francis
when the going was
good on the Orient
Express
(© Marlborough)

Francis Bacon and Lady Rose MacLaren on the author's balcony in Narrow Street (© Daniel Farson)

A title page from Muybridge with a rare drawing which Bacon gave to Peter Beard, courtesy Peter Beard

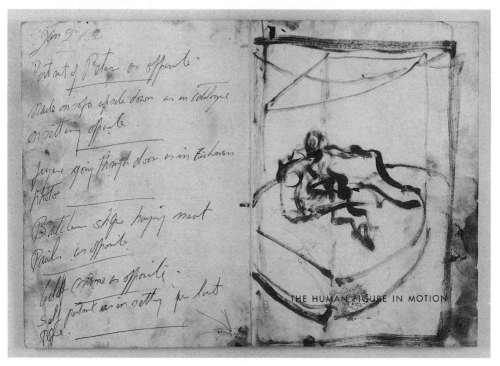

Francis Bacon
indignant outside the
French Pub, July 14
1989, when Gaston
retired (© Daniel
Farson)

A *happier* 'Cheerio!',
by Peter Stark
(© Marlborough)

Francis Bacon in the famous, chaotic studio in South Kensington (© Peter Beard)

*Two Studies from the Human Body*, 1975, in progress. The Artist peering through the door of his studio (© Peter Beard)

Francis and John Edwards embracing in Dean St (© Daniel Farson)

Francis Bacon and John Edwards (© London Weekend Television)

international days.' He was bound to have heard of Lacy. But when I asked him he misheard the question.

'Oh, yes,' he said vacantly. 'What I like is the way this bar's so well known. Everywhere. Istanbul, Detroit – you name it. Extraordinary.' *Detroit!*

Sutcliffe gazed fondly around his small club, dimly decorated as a tent. Seldom had I seen a room so moribund. It was empty apart from ourselves, the Moroccan barman and the unrecognisable Adonis on the wall – a large blown-up photograph dated 1937 with Sutcliffe in full military fig and gleaming breast-plate – 'I was almost in sepia,' he murmured. The real Sutcliffe seemed unsure if he was seventy or eighty, explaining that his nephew and co-partner was in Penge looking after his mother. Remembering that friends had assured me 'If anyone remembers Peter Lacy it's Sutcliffe', I tried again.

'Who? Lacy? No, I don't think so.' He shook his head slowly.

'He was a friend of Francis Bacon,' I persisted, and to my great relief this produced a tremor of recognition.

'Ah! The great Bacon.' Silence.

'What can you tell me about him?' I pressed him.

Sutcliffe looked ambushed: 'The great Bacon? Not a lot.'

'Where did you meet him?' I persisted. 'In the Tangerinn?' This seemed likely, as Francis stayed briefly in the Manuria Hotel above us.

But Sutcliffe giggled and looked at me with astonishment: 'Meet him? I'm not that old.'

I sighed inwardly. 'Who are we talking about?

'The man who wrote Shakespeare's plays – aren't we?'

'No, we're not,' I replied, exasperated. 'Francis Bacon the great British painter.'

'Never heard of him.'

Losing interest, Sutcliffe turned to his barman: 'A plane arrived from London today. I wonder who'll come in.' Turning back to me, he asked if I knew Don Collins.

Thinking at first of a drink, I shook my head.

'Antique dealer – West Country – lived here until last week – in fact died here last week. Extraordinary.'

The death of poor Mr Collins was the closest I came to Peter Lacy that night.

153

The atmosphere brightened with the sudden descent of a paunchy middle-aged Englishman with the beaky look of a spectacled penguin. He was staying upstairs in the Manuria and had made the concession to bohemianism of allowing his shirt-tails to hang outside his trousers, even though he still wore an old school tie.

'My dear,' he announced, 'I'm *stiff* from dancing!'

Sutcliffe whispered to me audibly: 'Dean at a university. Very important.'

The Tangerinn had opened at nine and it was now nearly midnight, so I crossed the railway tracks to the Miami Beach Bar which was run by a lively young Moroccan, Abdel Hamid, billed as 'a former exotic dancer', apparently the best in North Africa.

'Have you heard of Peter Lacy?' I asked him. 'I think he ran another beach bar.'

For a moment I was getting confused myself.

'Oh, yes,' he grinned. 'I speak to Peter.'

At last! But as I leaned forward my hopes faded as I realised that the exotic dancer was still in his twenties. There was no way he could have known Lacy, even as a child.

The penguin arrived with his handsome young Moroccan friend, who winked at me constantly when he was not indulging in a 'lover's tiff' which both seemed to enjoy. At one point, the Dean interrupted his dancing to inform me: 'At home I'm a man of discipline. I get up the same time every morning, eat the same breakfast – eight prunes – go home alone, put the lights out on the dot of ten-thirty. Here I'm *abandoned*!' He returned to the tiny dance floor where he danced stiffly, as a penguin would, while his friend shot me mischievous glances behind his back.

Over breakfast at the Minzah in the morning, I was wondering whether I should abandon my search – and then I remembered Paul Bowles. On my third visit to his unappealing tenement block the door was opened by his Moroccan companion.

'I'm about to have some tea,' said Bowles, as if my arrival had marred the occasion. There was no suggestion that I might enjoy a cup myself. The writer, now in his eighties, was seated on a banquette in the semi-darkness of his small, dour apartment, cluttered with papers and books which redeemed the gloom. It reminded me how different the rewards can be for a successful

154

writer, like Bowles, and a successful painter, like Francis Bacon, and I would have sympathised with Bowles if he had been less peevish. I persevered, asking him how much the film of *The Sheltered Sky* had changed his life.

'It has brought me a deluge of unwelcome visitors.' I got the message, as Muriel would have said.

It surprises me when the most awkward people become agreeable the moment they see a camera, and Bowles started to relax as soon as I produced my small Japanese camera with the built-in flash. He told me that the name of Peter Lacy meant nothing, though he remembered Francis Bacon and Lucian Freud at a Guy Fawkes party in Hampstead with urchins in the street outside. (*Urchins!*) The scene might have remained alert in Bowles's memory but hardly leaped across in the telling. At least he had a clearer impression of Francis in Tangier: 'He had a terrible studio which he rented in a building of such dilapidation that the matchwood lift finally plunged five floors to the bottom where it disintegrated into dust, killing a baby and crippling the mother – Francis told me about it with some relish.'

When he mentioned an artist called Ahmed Yacoubi, I recognised the name at once. Francis had spoken of him frequently and with unusual affection, and seemed surprised that I had not met him on my visit with Deakin. According to Francis, Yacoubi was the most sympathetic Moroccan in Tangier, and Michelle Green in *The Dream at the End of the World* claims that, like Jane Bowles, Yacoubi was 'powerful enough to walk into a room and charm everyone in it'. In another recent book, *Tangier –City of the Dream*, Iain Finlayson describes Yacoubi in 1951 as 'a handsome, intelligent, quick-witted, talented twenty-year-old'.

Jane Bowles encouraged his painting from as early as 1948 until he switched his allegiance to her husband, with whom he lived and travelled for several years. As far as Bowles could love anyone, it appears that he loved Yacoubi – as much for his talent as for his charm. Finlayson writes that 'it was taken for granted that Bowles and Yacoubi were sexually intimate [he wrote as if Bowles were dead] and no moral opprobrium was invoked by Tangier society to whom such a liaison appeared perfectly straightforward . . .' He added that Yacoubi, 'if an erotic element were to enter into his friendship with Bowles, would have accepted it as perfectly natural'. After all, Bowles was furthering his career and Moroccans were quick to acknowledge such favours. Finlayson concludes:

> If sexual relations, in whatever form, occurred between them, they were probably short-lived and both may have been relieved to have got the matter out of the way. Sex, for Bowles, appears to have been an embarrassment rather than a relief or a consummation of more delicate feelings. His fondness for young men can perhaps be better viewed as somewhat pedagogic and paternal.

If I had read this book beforehand, I should have shattered the gloom of that Tangerine apartment by asking casually: 'Did you have sex with Yacoubi?' Though that might have seemed rude on a first acquaintance, it would have settled the subject once and for all, if he was prepared to tell the truth. Probably Finlayson is correct in assuming that sex was secondary, if indeed it ever ocurred; Yacoubi was able to make Bowles laugh, and he supplied him with *majoun* mixed with a single drop of blood, both of which were ultimately more satisfying than the hurly-burly of the couch.

And there must have been an endearing side to Yacoubi unless it was calculatedly fey, for he enchanted Bowles by playing the flute to paintings he had just finished – 'to bring them to life'. Someone else said it was not surprising that Jane was angry, because Yacoubi was 'always trying to get money and other things out of Paul' – but that was the pattern of such relationships.

Judging by his affairs, which included a torrid interlude in New York in the early fifties with a former torch singer who was now a millionairess and who dropped him when she suspected witch-craft, Yacoubi had no difficulty in going with either sex.

Paul Danquah has been exceptionally kind in sending me a batch of letters saved over the years. My elation was tempered by the difficulty in reading them. Crumpled, scrawled with Francis's spider writing, with no punctuation and pages missing, they are hard to unravel. A typical missive from Barcelona, announcing that he is going to Aix-en-Provence with Peter Lacy and will take a train from Marseille, arriving home on Wednesday, is legible for once, which is surprising for it is written on lavatory paper with the

156

explanation 'Please excuse the paper it is Sunday and I can't get any.'

Many of the letters are mundane with references to rent due at 9 Overstrand Mansions, sheets and bedding, and keys to be left by or for a lodger. In Tangier Francis semed to be alighting on different addresses then moving on. At one point he rented a flat for a year with three rooms, a kitchen and bathroom: 'I have only a large bed a couple of table and chairs and a cooker and a lovely Moroccan sergeant who is one of the physical instructors but I am fraid he is going to be moved very soon to the South of Morocco.' Inviting Peter and Paul to stay, he says he will buy them beds and they will be 'terribly welcome' if they do not mind the discomfort.

Continuing with local news, he reported that 'Janie Bowles has been very ill. She had a stroke while Paul was in Ceylon and she seemed to recover but her sight was still very bad They have both been in London for a short time for her to see a specialist They are due back in a day or two.'

Francis then referred to Ahmed Yacoubi, usually spelling his name as 'Achmid', with whom he was unusually close. Bowles had introduced Yacoubi to Francis. Though he was unable to read or write, Yacoubi was immensely strong and played football, close to Francis's ideal. Apart from his physical attraction – John Moynihan reports that he was known to possess 'a gigantic member' – Francis genuinely liked Yacoubi and admired his work sufficiently to recommend it to Erica Brausen, assuring her that an exhibition of his work would be successful, especially if Yacoubi came to London, where his looks and personality would be bound to impress. Such an exhibition was never realised, probably because Yacoubi's love-life in Tangier was becoming fraught:

> Ahmed has been in a bad way [Francis continued] he had an affair with a German boy of 12 and the father found out and arrived at the flat with 2 Police he was arrested and put in prison for a couple of days until he was bailed out he had a preliminary interview with a tribunal on Saturday he is in an awful state as it has been dragging on for about 2 months and he does not know yet what is going to happen.

Yacoubi's arrest indicates that the letter was sent in late August 1957, after Yacoubi's first arrest in June. The scandal frightened the Tangerine expatriates out of their complacency. Though the

157

boy's age varies in different reports, from thirteen to fourteen, he was still a boy, but this time he was not Moroccan, and the crime could not be talked away with bribes in high places.

Paul Bowles stood bail for the sum of 200,000 francs, about 500 dollars, but was equally concerned about his own fate at the hands of the new authorities. Francis behaved impeccably, sending two canvases to Yacoubi in jail and keeping Paul Bowles informed when he left the country, with the warning note 'I think you should be careful . . . about coming back for your sake as well as Ahmed's. If you write to me please do not put your name on the back of the envelope.' On 14 May, after five months in prison, Yacoubi was taken to court and acquitted in five minutes. Francis wrote at once to Paul Bowles with the good news, adding that Yacoubi was eager to retrieve his possessions from Paul's apartment, but the new purge – even described as an inquisition – continued throughout the summer, prompting William Burroughs to send the depressing verdict to Allen Ginsberg: 'Tangier is finished. The Arab dogs are upon us. Many a queen has been dragged shrieking from the parade, the Socco Chico, and lodged in the local box where sixty sons of Sodom now languish. The boy(s), many beaten to a pulp, have spelled a list of hundreds . . .'

That was very Burroughs, very Tangerine, and a wild exaggeration.

It is a cliché to suggest that gregarious and promiscuous people are often lonely, but I believe that this was true of Francis, who was happiest in the company of the few he trusted, like Paul Danquah and Peter Pollock, which is why he hoped for their visit. Though Peter Lacy could be difficult, he was fond of him and ended his letter on a wistful note: 'I do not see much of Peter Now he has a flat of his own he is working again at Deans till the end of September . . .'

Another letter, a single page scratched in pencil, asks when a certain friend is coming out to join him, plainly in need of company as he refers to a forthcoming 'operation': 'I would be a bit less alarmed of the operation with a friend here. The first night Peter and Ron and me were in the Police station they both set on me in the taxi and the taxi driver called the police. Peter seems to be going a bit mad. I shall never be able to work with all this . . .'

This was confirmed in another letter, simply dated 2 July and hard to decipher:

> I realize once and for all I shall never be able to work here or really I believe outside england I shall really never try carting the stuff about again. I am also going to try and give up the flat. I am hoping my trouble is going to heal without an operation.
>
> All the Billy Hill crowd are here they being charming to me because they are trying to get me involved in something I will tell you when I get home so if he should telephone or someone called Charlie Mitchell would you say you don't know when I will be back as they are leaving tomorrow it is a terrible nuisance to be in this state as Charlie is a really handsome east-end thug and in the circumstances would not be hard to make as he likes giving the whip. This has really been a disastrous holiday but in ways quite interesting
>
> I shall be so pleased to be back and see you again – money wise it has been terrible it is quite as expensive here and has gone like water.

'A disastrous holiday but in ways quite interesting', a Baconian understatement, especially if Charlie Mitchell was related to, or conceivably an alias for, Frank Mitchell the 'Mad Axeman' who was rescued from Dartmoor and kept by the Kray Twins in London where they were desperate to have him hidden until he was disposed of.

Francis joined Burroughs's midnight parties at the Manuria though he flinched when he was offered a can from the trash bucket instead of a glass, explaining later that he was afraid of getting typhoid. Neither was he keen on drugs. When he held a party at his flat in return, Paul Danquah remembered that Yacoubi mixed a lot of *majoun* while Burroughs wandered around with a great spoon and the pot in an old-fashioned jamjar, growling 'Now have some of this.' Paul and Francis discovered that only a pinch of *majoun* made them high, and when they experimented with *kif* Francis's face blew up like a balloon because of his asthma – 'He never did it again,' said Paul.

Allen Ginsberg described Francis at that period as satyr with the looks of an English schoolboy who 'wears sneakers and tight dungarees and black silk shirts and always looks like going to tennis . . . and paints mad gorillas in grey hotel rooms dressed in evening dress with deathly black umbrellas – said he would paint a big pornographic picture of me & Peter (Orlovsky).'

When he asked Francis how he finished a painting, he replied that he did it with a chance brush stroke that locked in the magic – a fortuitous thing that he couldn't predict or orchestrate.

Ginsberg compared Yacoubi's paintings to those of Klee, surprisingly, and certainly he had the potential and the charm for Francis to make a rare exception when Bowles asked if he would allow Yacoubi to visit his studio and watch him paint.

'Yacoubi drew, but he was desperate to paint oils on canvas,' Bowles explained to me.

'Well,' said Francis, 'I don't *ever* allow anyone to watch me work, but in your case I'll make an exception and you can come and watch me slosh the stuff on.' Yacoubi went there every morning to learn, and Francis brought him paints and materials from Winsor and Newton when he returned from London. He also gave him some of his rejected canvases to work on, and these were stolen later and sold as Bacons. One of them was the picture he allegedly recognised in Bond Street, bought for £50,000 and then jumped on outside on the pavement. Anyway Yacoubi learned his lessons, and his work enjoyed a modest success in America, where he died in 1989.

As for Peter Lacy, Bowles remembered nothing whatsoever, as if he were a figment of my imagination. I made my excuses, and let myself out of his dismal flat with a gesture of dismissal from the silent Moroccan.

There are times when luck nudges you in the right direction. My driver told me that David Herbert lived on the 'Hill' nearby. On a sudden impulse, I decided to brave any memories of the Deakin fiasco and call. After interminable knocking on his front door, he emerged on his way to a cocktail party and invited me to drinks the next day at twelve.

David Herbert is everything an expatriate hopes to be. For one thing he is as happy as an animal in his natural habitat – 'Where else but in Tangier could I have developed my tastes to the same extent, my hopes and indeed the very concept of my life . . . no other town could have fulfilled my purpose so well.'

As a younger son of the Earl of Pembroke, David was bound for the Church, the Army or exile, but Tangier has been his home for forty years. Instead he has created a famous exotic garden of such overgrown luxuriance that he was offered $8,000 if he would allow a camera crew to film *The Naked Lunch* there. Wisely he refused, after consulting friends who warned it might mean the end of his privacy – though the money would have been welcome. The interior is close to Wilton House, though the rooms reflect the light and air of Morocco, leading doorless into each other with walls of vivid green. David is an unabashed snob, and the tables are adorned by signed photographs, inevitably of the Queen Mother and his nephew the Earl. Cecil Beaton stayed here after his stroke and started to recover, helped by Herbert's no-nonsense, nanny severity. Another drawing, by her mother, shows Diana Cooper as the Madonna in Max Reinhardt's *The Miracle*. The atmosphere is the right side of frivolous, though perilously close to camp.

Herbert is the consular warden of Tangier's Anglican church, St Andrew's, which has an English interior though the ceiling is made of cedar carved by craftsmen from Fez, and the Lord's prayer is scrolled in Arabic above the chancel.

'I love my church,' said Herbert proudly. 'I have a rod and accompany the ambassador up the aisle. He's coming to drinks with his wife on Sunday. Do come!'

I sighed with relief when he replied to my next question.

'Peter Lacy? Oh yes, I knew him well. Played the piano in Dean's. I don't think he had any money at all. He was awfully sweet but I remember him getting very drunk. Darling Francis was having his first show and Lacy was so blind drunk that they had a fearful row and Lacy slashed thirty of his canvases. Can you imagine!' David Herbert laughed at such audacity, and went on: 'Yet Francis told me, "You know, I rather enjoyed it." I believe the pictures were intended for his first Marlborough show in New York.

'Francis was always being beaten up. It got so bad that our consul general was very upset and got hold of the chief of police, who was a friend, and told him he had to do something about it and the wretched street lighting. He impressed on him that Francis was a very distinguished painter and kept on getting mugged. A few days later the chief of police returned, patently embarrassed: "*Pardon, mais le peintre adore ça!*"

'Of course Francis asked for it. He must have enjoyed it just as he enjoyed his lover slashing the pictures. Francis couldn't have

161

been more than thirty then [he was in fact in his forties] and was painting very hard.'

A picture of Bacon and Lacy in Tangier was emerging at odds with the popular conception of his saintly forbearance. I was aware that Francis Bacon was now such a legendary figure that many of the anecdotes could be apocryphal, even told by Francis himself with that ringing self-mockery which removed the malice and made them fun, so David Herbert's version could have been an exaggeration. I still needed a piece to complete the jigsaw, but doubted I would find it as I drove to the Las Conchas Restaurant in Murillo Street to meet Sally Wool-Lewis, one of two Englishwomen who manage it.

A few minutes later, as I looked through the glass partition that divides the bar from the restaurant, I could scarcely believe my luck. It was one of the few moments when I thought, to use the old cliché, that my eyes deceived me.

Paul Danquah was sitting at a table talking to a woman, and as my gaze shifted I saw Peter Pollock sitting opposite. In this momentary time-warp, both seemed unchanged – except that Paul's hair was grey. Peter looked as boyish as ever. What made the encounter so astonishing was my conviction that Paul worked for the World Bank in Washington – I had even thought of flying out there to see him and, though Tangier was a natural base to return to, they were the last people I expected to see. After cries of mutual surprise and greeting, I learned that Paul had retired from his job five years earlier, and their home was now in Tangier.

If anyone knew the truth of Peter Lacy, they would.

'Was it true that Francis used to get beaten up?' I asked later, when we were sitting in their garden.

'If you start beating up a Moroccan, he starts beating you up,' Peter pointed out.

'Peter Lacy used to get beaten up,' said Paul 'Lacy was impossible with Moroccan pick-ups when he was drunk.'

Evidently, in Tangier, Bacon and Lacy frequently went separate ways. I learned that Francis's great friend in Tangier was a Moroccan known as 'The Gorilla'. 'He wouldn't attract me,' said Peter, 'but he was a very nice man and still polite if I see him.

He had a relationship with the lesbian sister of a Scot called James Duncan who ran the Golden Beach Bar.'

'Surely Lacy was good for Francis?' I asked.

'Terrible,' said Peter.

162

'A horror,' Paul agreed. He explained: 'Francis had a need for that kind of affair. Francis was desperately in love with him. It was obsessional.'

'Peter Lacy was flinging pictures out of the window wherever they went,' said Peter, drily. 'He had an uncontrollable rage. Trails of canvas were flung from their hotels.'

'He was strikingly handsome,' Paul conceded in his favour.

'I always saw him as a romantic figure,' I ventured.

'*Any* fighter pilot was romantic,' said Peter sardonically.

'He had a *funny* arrogance,' said Paul, trying to be kinder, 'about everything and everybody. But when you heard him playing the piano like Sinatra sings, you'd think: "No, he *couldn't* have done anything so nasty." '

Peter sighed. 'He was drunk and desperate and self-destructive.'

I rememberd an odd occasion, not fully understood at the time, shortly after I met Lacy in London. For a time Peter rented a gentleman's ground-floor flat at the top of Sloane Street, a suitably genteel and impersonal residence. He and Francis invited me there for drinks one evening and the conversation turned to the subject of sadism, as if to test me out. I may be flattering myself in wondering if Lacy wanted to whip me, and have no certainty that this was the case, though I gained the impression that he would have liked me to 'join in' in some role. When I said that the thought of whips alarmed me because they might hurt, he lost interest. Later, when we were alone and Francis showed me the weals across his back, this confirmed my reluctance. So there was more to Peter the saintly. The masochist is stronger than the sadist, and Lacy's vulnerability may have explained Francis's obsession.

Paul concluded: 'One of the saddest times in Battersea, when the relationship between Francis and Peter Lacy was very strong and they were exchanging letters, was when he received a card which wasn't as warm as it should be. I remember him holding up the card, and he looked so sad that I realised he was very much in love with Lacy.'

With Lacy's death, the Tangerine days were over for Francis. He had enjoyed them, though he admitted to Peter Pollock that he thought the Beat poets, Burroughs and Ginsberg, and their entourage – 'romantically poor with their American Express cards'. Now that Lacy was dead the *raison d'être* was gone. And Francis was established as Britain's foremost artist.

# 11

# Francis and the Women

You know I also made love to Isabel Rawsthorne.
                                   *Francis Bacon in an interview in* Paris Match

Francis liked women. They loved him. Francis once told Grey
Gowrie that a centre of his being was that he had disliked his father
and greatly liked his mother, but that it was his father for whom he
felt attraction. Perhaps this was the pattern: relationships with
men being more intense, more difficult, and relationships with
women being more affectionate, more straightforward. Helen
Lessore of the Beaux Arts Gallery told me after his death of her
sense of loss: 'He was one of my dearest friends.' As I mentioned
earlier, Sir Robert Sainsbury believes that Francis was closer to his
wife than he was to himself, because he was homosexual.
Myfanwy Piper recalled how Francis walked along the towpath
from Henley, when he was staying at the Imperial Hotel, to call on
herself and John Piper – 'We loved him.' My own dear friend
Karen Lamey, who lived with Peter Bradshaw next door,
remembered how Francis clutched her arm one afternoon as we
moved from the French to the Colony. 'Come on,' he said, 'let's go
ahead. This lot can follow.' To start with he was 'so high up' that
she was in awe of him, but he spoke directly as if they were on the
same level and she was able to relax: 'He was such a nice man.
He's not like anyone, is he?'

Though he had a deep affection, even love, for Muriel Belcher,
and an absolute trust in Valerie Beston, he enjoyed a special
relationship with Isabel Lambert (later Isabel Rawsthorne). He
admired her for her intellect as well as her looks, which he painted
in a series of portraits; I know of twenty-two, and there could be
more.

Virtually forgotten today – though the painter Tony Smith was
preparing an exhibition of her work shortly before her death

in 1992 – Isabel enjoyed a life of uninhibited exuberance until the onslaught of age. She was born in 1912 in East London, daughter of a master mariner, and at the age of twelve was taken by her mother to Liverpool where her father's ship put in; in due course she attended Liverpool School of Art. Returning to London at the age of eighteen with a scholarship to the Royal Academy Schools, she had to make her own way as her father had died of unknown causes in some far corner of the world, and her mother had emigrated to Canada. She was described as possessing 'a fierce, animal confidence in her right to do as she pleased' and never stopped studying and painting. As an assistant to Jacob Epstein, by whom she had a child, she posed for numerous works. Isabel moved to Paris when she was twenty-two, though she told me that she liked to consider this period of her life to be her adolescence. The first artist to help her was André Derain, who allowed her to work in his studio and painted a series of portraits. The picture she lent to the Fitzwilliam Museum in Cambridge shows a vivacious girl with dark falling curls and the promise of laughter on her lips. She was now twenty-six, and it is easy to understand why she was sought after as a model and a mistress.

'I adored Derain – he was the most French person you could ever meet. That's how I learned the language.'

Giacometti was her next challenge. His portrait of her, *Isabel dans l'atelier*, and his bronze head are now in the Sainsbury Centre for Visual Arts in the University of East Anglia.

'Alberto worked all night, but at five every evening we drank at the Lipp. Picasso used to sit at the table opposite and one day, after staring at me particularly hard, he jumped up and said to Alberto: "Now I know how to do it." He dashed back to his studio to paint my portrait with little red eyes, wild hair and a vertical mouth – one of five he painted from memory.'

She dismissed Hemingway as 'a selfish man with a certain charm but a craving to make an effect', and married a rival war correspondent, Sefton Delmer. He took her with him to cover the Spanish Civil War, until one day he commandeered a taxi and told her: 'I think it is time for you to leave. The bombardment of Barcelona is becoming serious.' Then in Poland in 1939 he put her on the last plane to Paris, and when France fell she sailed on the last boat to England. 'I seemed to be on the last thing from

165

everywhere. That was the end of my adolescence. How I loved Paris – it gave me everything.'

In 1947 she married the composer Constant Lambert for the worst of reasons: 'I thought that if he married me, I would bring him back to life. He was a sad and lonely man.' He was described as 'the English Diaghilev' by Ninette de Valois, who was possibly unaware that Diaghilev had commissioned him to write for the Russian Ballet when Lambert was only twenty. He was noted for his wit, and his fellow composer and greatest friend, Alan Rawsthorne, said that when he was with Isabel it was quite fantastic. After Lambert died from DTs in the London Clinic in 1951 after turning on her in his drunken madness – 'We've seen enough of *you*' – she married Rawsthorne and designed his ballet *Madame Chrysanthème*.

Writing her obituary in 1992, I mentioned that 'she wore the surprised expression of someone who has just heard a marvellous joke and wishes to share it'. I met her one midday at the Intrepid Fox at the beginning of Wardour Street, around the corner from Old Compton Street, and when she asked what I was doing I told her I was preparing a book called *In Praise of Simple Food*. 'But that's splendid!' she cried with her usual gusto. 'That's everything I need, I'll buy it!' But when we discussed what recipes I should use we realised they would, inevitably, be disconcertingly brief – 'Take one Cox's apple and a slice of Cheddar.' We laughed so much that the book remained unwritten.

Whenever I see Francis's astonishing full-length painting done in 1967, *Isabel Rawsthorne Standing in a Street in Soho*, now in the Nationalgalerie in Berlin, I remember her fun that morning. It is not surprising that Francis, who knew her so well, should have loved her. Her joyful company always enhanced the occasion, though there was a poignant mistake one lunchtime at Wheeler's when I remarked that, fond as I was of Alan, I found him rather silly. 'That's just how I feel,' said Francis. We were startled when Isabel agreed, though she did so tearfully: 'It sounds so terribly cruel but I do know what you mean.'

'I didn't realise you knew Alan,' I remarked, puzzled.

'Know him? I'm married to him!'

Francis and I had just met another man called Alan in

the French and explained the confusion, but our laughter was embarrassed.

There is no doubt that Francis was impressed by the lustre of her lovers, particularly Giacometti, whom Francis called 'the greatest living influence on my work' when he introduced us in the Colony. Most people have their snobbery and would be dull without it – class snobs, money snobs, and in my case a celebrity snob. Francis was an artistic snob if the names were distinguished, as they were in Isabel's case. This helps to explain the claim he made in an interview with *Paris Match*: 'You know I also made love to Isabel Rawsthorne, a very beautiful woman who was Derain's model and Georges Bataille's girlfriend.'

It is impossible to know if this claim is true, though Ian Board remembers them consuming a bottle of Fernet Branca in the Colony one afternoon: 'They looked like clowns and acted like clowns, their tongues down each other's throat.'

Though he declared a special admiration for Alberto Giacometti, Francis arrived drunk at the restaurant for a dinner arranged by Isabel. As he became progressively drunker, his discourse on art deteriorated into a meandering monologue about life and death, as it was wont to do. Giacometti drank sparingly and listened patiently with the occasional shrug – 'Who knows?' Probably aware that he was boring the man he considered 'the most marvellous of human beings', Francis silently raised his edge of the table higher and higher until all the plates, glasses and silverware cascaded to the floor. Apparently Giacometti was delighted 'by that kind of answer to the riddle of the universe and shouted with glee'.

Though Francis was passionately interested in the original work, travelling abroad with Lucian Freud to see an Ingres exhibition, it is significant that he was just as inspired by reproductions. When he was in Rome he did not see the Velasquez *Pope Innocent X* because he could not be bothered. He was as excited by the *idea* as by the paint, though he admitted to a fear of 'seeing this marvellous painting and thinking of the stupid things one had done with it'. Perhaps such a confrontation might have *un*-inspired him.

Though Francis commissioned John Deakin to photograph

various friends he refused to appear in a documentary on Deakin shown in March 1991 by Channel 4 – *Salvage of a Soho Photographer* – on the surprising grounds that he scarcely knew him. When the director, John Christie, suggested they had been exceptionally close, Francis repeated his assertion, adding: 'Anyhow, he was not a particularly good photographer and photography in itself is of no importance', or words to that effect. He implied, also, that if he had commissioned Deakin this was simply a means of giving him money.

This was an old man's self-deception. It is understandable that he did not wish to appear in a television documentary, but equally plain that he wished to distance himself from any contribution that Deakin's photographs might have made. Fair enough. He did not paint *from* Deakin's portraits but they served as a trigger, even for his distortion. One of his subjects was Henrietta, the laughing girl with the tossed back hair whom I met on my first day in the French.

At this time she was living with Michael Law, who worked for the Crown Film Unit. Subsequently she married the Indian poet Dom Moraes, and the actor Norman Bowler. A volatile character, Henrietta Moraes, as she is generally known today, admits that she went through a phase when she was a cat burglar – this she told me with the nonchalance of someone who says they prefer to shop in Harrods rather than Fortnum's. 'Of course I was caught and went to prison for ten days. When I came out, I found that Muriel Belcher had organised a whip-round and £1,000 was waiting for me in the Colony, which was sort of amazing. Muriel was like that, if she liked you.'

Francis told her one morning in the French pub that he would like to paint her. 'Yes, of course,' she replied, with a toss of her head. 'Fine.' He explained he was unable to work from live models because people were shocked by the results, and there was some truth in this, though of course he preferred to work alone. Deakin, Francis told Henrietta, would take some photographs instead.

'Deakin came over to my flat a week later and told me to take my clothes off, and I sat on the bed with my arms and legs crossed. Deakin said: "For God's sake, he doesn't want a *pietà*. He wants you naked and lying on the bed and he's told me the exact position. Throw yourself back and abandon yourself." He was very sure of all the angles, but they didn't seem right to me. I thought they were rather extreme – er, *intimate* – that Francis couldn't possibly want to paint me like that, hundreds of close-ups of my private parts! But I said: "All right, go ahead – it's only images, after all." '

A week later Deakin came into the French pub to show them the results. 'Francis took one look and said they were absolutely *useless*! Taken from the wrong angle. So I had to do it all over again, this time upside down.'

In between, Henrietta went to a drinking club in Soho which she described as 'really low and loathsome', full of sailors; Deakin was flitting about furtively with bits of paper which he tried to hide from her. Seizing one, she realised he was selling the rejected photographs of herself naked on the bed, concealing nothing, and charging the sailors ten shillings a shot. 'I was really furious at the time. Then I thought it was *so funny*! But only ten shillings! How dare he!'

Apart from several portraits, Francis's most famous painting of Henrietta is *Lying Figure with Hypodermic Syringe* of 1963. 'I'd never heard of hypodermic syringes or serious drugs at that point,' she said. 'It caught up with me later. How did he *know*? It was something he must have *seen*.'

Henrietta says that Francis promised to give her one of the pictures, but he never did. 'I waited about twenty years and then I asked him. He said, "Oh darling, you'd have sold it long ago, wouldn't you!" I had to admit that I probably would have.' He gave her money instead: 'He was a very generous person.'

Francis admired Deakin's photographs at the time, allowing their use as illustrations in David Sylvester's *Interviews* in 1975. The images used included Henrietta writhing on her bed; Lucian Freud, also in bed though fully clothed; and a powerful close-up of Isabel Rawsthorne which is echoed in the Bacon portraits – astonishing swirls of paint which achieve an instant recognition while capturing her personality. 'If you look at the details,' she told me, 'they are fabulously accurate and extremely difficult to do. Practically no one else could do them.'

If Princess Margaret has a memory of Francis Bacon it is unlikely to be happy; his presence at a party could be a time bomb, and in this case it went off. The posher the occasion, the more outrageously he could behave.

Lady Caroline Blackwood, who married Lucian Freud, remembers the ball given by Lady Rothermere. Champagne flowed so abundantly that the Princess was 'seized by a desire to show off'. She grabbed the microphone from the startled singer of the band, whom she instructed to play songs by Cole Porter. 'All the guests who had been waltzing under the vast chandeliers instantly stopped dancing. They stood like Buckingham Palace sentries called to attention to watch the royal performance.'

Princess Margaret knew the songs by heart but she sang them hopelessly off-key, egged on by her sycophantic audience of ladies laden with jewellery and gentlemen penguins in white ties and tails. 'They shouted and they roared and they asked for more.' Unfortunately, according to Lady Caroline, Princess Margaret 'became a little manic at receiving such approval' and 'started wiggling around in her crinoline and tiara as she tried to mimic the sexual movements of the professional entertainer. Her dress with its petticoats bolstered by the wooden hoops that ballooned her skirts was unsuitable for the slinky act but all the rapturous applause seemed to make her forget this.'

She was starting on the familiar lyrics of 'Let's Do It' when

a very menacing and unexpected sound came from the back of the crowded ballroom. It grew louder and louder until it eclipsed Princess Margaret's singing. It was the sound of jeering and hissing, of prolonged and thunderous booing. Princess Margaret faltered in mid-lyric. Mortification turned her face scarlet and then it went ashen. Because she looked close to tears, her smallness of stature suddenly made her look rather pitiful.

The Princess abandoned the microphone and was hurried out of the ballroom by her flustered ladies-in-waiting as the band stopped playing, uncertain what to do, and Lady Rothermere's guests asked each other what had happened.

A man whose face was already red, but was now apoplectic with rage, told Caroline: 'It was that dreadful man Francis Bacon. He calls himself a painter but he does the most frightful paintings. I just don't understand how a creature like him was allowed to get in here. It's really quite disgraceful.' Afterwards Francis said: 'Her singing was really too awful. Someone had to stop her. If you're going to do something, you shouldn't do it as badly as that.'

Also, of course, he was drunk. Considering that it was gallant, if vain, of the Princess to get up and sing in the first place, his reaction was cruel. Yet Francis had 'an anarchic fearlessness which was unique,' Caroline wrote admiringly.

> I can think of no one else who would have dared to boo a member of the royal family in a private house. Among all the guests assembled in Lady Rothermere's ballroom, more than a few were secretly suffering from Princess Margaret's singing, but they suffered in silence, gagged by their snobbery. Francis could not be gagged. If he found a performance shoddy no conventional trepidation prevented him from expressing his reactions. Sometimes his opinions could be biased and perverse and unfair, but he never cared if they created outrage.

Presumably, Lord Rothermere had forgotten the incident when introduced to Francis at an anniversary party for the *Daily Mail* in 1990. 'And what do you do?' he asked.

'I'm an old poof,' said Francis.

# 12

## The Lost Soul of George Dyer

I would rather have torment than annihilation. If I was in hell, I would always feel I had a chance of escaping.

*Francis Bacon*

Once, in the Golden Lion, a young hustler proudly showed me the trousers he had just been given, explaining that they were '*Calvary* twill'. His mistake was heartbreaking. I sensed that, whatever hill he landed on, he was bound to be crucified. George Dyer used the Lion too and I saw him there frequently, usually sitting on his own, staring into his glass with the same vulnerability. Though he had been a minor 'villain', I understood that his crimes had been petty, and though his looks were hard he was hopelessly weak – fulfilling Oscar Wilde's 'tyranny'.

There was an innocence about George, even a sweetness, which was touching; but his hopelessness made him dangerous. He had old-fashioned manners and would stand up when he saw me, asking if I wanted a drink. Relishing his role as confidant, Deakin had a genuine affection for George, apart from his usefulness as a 'meal-ticket' in his capacity as Francis's new friend. Deakin also teased him, which George enjoyed – I doubt if anyone had teased him before because of his air of latent violence.

George had a slight speech impediment, as if the words were struggling to break free, which added to his emotional if not physical vulnerability. Wearing excellent, soberly cut suits paid for by Francis, he could have been a City businessman until you heard his strangled East End accent. The combination had considerable charm.

Peter Bradshaw recalled an afternoon when George sat beside him in the Kismet Club on one of the banquettes and poured his heart out: 'I don't know, Peter. I can't cope with it all. Everyone finks I'm on to a good fing – finks George has got it made. They don't realise how difficult it is. I don't know what to do. It's like I'm using him as a walking-stick.' Peter imitated the pronunciation – '*war-kin*' stick. He, too, was fond of George and said it was sad to see him so unhappy – 'Next time I saw him in a Chelsea pub and he borrowed a pound off me.'

Usually, George was 'loaded' with money, supplied by Francis even if only to keep him quiet. That was the trouble, for George inevitably acquired a coterie. 'He always had hangers-on in the Lion,' said Peter. 'He didn't like it, but he couldn't shake them off. Sometimes there were as many as six blokes, but he wasn't strong enough – he felt trapped and couldn't see any way out.' Also, he was lonely and grateful for their company. If he paid for everyone it gave him a semblance of self-respect.

So, with nothing to do, George drank prodigiously all day, assisted by Deakin and the hangers-on. The hangers-on were not vicious – their own crimes could hardly be more petty; but they knew they were 'on to a good thing' and gave George the attention he needed. Jack Murray, who ran the Apollo Club in Wardour Street, complained to me with a sigh: 'I'm very fond of dear George and I don't mind him falling into the club in the early evening with his chums, but he's drunk so much everywhere else that by the time he gets to me he can't order a drink, let alone pay for it!'

Some people may wonder what Francis saw in him. After all, he was hardly the 'Nietzsche of the football team'. Presumably, the answer is simply the threat and the actuality of violence – to start with at least. There is an irony that, in the pursuit of rough trade the pursuer is both victim and ringmaster. The fantasy of a relationship with 'a real man' – such an elusive quarry needs to be put in quotes – prompted Francis's generation to set out in pursuit of Guardsmen and sailors who offered the illusion and sometimes a fleeting satisfaction. The game was played with such conviction by both pursuers and pursued that one man whose real name I never knew, a friend of Cecil Beaton, Lady Diana Cooper and Stephen Tennant, wanted to change his name by deed poll to Simon Sailor until he was persuaded to change it to Simon Fleet instead.

Francis was always a law unto himself, but some of the rules applied, namely that any guilt in being homosexual was assuaged if the pick-up was paid for. It was an encounter which satisfied everyone until it became a serious 'affair' and then the waters of friendship generally proved treacherous. A homosexual relationship might succeed if both parties were wholly homosexual, yet even this could be fraught.

Peter Watson, the wealthy American who patronised artists and backed Cyril Connolly's *Horizon*, was found drowned in his bath; and there were rumours that, far from this being an accident, he had been murdered by the handsome young American lover whose money Francis stole in the south of France and who died in curiously similar circumstances in the West Indies a few years later. Francis introduced me to Watson, whom everyone adored; I thought he was rather a cold fish compared to the lover, who was bright and friendly – though everyone hated him as the bad influence he proved to be.

Then there was Brian Howard and his devoted sailor-friend Sam, who tried his saintly best to cope with Howard's bad temper and his alcoholism. Both men took to heroin which weakened their resistance at the end. Sam died in his bath due to gas fumes from a faulty geyser; Brian Howard died from an overdose three days later. They were buried together. The only time I met Brian Howard was at a small drinks party in Dolphin Square which he gave for Christopher Isherwood on a visit from California. Francis took me along, and I think we were the only other guests to turn up. I disliked Isherwood for his absurdly bushy eyebrows and disagreeably shrill voice as he spoke with the pedantry of an American university lecturer, whereas the flamboyant Howard made no impression on me whatsoever. Only now, as I read the countless reminiscences of the thirties and forties, do I regret the lost opportunities to study characters who emerge in the memoirs of their time.

Francis met George Dyer in 1964, the year in which I abandoned my job in television and moved to the Grey House on the North Devon sands, which had been left to me by my parents, to find out if I could write. It proved a rash impulse, and within a year I was so poor that my visits to London were rarer and I began to lose touch.

One morning I was irritated to hear a car draw up on the drive outside soon after six o'clock. I dread such intrusions at the best of times, and these were the worst of times financially. Going to investigate, I was aghast to see the hangers-on disgorging from the car, followed eventually by George who looked around him, bewildered.

'I fort we was going to Brighton,' he explained.

George had become a liability, the threat of violence a reality as he and Francis fought in the mews cottage, with Francis flinging George's clothes and belongings into the cobbled street to be retrieved by dustmen who could scarcely believe their luck. Discreet as they both are regarding Francis's private life, even Valerie Beston admits that George could 'be very bad indeed' when drunk, and Sir Robert Sainsbury described him as 'absolutely ghastly', having had the misfortune to sit next to him when Francis brought him to dinner at his home.

George spent recklessly, as if he hated the money – which is understandable. At one point Francis tried to buy him off with £20,000 (the equivalent of about £100,000 today), on condition that he lived in Brighton. Francis must have known this was a hopeless solution, for George was bound to come back. Meanwhile, he was followed by his entourage whom he invited to English's oyster bar in Brighton in a parody of Francis playing host at Wheeler's. Brighton was close enough for them to carry on to London, and it was after one of these nights that the entourage decided to continue to Devon, though I have no idea how they knew where to go. George was drunk, but evidently woke at one point during the journey to spot a signpost which he mistook for London's Bow – 'Wot the bleedin' hell we doing in the East End?' he asked before he fell asleep again.

Unable to cope with their arrival, I gave them breakfast and took George aside to say they would have to leave. I was on my own and anxious to be rid of them, sensing trouble. Sober by now, George understood the situation and behaved impeccably, apologising. Though I knew a couple of the hangers-on by sight, I had no idea of their names or who they really were, and hoped they had merely acted on the spur of the moment with the thought that it might be fun to drive through the night.

After breakfast they raced off in the direction of Ilfracombe, where I have the uneasy feeling that they intended to 'do a job', and I had no wish to know what kind of 'job' it was. Neither

George nor I referred to the incident afterwards, as if it had never happened.

Accompanied by Deakin, Francis and George set out for Athens by train and then took the ferry to Crete. Francis remained on deck next to the lifeboats for most of the crossing in case one of the Aegean squalls sprang up and put the ship in danger. Having made their way from Heraklion to the port of Chania, they stayed in the pleasant old-fashioned hotel at the end of the promontory in the middle of the harbour until their scenes became so violent that they were asked to leave. Despite some cheerful photographs by Deakin taken at the start of their train journey, with Francis gesticulating over a regiment of wine bottles, this was one of those holidays that people do not talk about afterwards, except for Deakin's terse dismissal: 'It was unbelievable rows, arguments and fights all the bloody way.'

Desperate for a solution, Francis resorted to the deceptive calm of the English countryside, even though he detested it: he bought or rented a modern house near Newbury which was conveniently close to the racecourse where both of them could gamble. This would be good for both of them, particularly for George. Francis even deluded himself that he would be able to paint there, as he explained when I chanced to meet them on the train from Exeter which they joined at Newbury, inevitably in the buffet car. I sensed the swift disillusionment – 'I thought I'd be able to do some work there, but I've discovered that the light is entirely wrong. The studio's facing the wrong way.' He said this indignantly as if it was the studio's fault, and tugged testily at his collar. 'Well, there it is. Anyhow, the whole idea was madness.' George nodded despondently.

The *Spectator*'s art critic, Giles Auty, coincided with Francis and George in the restaurant car of the same train:

In days when Britain was less affluent, I suspect many users of restaurant cars seldom dined out other than when travelling. There was a subdued hush in the dining-room broken only by the tinkle of cutlery and whispered discussions between long-married couples as to whether to order a half-bottle of beaujolais. The waiter motioned me to an unoccupied seat at a table . . . 'If you wouldn't mind joining the other gentlemen, sir.' Almost as I did so, Mr Bacon's new companion, sporting

176

a bright ginger crew-cut, complained very loudly of the heat: 'Cor, Francis, it ain't 'alf fuckin' 'ot in 'ere.' Throwing off his coat, he revealed a short-sleeved shirt, impressive musculature and brilliant braces. Several delicately poised fish knives clattered to the floor.

I do not remember George's hair as particularly ginger, though there was a period when it was crew-cut; he wore braces, as East End villains did, and his language is instantly familiar.

When the English countryside failed him, Francis sent George to Tangier, accompanied this time by Denis Wirth-Miller. This was at the time when Peter Pollock was running the Pergola Beach Bar there. Pollock grew to dread George's arrival: 'He would come to the Pergola in the middle of the day in a full city dress suit and get steadily drunk and didn't know how to cope, getting more and more sloshed as he sat there during long lunches. I disliked him very much. Francis was never here at the time – he'd go flying off – but George was sent out here to get him out of the way, chaperoned by Denis who got equally drunk.'

'Didn't George enjoy himself at all?' I asked wistfully. 'Did he make any friends?'

'George didn't want the Moroccans,' Paul Danquah intervened. 'He liked little boys.'

'Really?' said Peter with a lift of the eyebrows. 'I never thought of him like that. I didn't think he was interested in sex. I do know that on one of the visits he was so drunk that I drove him to the airport terrified that British Airways wouldn't take him. I was thankful to see him go.'

Francis also took George to New York, where they checked into separate bedrooms at the Algonquin Hotel. Jeffrey Bernard was there at the same time. 'I must have been mad, for I was dead broke and it was freezing. Francis bought me an overcoat and every morning I joined him for breakfast at the Algonquin, which consisted of a bottle of Dom Pérignon, and every morning he gave me a crisp hundred-dollar bill.'

'Did George join you for breakfast?'

'No, I hardly saw him.'

I asked about the legendary incident when the manager phoned Francis to warn him that George was trying to jump from his bedroom window: 'He's on the 19th floor isn't he? Then let him jump, he won't feel a thing.' Jeff laughed: 'I'm not sure about that, but what I do know, because I was there, is that a phone call came through to say that George had tried to commit suicide, but that Francis would be glad to hear he had been saved by the house doctor. Francis asked what George had done.'

'He took an overdose of sleeping pills,' said the manager.

'Is the doctor still there?'

'Yes, Mr Bacon.'

'Then tell him to write another prescription so he can do the job properly.'

Unable to dispose of him, it would not be surprising if Francis wondered aloud if there was someone who could rid him of this turbulent priest. If so, it prompted one of the most bizarre and regrettable episodes in his life.

Often described as 'a difficult person', Sonia Orwell was also vaultingly ambitious. As Sonia Brownell she was one of two secretaries at *Horizon*, and Cyril Connolly acknowledged his indebtedness to her for typing out the manuscript of *The Unquiet Grave*, which he published under the name of 'Palinurus'. Later she married George Orwell when he was dying, and finally Michael Pitt-Rivers, who was implicated with Lord Montagu and Peter Wildeblood when they were charged with a homosexual offence involving three young airmen. Like Anne Fleming, though infinitely poorer, Sonia Orwell became a voracious lion-hunter on a constant social safari as she aimed her sights and bagged two of the biggest cats in the jungle – Lucian Freud, with whom she had an affair, and Francis Bacon.

To start with, Francis barely tolerated her, though he took me to one of her parties at her flat off Sloane Square. She had no time for me, and I never liked her on the few occasions we met afterwards. Peter Pollock's sister, Claire, found her 'cold, ill-mannered, indifferent, belligerent', and so did I. Conversely I appreciate that she could be charming to those whom she admired. She had an interesting face, lovely eyes and hair, and laughed a lot, which was all in her favour; but she was also possessive and highly strung, crazy enough to take it on herself to solve Francis's problem once and for all by hiring someone to kill George Dyer.

She chose a young man known as Blond Billy. I cannot remember him – probably because I was stuck in North Devon struggling to survive – but Ian Board described him as a doorman at a Soho nightclub: 'He adored Francis and Francis was fascinated by him – they may have had some walloping thing together. On his nights off he came to the Colony and I'd say, "Let's all go on to your club," and we'd be allowed in if Francis was there.'

Someone else remembered that Blond Billy and another Runyonesque Soho figure called French Henry went gambling at Charlie Chester's with Francis, who gave them £50 each in £1 chips when he was £2,000 ahead. Blond Billy won £450 and suggested they celebrate the New Year by going on to the Trattoria Terrazza in Dean Street. Waking the next day with some of his chips, he returned to Charlie Chester's where he was told: 'You're barred. You took Francis away when he was winning.'

'Isn't he allowed to win?'

'No.'

Apparently Blond Billy, who was 'just out of nick', was prepared to do anything for Francis, perhaps an ideal hit-man in Sonia Orwell's feverish imagination, although there is no indication that he contemplated the madness of her suggestion that George should be disposed of. In fact the plan was quickly abandoned when word reached Lucian Freud, who was so shocked that he wrote to Sonia saying she must drop the idea at once and on no account proceed with it. He ended his letter: 'With friends like you I really don't need enemies.' She replied pathetically that Lucian did not understand her alcoholism. Inevitably, Francis heard of the 'contract to kill' and, with an ironic twist, became closer to Sonia – though Lucian stopped seeing her.

Peter Pollock summed up the situation exactly: 'Sonia had an important view of herself and I can see her saintly attitude in this, unable to realise that Francis wanted George to be part of him.'

The painter Robert Medley remembers George Dyer at this time. 'I knew him quite a lot, first of all through Francis, then through Vera Russell [first wife of the art critic John Russell] who met him at the Cornwall Arms in Queen's Gate after they separated. He was rather nice, actually. But he had quarrelled with the Kray boys and was anxious to avoid being beaten up by them. One night George hammered violently on Vera's door: "Let me in, they're coming to get me!" Vera let him through into her back garden. She was a great supporter of George and never forgave Francis for the affair being mishandled when he broke it off.'

Francis was committed for trial at the Inner London sessions when he appeared at Marlborough Street in October 1970 accused of unauthorised possession of cannabis at his mews home. Though George no longer lived there he returned constantly, trying to batter down the door, and his latent jealousy exploded when he discovered that Francis had a new friend, the model for the *Triptych 1970* which is now in the Australian National Gallery in Canberra. As with all Bacon portraits, the face and sleek, black hair are instantly recognisable, especially in the right-hand panel in which he poses naked.

Enraged, George tipped off the police. Led by Detective Sergeant Carol Bristow, they raided his studio at 8.25 one August morning. Shown their search warrant, Francis asked: 'May I ring Lord Goodman?'

The police searched the studio with two dogs trained to sniff out drugs, and 'Colonel' led them to a pipe stem containing 2.1 grammes of cannabis in silver paper in the bottom of a paintbox underneath a pile of underclothes. Given the chaos of the studio and the likely state of the underwear the raid had an element of farce – especially as 'Colonel' was Ronnie Kray's nickname.

The case was serious for Francis – if he was convicted of possessing drugs he would be prevented from entering the United States. The Marlborough Gallery was alarmed and in due course Basil Wigoder, one of the most brilliant QCs in the country, was retained to defend him.

Francis handled himself with dignity throughout, though it must have been an ordeal with the likelihood of nasty revelations on the way. Sergeant Bristow testified that, when he was shown the pipe stem, Bacon said: 'Look, I have various people here and it must belong to them. It must have been here for years. It is not mine. What is it used for? I do not smoke cannabis, I do not smoke at all. I am an asthmatic.'

Remembering when Bill Burroughs gave Francis his first joint of 'jam' in Tangier, I am sure Francis told the truth, though I have a photograph of the two of us at the Soho Fair in the early 1950s and he is holding a cigarette. This was unusual. I doubt if he smoked cannabis at the studio, though it is likely that friends did, including the latest friend and model.

In evidence, Francis confirmed he had made two attempts to smoke cannabis in Tangier in 1956 but suffered from such severe asthmatic attacks that he had never smoked it since – presumably a reference to the joint supplied by Burroughs. 'I would not allow people to smoke it in my premises if I knew what they were smoking, with the law as it stands.' Writers, artists and students were frequent callers at his studio. As for the mysterious pipe stem, this belonged to a man who had visited his flat years earlier and was now abroad. Francis found the stem on the floor afterwards and put it away and forgot all about it.

In reply to Basil Wigoder's questioning, Sergeant Bristow agreed that she had obtained her information about the presence of drugs from George Dyer. Wigoder was a formidable defence counsel and the entire episode was unsatisfactory from the police's standpoint, based as it was on information supplied by Dyer, who was described as having been in the employ of Francis Bacon for the last eight years as a model and general handyman.

Poor George. If he was trying to attract attention, he succeeded to his own detriment. Francis testified that Dyer was ill through alcoholism and often made allegations against him when drunk. Dyer had been to borstal and jail. 'When he is drunk he feels I don't pay him enough. Sometimes he has broken down my front door and broken into my flat. I pay him a regular wage but that doesn't suffice because of his drinking, and he comes and asks for more. Sometimes I give him some, sometimes I don't.' On 27 August he had refused. It was then that George Dyer went to the police to make his allegations.

As a police informant George was unreliable, and Francis was acquitted on both charges. 'I bear no animosity towards Mr Dyer,' he said as he left the court.'He is a very sick man. I still employ him, and I have kept contact with him while he was in hospital. I shall continue to employ him. Naturally I am relieved this whole business has cleared my name. It has been a great strain.'

His application for costs was rejected. 'I have considered the circumstances,' said Judge Leslie, 'and decided it would not be appropriate to make such an order.' Basil Wigoder took a chance in applying for them, presumably to stress the point that his client was blameless; but Judge Leslie proved the wiser, possibly sensing that this was largely a homosexual quarrel redolent with vindictiveness. Paradoxically, I suspect that George acted as he did because he loved Francis.

Needless to say, it changed nothing. Their relationship continued as turbulently as before.

Probably through feelings of responsibility, loyalty or even lingering vestiges of affection, Francis took George to Paris for the grand opening of his exhibition at the Grand Palais in October 1972, the most important moment in his career since the Tate retrospective. By then I was so out of touch that I had not been invited and I was too broke to make it on my own. Possibly with a degree of gloat, Deakin kept me informed. His own invitation hadbeen withdrawn after a strained lunch at Wheeler's – 'George morose and not drinking in readiness for Paris' – which ended in a quarrel, but this did not prevent Deakin from joining the entourage that crossed the Channel. It represented a volatile mix of friends and rivals including Denis Wirth-Miller and Dickie Chopping; Muriel Belcher and Ian Board; Thea Porter; John Moynihan and his wife Claire. Francis was accompanied by Isabel Rawsthorne, his sister and Sonia Orwell.

They stayed in the Hotel St Peres, where George Dyer's body was discovered in his bathroom on the morning of 24 October. It has been suggested that the news of his death was brought to Francis later in the day as he waited to receive the Minister of the Arts on top of the steps leading to the Grand Palais, with the flags waving, the band playing and the guard of honour saluting. As they went inside, one of the first paintings to attract the Minister's attention was one of George Dyer on the lavatory, a brutal echo of George's death on the hotel lavatory, apparently with blood streaming from every orifice. It has been claimed that the President flinched; one can only imagine the feelings of Francis.

In fact the official opening took place thirty-six hours after George's death. The confusion has been explained to me by Pathe Lambert, a close friend of Isabel though no relation, who arrived the day afterwards and was told the news by Isabel. Sonia Orwell invited her to have dinner with Francis, his sister, Isabel and Marguerite Duras in order 'to keep Francis occupied'. Years later, when asked by *Paris Match* if he had been close to any writers,

Francis replied: 'Close? No. I once met Marguerite Duras thanks to Sonia Orwell, her translator. She's charming, but what purpose does it serve to read her books?'

On the day of George's death, Francis attended a lavish reception hosted by Madame Pompidou; it was then that the band played and everyone appeared in full fig flanked by a guard of honour. The news of the tragedy was brought to him there, or he learned of it a few hours, or perhaps even minutes, earlier. This remains unclear.

John Moynihan remembers that 'Deakin was very much with us, drinking quite a lot, acting as the go-between and court jester.' This was after Deakin had been forgiven by Francis, greeted 'at the top of the grandest of all grand staircases'. He saw less of Francis, who was occupied with the VIPs and officials attending the reception, which he entered arm-in-arm with Isabel as they were led inside to be introduced to the 'high-ups'. 'It was the very moment George died,' Isabel told Tony and Pipi Smith, 'and there was a great to-do. I was sworn to secrecy but said I didn't have any secrets.'

'It was all hushed up,' says Ian, 'very hush-hush, you know! It could have fucked up the whole exhibition with more about George's death than the show.'

Francis's reaction was more astonishing than I could have believed. I asked John Moynihan if Francis was 'grief-stricken': 'He acted *elated*. He decided to push it away – the Pompidou reception and the guard of honour, oh yes, he loved it. He was swollen from the adulation, a great peacock. It was no good trying to be sympathetic or say one was sorry – instead it was more and more champagne. We met in the Coupole with Deakin, Claire and Sonia the night of the second private view, and Francis came in. He was wired up, didn't show any grief at all, laughing a lot. And so were Sonia and Deakin, enjoying his red wine.'

David Hockney was there too, and went across in the Coupole to tell Francis, whom he had met a couple of times before, how sorry he was to learn of George's death: 'He just picked up the serviette, screamed and said: "Well, you know, you can only laugh or cry. Ha! ha!" And then kind of mock tears, very loudly. Dramatic really, like the paintings.'

Did George commit suicide? There were rumours at the time of an overdose of drugs taken in a confused, drunken state, or an accumulation of pills and drugs which rebounded. The critic Robert Melville enraged Francis when he referred to George's 'suicide' in his review of the Grand Palais in the *New Statesman*, denying the convenient verdict by the French authorities that it was 'death by misadventure'.

'That was an awful thing to have done,' Francis accused him. 'What will people think? After all, they are only simple folk and won't understand.'

Melville protested that he had not realised that Francis was against suicide, and Francis explained he was thinking of George's parents. 'This sounded a bit odd to me,' wrote Melville, who added that John Russell complained in a letter to the *New Statesman* that their art critic had done a despicable thing in calling it suicide when it wasn't. 'But of course, it *was*.'

'Of course it was,' Francis confirmed to me on the one occasion he referred to it. 'Are you foolish or something? Think of the timing. Of course it was deliberate.'

Did he feel no grief or shed no tear except the tears of mockery produced for David Hockney? If he felt guilt perhaps he purged himself as only writers and artists can, by painting a posthumous 'narrative' triptych which depicted George's death. It can also be seen as a form of tribute or, more callously, as an exploitation because he was fascinated by the starkness of the subject. Probably both.

The *Triptych – May–June 1973* shows George in the right panel on the lavatory; in the central panel he is caught in drunken despair under a light-bulb as naked as himself; on the right, he vomits blood into a washbasin. As a final tribute, George's face was featured on the poster and the cover of the catalogue for the second Tate retrospective in May 1985.

When President Pompidou was shown around the Grand Palais, George was more in evidence that night than ever before. As a model he had served Francis well: *George Dyer Crouching*; *George Dyer Talking*; *George Dyer Staring at a Blind Cord*; *George Dyer Riding a Bicycle*; *George Dyer with a Dog*; *Study of George Dyer and Images from Muybridge*. His presence was inescapable. There was also the *Triptych* of the man who usurped him, prompting George in his jealousy to inform the police of drugs in Reece Mews. George was deplorable in that respect, but no one provided Francis Bacon with such inspiration as George Dyer.

The only time we came close to discussing Francis's cruelty to George by giving him the money to drink himself to death, an obliteration which would render him harmless, was an evening when I was due to meet David Lewis Jones of the *Daily Telegraph* to discuss the obituary I had been asked to prepare on Francis. We had not met before, and arranged to meet in the Colony around six-thirty. By chance Francis was in the club that afternoon, and I was careful not to mention my appointment. Few people relish the news that their obituary is being written in advance, even though that is the usual practice. I realised also that, though Francis was in an exuberant mood, he was drinking heavily and it could change.

Suddenly he decided to move on to the French and I left a discreet message for Lewis Jones to follow me. But as soon as he entered the French, Francis wanted to go to the Golden Lion next door. After leaving a further message, I followed him. It was now six o'clock and Francis was at his most expansive, dropping his trousers to reveal some bruises sustained when falling down the stairs of the house he had bought in Wivenhoe in Essex on one of his visits to Dennis Wirth-Miller and Dickie Chopping. He surprised the hustlers in the Lion with his explanation for the bruises: 'I think they polished the stairs on purpose in order to kill me before I changed my mind. You see, I've promised to leave them the place.' He shook with laughter at this idiotic fantasy.

I saw the new landlord eyeing Francis with suspicion, especially when he ordered champagne, which had rarely if ever been known in the Lion before. He had no idea who Francis was, nor did Francis look particularly respectable in his black leather jacket and tight trousers around his ankles until he hoisted them up and pulled out some £50 notes from a pocket. Somehow, a warm bottle of champagne was unearthed from the cellar and Francis slopped it into the glasses of the hustlers – who complained that they preferred cider.

At this moment, I sensed that Lewis Jones was standing behind me – and so did Francis.

'And who might you be?' he demanded, swinging round like a discus thrower. A dark-suited Mr Lewis Jones introduced himself, explaining, politely, before I had the chance to intervene: 'I'm the obituarist for the *Daily Telegraph*.'

Francis's gaiety changed to thundering rage as the word 'obituarist' penetrated his fuddled brain, no doubt transforming the inoffensive, diminutive figure of Mr Lewis Jones into a towering grey-bearded Nemesis with a scythe, alerted by the news that Francis was revelling his last hours away in a dubious Soho pub. After glaring at him with unconcealed hatred, Francis declared he wanted some snails. We left the pub after I managed a quick word to say I would contact Lewis Jones the following day. Luck was against us by now, and L'Escargot only offered us snails wrapped up in pastry. We continued to the Jardin des Gourmets where Francis turned on me as we sat down, blaming me for my failure to look after a particular friend as well as I should have done. This was hurtful, as it was meant to be, for I had done my utmost, frequently against the odds, to behave as honourably as I could. I retaliated harshly that in lavishing £20,000 on George he had done him no favour by destroying any lingering incentive he might have had.

Today, I am not sure what else Francis could have done. Possibly George was that rare and desperately sad creature who is beyond help, but it was certainly alcohol which became the 'walking-stick' rather than Francis, who was unable to give George the necessary emotional support.

George's illustrious supporters also included Robert Medley and Giacometti, who, surprisingly, patted him on the knee in a London taxi, declaring: 'When I'm in London, I'm homosexual!' Francis told Michel Archimbaud that he had a friend who came from the East End of London – 'an atonishing person' – who was plainly George Dyer, and that Giacometti was determined that he should paint him. Francis encouraged this but because it would have involved a visit to Paris it never occurred. Francis tried to persuade George because he preferred Giacometti's drawings above his sculpture – 'Especially those he did in crayon or fusain. I know he said that the great adventure for him was to see something unknown rising up, each day, in the same face. I find that very apposite.' That Giacometti should contemplate such a portrait shows that George Dyer interested people more than is generally credited.

In retrospect the tragedy of George's death should not diminish the good times they had together. 'Ghastly' though he could be when drunk, he was loveable too. I felt this when Miss Beston showed me the photographs taken by John Deakin on the Orient Express on the way to Venice. The rapport between George and Francis is undeniable and touching. They look totally attuned. The trouble was that when Francis was working hard, George was on the rampage; and when George was drying out in Putney, Francis was 'Blotto'. Ultimately, work came first with Francis, but the photographs also reveal the surprising force of George's looks which made him so useful as a model. Jane Willoughby liked George, so did my agent, Irene Josephy, who remembers his politeness. He may have been trouble – the nicest people often are. But after George's death in Paris the ranks closed in favour of Francis. The turbulent priest would trouble him no more.

In 1985 Francis told *The Times*, in reference to the *Triptych 1973*:

This picture – it is of somebody – a great friend of mine. When I had a show in Paris in '72 he committed suicide. He was found in the lavatory like that and he was sick into the basin. And I suppose in so far as my pictures are ever any kind of illustration this comes as close as any to a kind of narrative.

The *Triptych* was bought at auction in New York for £3.9 million, and is now in a private collection in Switzerland.

# 13

# Why Does Death Have to Be so Bloody?

> I always go back to Shakespeare . . . take the last great speech of
> *Macbeth*, those so famous verses on death and the fleetingness of life,
> time which is passing and which no longer has any significance.
>> *Francis Bacon in an interview with Michel Archimbaud*

Writing from a homeopathic ward for tropical diseases in the East
End of London, Deakin described his own four days in Paris in
1972 as a blur of brandy, illness and purple hearts:

> The Paris *histoire* could not have been less like your imaginings. Far from
> nightly dancing the *Merry Widow* waltz at Maxim's until dawn, ospreys in
> my hair and my throat ablaze with diamonds, it is a tear-jerker of
> unparalleled misery. To begin with, my illness had reached its climax
> (necessary details to give you the true picture), mouth and throat full of
> ulcers, unable to eat, big toe oozing pus, itching blisters around my arse
> and my prick skinned and raw. I had been having treatment for eight
> weeks and was due to be hospitalised but put it off until after the opening.
> After two weeks here now everything under perfect control and much to
> Francis' annoyance had nothing to do with drink, or as the doc put it so
> delicately, my social life.

It was hard to excuse Deakin's vindictiveness over the last
few years when he did his utmost to estrange me from Francis, and
succeeded intermittently. My lowest point in my relationship with
Francis was reached when I returned to television to interview
celebrities. On the night before an interview with Godfrey Winn I
argued with the taxi driver on my way home to Narrow Street,
where I kept a room, and he drove me straight to Limehouse
police station where I spent the night in a cell instead. In the
morning I was taken with the others who had been arrested in a
Black Maria to the magistrates' court. Here I was fined the
nominal fee of ten shillings, which I paid at once. Then I hurried to

188

TV House to interview Winn, who looked aghast but was sympathetic when I told him confidentially what had happened. I joined Deakin at the Kismet in the afternoon.

My appearance in the magistrates' court was negligible unless it was reported. As the afternoon wore on I dashed out to buy every edition of the *Evening Standard*, thankful each time to see no reference. But the last edition ran the news item that I had been arrested for being drunk and disorderly, with the dismaying addition that I had asked for time to pay the ten shillings, as if I were destitute.

'How the mighty have fallen!' said Deakin, and friends wrote to me when I was back in Devon to say that he carried the cutting with him for days, producing it like a writ.

Meeting him in the Golden Lion a few months later, at opening time, he admitted: 'I haven't done much to help, have I?'

'No, John,' I agreed, 'you haven't.'

This was the closest he ever came to an apology, and I left it at that. His jealousy was understandable but it was hard to forgive.

Death is invariably bloody. I was confined to Devon when Deakin had a lung removed in Westminster Hospital – he sent me hilarious letters from a ward with the disconcerting name of Marie Celeste. Then my financial fortunes started to rise again as the late John Anstey, the impressive editor of the *Telegraph Magazine*, commissioned me to write and photograph a feature on graveyard art. This took me across Europe to a 'happy cemetery' in the north of Romania, where I simultaneously researched my biography of my great-uncle, Bram Stoker, who wrote *Dracula*.

It had been arranged with Deakin that I should fly from Bucharest to Athens and catch a ferry to the island of Poros, where he was supposed to be convalescing with an American friend with one eye, known as Black Patch. After a sleepless, flea-bitten night in a small hotel in the port of Piraeus, I searched the harbour as the boat docked at Poros, expecting to hear Deakin before I saw him. There was no sign nor sound, so I swam interminably, holding my breath under water to rid myself of any persistent lice. Disappointed to find no trace of Deakin that evening, I went to the local gendarma in the morning – they would be bound to know of an American who wore a black eye-patch and was accompanied by a noisy English friend. But they shook their heads suspiciously.

189

Returning directly to London, I opened the door of the Colony to be greeted by Muriel: 'Buried her yesterday, deah!' as she gave a sardonic toss of the head.

Released from the Marie Celeste, Deakin had been driven at Francis's expense to convalesce at the Ship Hotel in Brighton. He had wanted to fly to meet me, but the airlines had refused to fly him to Greece in such a weak condition, and probably they were right. That evening he met Rex Crutchfield, a mutual friend who lived in Brighton and whose drinking capacity was even greater than his. Together they did the bars and clubs of Brighton with a vengeance, and it did for Deakin. When Bruce Bernard telephoned him at the Ship the following afternoon to ask how he was, Deakin admitted he had drunk too much on the night before and was feeling weak. He had just rung down for some tea, and when the maid brought it a few minutes later he was dead. 'I must have been the last person to speak to him,' Bruce told me.

True to himself, even now Deakin continued to haunt his friends. When asked to name his 'next of kin' at the Marie Celeste, he wrote 'Francis Bacon'. This may have been intended to impress, but it led to repercussions. It was Francis's unpleasant duty to identify the body. 'It was the last dirty trick he played on me,' he said.

'They lifted up the sheet,' Francis told me, 'and asked: "Is that Mr Deakin?" I replied: "It most certainly is." There she was with her trap shut for the first time in her life, and do you know,' Francis started to laugh, 'it was all so extraordinary. Through some stupidity in the law which I couldn't understand, he had to be buried in a pauper's grave. I could just hear them in Soho saying what a mean bastard I was for not giving him a decent send-off. Well, there it is.'

Francis had done enough and could not face the funeral. A few friends, including Marsh Dunbar, Graham Mason and Deakin's doctor, Neil Perrett, drove down specially but were held up in a traffic jam and arrived late for the service – if, indeed, there had been one.

'We all peered down into this hole that was Deakin's pauper's grave,' Marsh gestured a tiny space like that of a large napkin, 'and there he was at the bottom in a box. Oh, I do miss him so much,' she laughed.

'You know,' Francis told me with greater hesitation, 'it was even more extraordinary than that. There was no will or anything, and I suppose that explains the pauper's grave, but he left several thousand pounds. . . .'

'You're not serious!' I exclaimed.

'Well, you see,' he explained diffidently, 'I gave him the proceeds of a picture a few years earlier – and he never spent much, did he? Of course he continued to pretend he had nothing, because it suited him. I suppose the news of the money will come as an awful shock to a lot of people.'

'Certainly to me,' I agreed.

'Well, they advertised for someone to claim it and discovered Deakin had a perfectly good brother all the time. He's given Bruce all Deakin's photographs.'

'I can't believe it!'

We started to laugh – which is not a bad way to remember John Deakin, who made us laugh so often.

Robert Colquhoun died in the arms of his friend MacBryde in 1962. The solitary Robert moved to Dublin where a few years later he was struck and killed by a car as, staggering back from the pubs, he danced the Highland Fling in the middle of the street.

After a drinking marathon in the Fitzroy, Nina Hamnett fell and fractured a thigh bone. When she returned to hospital to have the pin removed, they bungled it, leaving one of her legs four inches shorter than the other. This was why she supported herself with a stick. It became her scaffolding, though she felt insulted when Augustus John advised her to go to a home for aged artists. After a radio play about her life in Charlotte Street, which she considered a betrayal, she threw herself from her bedroom window, impaling herself on the railings forty feet below.

Lucian Freud looked down at the emaciated figure in Paddington General Hospital, by now barely sustained by tubes and traction. He was joined by a relative, who disapproved of Nina's bohemian lifestyle but tried to be agreeable. 'Well,' she remarked cheerfully as she stared at the ruins, 'still the same old Nina!'

Nina's last words – and she was neither the first nor the last to

191

use them – were: 'Why can't they let me die?' She did so on 16 December 1956, aged sixty-six.

John Minton loved Henrietta, even if she was not in love with him. Then the predictable occurred. He found the ideal man he had been looking for: young, attractive, original, whose good humour made him popular with everyone, and the young man fell in love with Henrietta. One day Minton made the mistake of telling him: 'You must choose between us.'

'My heart fell to my boots,' says Henrietta, 'for I dreaded that he was going to choose me.' And he did.

Julian Maclaren Ross said that Minton was 'torn to pieces by tiny marmosets'. In 1957, Minton's newest friend phoned from a party to say he might be staying there overnight; his lodger tiptoed into Johnny's bedroom to report that he was fast asleep. The friend phoned again in the morning, and the lodger confirmed that Johnny was 'still sleeping it off'. So the friend stayed on for lunch.

By the time he returned it was too late. Minton had taken a massive overdose. If he did so in the belief that there would be a reconciliation when the friend arrived in time to save him, it all went wrong. Such a waste. Minton had the last vengeful laugh: he left his splendid Chelsea home to Henrietta instead of to the young man who had chosen her.

Since I dread hospitals, Ian Board had to insist that I visit Muriel Belcher in the Middlesex, where she was transferred from a private nursing home after complaints that her behaviour was obscene and uncomfortable. I was relieved to find her calm and reasonable, though Michael Clark's portrait of her on her deathbed reveals the haunting terror beneath the dignified façade which she presented that afternoon.

Muriel died in 1979. Jeffrey Bernard and I were asked to give an address at her memorial service in St Paul's church, Covent Garden, on 29 November.

Francis and I had an early lunch at Wheeler's to discuss my notes. He was subdued yet he went through them with exemplary patience, suggesting cuts and passages which were ineffective. This was Francis at his kindest. I assume he had been asked to give the address himself, but felt unable to go through with it.

I began by saying: 'I cannot imagine a finer opportunity than a service like this to give thanks as we do now for our great good luck in knowing Muriel Belcher, who turned life into a marvellous party.' At least the platitudes were genuine. Afterwards, Francis was generous in his comments for he knew that I am the worst of public speakers and hate such occasions. He left on his own, more ashen and distressed than I had ever seen him.

Shortly after the opening at the Grand Palais, I was dismayed to read a letter in the *Standard* which pointed out that it was incorrect to claim that Francis Bacon was the first British painter since Gainsborough to be honoured with an exhibition in Paris. The writer himself had been given a previous exhibition in some gallery whose name I have forgotten. It was signed 'Graham Sutherland', and I flinched on his behalf.

There was no need for such a demeaning letter: his pictures continued to fetch high prices – even higher when he, too, joined the Marlborough. He painted portraits of the rich and famous, and though he was accused of snobbery for doing so, that has been the prerequisite of portraitists through the ages. His lifestyle was enhanced, and he could afford lavish extensions to the Villa Blanche above Menton. Yet international fame eluded him, and Francis Bacon had usurped his right to the title of Britain's 'greatest painter'. When he received the Order of Merit, which he valued so highly, it was an added twist of the knife that Francis rejected such honours with a quip and a shrug of indifference. Graham was not a bitter man by nature, but it is understandable that he became bitter now and found the constant comparison odious. It was a classic example of the pupil surpassing the teacher.

There can be little doubt, as we have seen, that Sutherland influenced the younger Bacon with such paintings as the *Red Tree* of 1936, but it is equally plain that Bacon's imagery had a strong influence on him too. To give an obvious example, the famous portrait of Churchill in which the feet are a blur had an affinity with Bacon's trapped and gasping businessmen. This did not escape the critics: Pierre Jeannerat, who had condemned Bacon's 'nonsense art' at Agnew's in 1937, now referred to Bacon's 'Svengali' spell over Sutherland. By the mid-1960s the strain on their relationship had become too much and they stopped seeing each other.

Sutherland wrote to Michael Wishart on 28 February 1978 to congratulate him on *The High Diver* – 'a marvellous piece of writing because it embraces quite simply your feelings to a point which astonishes and hurts'. He wrote that Kathy and he regretted that they had lost touch:

> It would be idle to say that we have not missed seeing you and seeing your work grow. We could have done – but did not. I regret it. I don't really regret our break with Francis – the association was becoming too acid and boring to support and I had my own thoughts to try and expand in peace. But we have many new friends here [France] and in Italy and as we get older we have ourselves. K as beautiful as ever and who has been more than wonderful to me always.

At the end of another letter he concluded: 'What you say about F.B. one cannot but admit. Certainly my image (to quote you and "in-so-far as he was able") was firmly and persistently rubbed out in England. Fortunately other countries think otherwise!'

Sutherland is unfashionable today, eclipsed by Bacon's grandeur. He deserves better, but at times he laid himself open to criticism. Complaining that Bacon received higher prices, he ignored the obvious: that he himself painted too many, smaller pictures, diminishing their impact. Many of his portraits are squared, a practice he did not bother to conceal; it made them look stiff and laborious. At times the outlines around the face seem overworked.

The critic and editor of *Modern Painters*, the late Peter Fuller, wrote in 1988: 'It isn't just that Sutherland was a "nature" painter, whose principal subject was landscape whereas Bacon is, first and foremost, a painter of the human figure. Sutherland's paintings are haunted by a yearning for spiritual redemption; he is the last serious artist who has practised an aesthetic rooted in natural theology.'

But Peter Fuller detected the Baconian influence on Sutherland in the pessimistic painting of *Christ Carrying the Cross* of 1950, which shows Christ at his moment of collapse:

> He is shown falling to the ground amid strange architectural ruins. An odious thug, with grinning teeth – explicitly recalling similar figures by Francis Bacon – boots him mercilessly. In this picture, at least, we are

offered no hint of resurrection. It is tempting to read the work as an allegory which expresses Sutherland's growing doubts about the Baconian culture which was emerging in post-war Britain.

Ironically, Sutherland's foremost admirer did his cause more harm than good. In his monograph in 1961 Douglas Cooper declared that 'Graham Sutherland is the most distinguished and the most original English artist of the mid-twentieth century.' So it seemed that at long last Cooper had come down emphatically on the side of Sutherland rather than Bacon, having known them both since before the Second World War, and it is hard not to suspect that personal malice was just as responsible as his undoubted artistic judgement. Consequently, the alliance was prejudiced and bound to break apart. Ironically, it did so when Sutherland made the mistake of painting Cooper's portrait in 1967. The version I have seen in reproduction looks as attractive as Cooper would have wished, without descending to blatant flattery, but there was no pleasing of such a vanity. The other showed him in a pink shirt cleaning his spectacles, and sold for $46,200 as part of the Cooper Collection at Christie's in New York in May 1992. Cooper hated it, claiming it made him look like 'a gross and cruel monster', and threatened constantly to 'do' a Lady Churchill and destroy it. It helped to destroy his friendship with the artist, but there were other factors too: Sutherland could be difficult in his meticulous integrity.

Shortly before his death, one of his earliest and most powerful patrons, Lord Beaverbrook, dictated a letter when Sutherland complained about the quality of a reproduction of a portrait in the *Daily Express*: 'Here is a Graham Sutherland letter, complaining, complaining, complaining, complaining. Send it down to the archives at Cherkley.'

Kathy Sutherland made matters worse when she sprang to her husband's defence in 1974 after learning that he was being left out of Cooper's proposed exhibition, never realised, of the greatest paintings of the first half of the twentieth century. Writing that Graham did not care because he was used to not having a real supporter, she accused Cooper of being an arrogant snob who could be written off as someone who had decided to break a long and intimate friendship. Afterwards, they coincided at a lunch given by Princess Grace at Monaco, and Cooper merely nodded to them. The following year he sold thirty-seven paintings, drawings and lithographs by Sutherland, exhibited at the Redfern Gallery.

Probably because he was the nicer man, Sutherland attempted a rapprochement with a letter admitting that the row did not reflect much credit on himself or Kathy. Wendy Reeves tried to bring them together, and a date was fixed for dinner. Cooper agreed, but Sutherland changed his mind at the last moment, explaining that Cooper had 'always wanted to guide and steer him'.

Unfortunately, Cooper was a formidable adversary and the withdrawal of his support was nearly fatal. After Sutherland's death, Cooper wrote to *The Times* that he thought he saw a gifted painter and creative artist who was misunderstood – for a short period. 'Subsequently, Sutherland's work had become progressively weaker and more repetitive, and he had lost interest in it.' He had never believed or claimed that Graham Sutherland was, in the historical perspective, 'an artist of major stature'.

However, it is good to know that Sutherland found himself again when he returned to the Pembrokeshire landscape in the 1970s. This was his natural terrain, rather than the brighter skies of the South of France. Peter Fuller wrote that the remarkable paintings of these years were more 'than an old man's spiritual home-coming; he finally fused his English nature with what he had learned from the best twentieth-century French painting, to produce some of the most original and elegiac British paintings of recent years'. In a memorable phrase, he said that one picture bore witness 'to Sutherland's Ruskinian capacity to see in a pebble the grandeur and scale of a mountain range'. This was Graham Sutherland's genius. Fuller also found them 'heavy with presentiments of a return to the earth, of impending death'.

Despite his loyalty to Sutherland's work, and his reservations over Bacon's, Peter Fuller was anxious to meet Francis Bacon and asked me to introduce them. Tragically, this sympathetic and gifted man was killed in a car crash before I could arrange it. However, I did succeed in reuniting Francis with Graham and Kathy. They had been the best of friends in the early days when both men were poor, starting their great ascent. They shared a studio and enjoyed an intimacy which was sensual rather than sexual, though Robert Medley believes there was 'a strong streak of homosexuality' in Sutherland though Kathy never allowed it out. Graham, the Catholic convert, may have disliked Francis's hedonistic atheism, but was too kind to disapprove and he was selfless with his encouragement when Francis was unknown. The falling-out of friends is always to be regretted; it was time they met again.

They did so in the old Jules Bar in Jermyn Street, because Kathy and Graham Sutherland insisted on meeting outside Soho which they regarded as alien, if not enemy, territory. At first the three of them were restrained, formally polite; then they leaped on each other like dogs recognising their master as he returns home after a long absence. The champagne and the laughter flowed as I listened with pleasure. After an hour, Francis suggested that we move on to dinner at Wheeler's, an outcome the Sutherlands anticipated and had been determined to avoid. Graham looked nervously at Kathy, his expression indicating 'Well, why not?', like a schoolboy hoping for a 'treat'. I sensed her reluctance, but she agreed.

When we arrived at the familiar stamping-ground she retired to the ladies' cloakroom while we sat down at a ground-floor table, lulled by the success of the reunion. I noticed Francis's mood change as if a cloud had obscured the sun, though this was imperceptible to Graham, who leaned forward with a confidential smile: 'Francis, you may have heard that I've been doing some portraits recently. I think they're rather good. Have you see any of them?'

I cringed.

'Yes,' said Francis lightly, with a lethal certainty. 'Very nice . . . if you like the covers of *Time* magazine.'

Kathy came back to the table, and they made their excuses and left. The three of them did not meet again.

In the spring of 1972, as I was driving through Europe with Peter Bradshaw and my god-daughter to prepare the feature on graveyard art for the *Telegraph Magazine*, I wrote to Graham from Cannes asking if I could meet him and received a warm letter inviting us for drinks. The modest bungalow on the hills above Menton, which we saw together for the first time when they were looking for a home in the South of France, was now sumptuous with walls of sliding-glass windows and floors of Italian marble. I found it impersonal, like a museum, but Graham welcomed me with the old warmth and a smile which suggested a conspiracy as he came straight to the point:

'How's the monster?'

'Haven't you heard? He's dead.'

'*Oh no!*' He looked shocked and amazed. 'But I've read nothing in the papers.'

'Why should you?' I asked, equally perplexed.

'Who are we talking about?'

'John Deakin – aren't we?'

'No!' cried Graham, 'I was referring to *Francis*!' We laughed nervously, and I detected a slight note of regret as well as his obvious relief. It had not occurred to me that he thought of Francis as a 'monster', though it should have. He could hardly wait for news about him.

Time had passed and we had changed. The spontaneous rapture of my former friendship with Graham and Kathy had gone. Graham asked Peter Bradshaw if he was a painter, and Peter always regretted that he was too bashful to admit it. Kathy looked at my god-daughter, who wore a nearly transparent dress, with the basilisk stare of an older woman who might be able to afford Balmain but could no longer afford to appear in anything so brief. 'Surely you must be frightfully cold?' she kept on repeating.

When we left, I asked naively if Graham had any message for me to pass on to the 'monster', thinking that he might wish to send his good wishes. This time I received a basilisk smile. 'No, I don't think so, do you?' He followed us in his car to buy the English papers in Menton, the evening ritual of the expatriate. They appeared to be wonderfully, dreadfully dependent on each other.

Graham Sutherland intended to enter a Catholic retreat if Kathy died before him, but he died first, on 17 February 1980. With his customary shrewdness, Lord Goodman anticipated that Sutherland's paintings would slump and advised Kathy to sell immediately the large number she had inherited, while the prices held. As any reminder of Graham was painful, she agreed; the forecast proved correct. With the proceeds, he arranged for her to live in comfort at the Connaught Hotel. It seems that at first she enjoyed London and the novel experience of riding on a public bus, but she grew increasingly lonely. Seeing Francis in the hotel foyer one evening, she went across and made the surprising remark, as he told me afterwards, 'G always said that you were the best.'

Possibly she was unable to forgive herself for such a betrayal, true though it might have been. Afterwards, whenever she saw Francis she asked a porter to help her into the lift so she could retire to the safety of her bedroom. Wondering if she wanted to see me, I wrote to her at the Connaught and received a card in her now faltering hand, dated 22 March 1985:

> So kind to write.
> G told me to live here as it was so safe but I have had awful bronchitis and general breakdown and don't care if I live or die. All was only possible with GS and I did have a good innings, but sick of everything now, and see no one – a recluse, reading and telly if good or funny and the effort of getting through each day. Nice to hear Love K.S.

I assumed that she saw no one because she did not wish to do so. I should have persevered. Her death shortly afterwards passed virtually unnoticed.

# 14

# Soho in the Seventies and Eighties

How can I trap this transient thing?
*Francis Bacon in conversation with the author*

During the seventies the original hurly-burly of the Colony Room changed. There were still tumultuous days, but inevitably the membership had moved on and the so-called School of London or Muriel's Boys no longer came there. By now, when Francis flung open the door to see who was inside, it was more a case of lucky dip. If he recognised someone he liked, the smile burst across his face. When the television personality Michael Parkinson told a mutual friend that he would never go to the Colony because it was 'full of failures', it amused me to enter it that same afternoon and find Francis with the fashion designer Thea Porter and the actor Tom Baker. Though when I asked Francis if he would appear in a series I was preparing called *Success Story*, he recoiled: 'Are you mad? I'm not a success. Now if it were failures you were doing, *then* I might be interested.'

Francis continued to be unpredictable. Jeffrey Bernard remembers the conversation one Friday, which hovered around sex and death.

'Francis seemed amused by both subjects, and he used to quiz me about being heterosexual as though I was a creature from outer space. He cleared a table of American tourist matrons with one of his loud, outspoken remarks during a natural lull in the lunchtime noise. "Which woman do you most fancy in the entire world?" he asked me.

' "I don't know. What am I supposed to say? Ava Gardner? Cyd Charisse? What a daft question! Anyway, who do you most fancy in the entire world?"

'He replied with a languid yet loud tone: "D'yer know, I think I'd really like to be fucked by Colonel Gadaffi." Exit the Americans.'

During another lull he asked Jeffrey: 'Now that you've lost your looks, what are you going to do?' With so many 'queer' friends like himself, he considered Jeff, like Graham Sutherland, an 'honorary queer'. One thing they had in common was gambling, though Jeff preferred the horses to the green baize.

A few, a very few, were able to stand up to Francis. Fred Ingrams was delighted when Francis left the Colony to see a mixed exhibition at the new Birch and Conran Gallery next door, where he bought one of Fred's pictures 'because it's the only good thing there'. 'I felt eighteen feet off the ground,' says Fred. Francis had given the gallery an encouraging send-off, though James Birch feared Francis was so drunk that it was unlikely he would remember it the next morning. However, he came in as promised and wrote out his cheque for £450. Several months later I was talking to Fred in the French when Francis sidled in. As he failed to recognise Fred, I introduced them, adding provocatively: 'You remember, Francis – you bought one of Fred's paintings.'

'Really!' Francis shook himself indignantly like a dog coming out of the water. 'I suppose I was pissed. I wonder what's happened to it.' Fred may have been hurt, but he had the wit to list Francis Bacon as one of his 'collectors' in the catalogues to his recent one-man shows. Today he is established as one of our most promising young artists, but occasionally he lets out a sigh as he remembers Francis's rejection – 'I wonder what happened to my picture?' No one seems to know.

In spite of the element of risk, Francis was always welcome at parties. Suzi Bardolph hugged him in the Colony, turning pink as she confessed she had only just discovered the dozen bottles of vintage wine he had brought to her house-warming a few nights earlier.

'Francis, some idiot hid the wine in a broom cupboard. And when we ran out of booze and sent to the off-licence for some plonk, you contributed. Oh, dear! What can you have thought when I failed to produce your wonderful present?'

'I thought you were saving it for a special occasion.'

'Special occasion!' she groaned. 'But I'll never have an occasion so special ever again!'

'Anyhow,' Francis reassured her, 'I hope you enjoy the wine – it's rather special.'

Francis, like Cocteau, Picasso and Dali before him, had been asked to design a label for the latest vintage of Château Mouton Rothschild. They found the idea entertaining, especially as they were reimbursed with rare and costly bottles. Francis's attempt was never used, but the failure resulted in a growing friendship with Baron Philippe himself which explained Francis's new expertise in old wine.

Apart from sudden dashes to Charlie Chester's gambling club on the corner of Brewer Street, Francis was reluctant to leave the Colony once he was installed, and equally loath to see me go. I was easily bribed with champagne, but it was his company which was so intoxicating and this was what made me put off leaving until the last possible moment. One Christmas I had a crucial meeting with Alan Yentob, the Controller of BBC2, at Television Centre to discuss a script on my great-uncle Bram Stoker, author of *Dracula*. I phoned from the Colony with the warning that I might be late. I was about to add that it would be safer to fix another appointment when his secretary assured me there was no problem and said I should just arrive as soon as I could. Francis was at his best that afternoon, my friends were mesmerised, and when I tore myself away I found myself stuck in a taxi in a Christmas rush-hour. I burst into the BBC bar half-hysterical, three-quarters drunk and an hour late. The programme on Bram Stoker has yet to be made.

This happened on countless occasions, and the weakness was mine. I do not deceive myself that he wanted me to stay because he enjoyed my company; in fact he was shockingly indifferent to what I was doing, and if I showed him the advance copy of a new book he was apt to fling it on the floor with a dismissive: 'Very nice, I'm sure.' I never minded this – it became a ritual – though others were startled. But I realise that when he kept me in the Colony he gained a sadistic pleasure in seeing me sink to the occasion.

I was looking forward to Lucian Freud's private view at the Hayward Gallery in 1988, not just for the excitement of seeing the work but also because I had been invited to a private dinner party by his dealer, James Kirkman, at his elegant home in Brompton Square. This was a special occasion, with Mr and Mrs Andrews and Mr and Mrs Auerbach among the guests, and I was flattered to be included in such a closely knit group. I determined to behave myself.

Unfortunately I met Francis in the Colony in the late afternoon. As usual, the heady mix of Francis and champagne could not be denied, and I made the mistake of telling him about the party, possibly to impress him – though I should have been wiser by then, for he and Lucian were no longer friends. With the vain hope – vain in every sense – that I might bring them together, I wondered if Francis would like to come to the Hayward with me, forgetting that his arrival would create such a *frisson* that the paintings would cringe with outraged loyalty towards their maker. I also told Francis that Lucian himself had told me that he would not be going there; Lucian had given me a wide-eyed stare when I expressed surprise. 'Why should I want to do that? I'm not on exhibition myself. My life isn't interesting, though I hope my pictures will be remembered. I want to keep well out of it.'

Francis felt the same. 'I won't be going anywhere tonight,' he declared emphatically. Then, deceptively casual, he added: 'You know, the trouble with Lucian's work is that it's *realistic* without being *real*.' He tugged at his collar and beamed. 'You know what I mean?' This needed no answer and he called for champagne. After several more bottles and abortive attempts to leave, I staggered into a taxi, lurched into Lord Gowrie at the entrance to the Hayward, and made the disastrous error of returning to the Colony in case Francis was still there, as he was.

When at last I made it to Brompton Square I realised to my dismay that everyone was sober. I was startled, almost haunted, by the sight of several Bacons looming at me from the walls upstairs before we descended to the dining room, laid out with separate tables, below. I sat next to Mrs Auerbach, who was nice and jolly, but no one knew if Lucian himself would appear. A few days earlier we had lunched at Harry's Club, where the bill was so astronomical that I felt guilty over the cost of food for the first time in my life when I seized the bill. Sensing I could ill afford it, Lucian came directly towards me after a dramatic entrance through the french windows leading to the garden, and with a confiding stare handed me an envelope which contained a couple of hundred pounds. I have an image of him dressed in a cape with a top hat and silver-topped cane, but that was probably due to the champagne in the Colony which had gone to my head, leaving me just enough sense to realise it was better to leave the party than collapse unconscious in the fish. I have regretted my behaviour at that dinner ever since.

Worse was the launch for my book called *Gallery*, based on the television art quiz which I devised for Channel 4. My then publisher, Bloomsbury, decided to stake the party in Leighton House, the home of the great Victorian painter, Lord Leighton, in Holland Park. In order to be sober, I came directly from home with my friend Bradshaw, but at the last moment we were joined by three friends from North Devon who took a day return to London in order to attend the party: a lovely, bubbly woman called Daphne; her ex-husband; and his best friend, her current husband. We lunched at Ming's, opposite the Coach and Horses. It is a fallacy that Chinese food acts as blotting paper. When we entered the Colony, my spirits leaped when I saw Francis sitting there: this was a treat not only for myself but for Peter and my friends. He was the only person there, and it was obvious within seconds that he was in a vile mood – I have seldom known a viler. The habitual champagne was ordered, but this time it was more blackmail than a bribe: and, not to be outdone, I matched him bottle for bottle to show I could pay my way for once and was not beholden. This was foolish, for Francis disliked being bought drinks in return. I did not make the mistake of telling him that Daphne's former husband was a painter, for Francis was in a mood to demolish. There was no charm that afternoon. Instead he resorted to the foulest obscenity – most unusual for him.

'He may be a very great man,' said Daphne afterwards 'but – my God! – he's not a nice man.' Curiously, I felt ashamed for Francis. By the time I reached Leighton House I had lost the game.

When I related the episode to Gilbert and George, Gilbert exclaimed with glee: 'But don't you see? That's how Bacon is. He's absolutely right to behave the way he wants.'

It was a slight comfort that he was rudest to his closest friends, such as Denis Wirth-Miller, whom he baited so mercilessly that once even Denis protested in the Colony: 'I say, Francis! That's a bit below the belt!'

'From what I've heard,' said Francis, 'there's precious little below your belt!'

For once I got things right with my launch for *Soho in the Fifties*, helped by the owner of Kettner's, Peter Boizot, who sent up magnums of champagne to my private bar in the corner – a wise precaution after the bright PR girl assured me that the publisher was providing 'an assortment of soft drinks and beers' as well as the traditional warm, medium-sweet 'dry' wine.

The elegant room once used by Wilde was decorated with blown-up photographs provided by Tommy Hawkyard, and a piano was brought in for Mike Mackenzie, who had moved to the Dorchester after enhancing countless evenings in the Colony. All was set for a good party; but when a photographer for the *Express* gossip column wandered in five minutes early, oozing boredom from every pore, there was no one there apart from Lindsay Anderson, dressed for the North of England, and myself. After taking a few shots of the two of us, the dispirited man wandered off again, muttering: 'No story here.' If he had returned an hour later he could have snapped both Auberon Waugh and Peregrine Worsthorne, or Peter Bowles and John Hurt, or a lively group consisting of Francis Bacon arm-in-arm with Dorothy Hudson, the President of the Soho Society, together with her adversary Paul Raymond, whose Revue Bar represented the seamier side of Soho's sex life.

Francis told me he had been waiting downstairs – 'I didn't know you were up here' – and delighted everyone with his good humour, including three students who were startled by his comment: 'I'm told Dan is now our leading expert on art', for the sarcasm escaped them.

Francis was a prince on such occasions.

On 28 October 1982, when I returned with my friends Peter and Karen from a holiday in Turkey, they went up to the Colony while I stayed in the French. A few minutes later Peter came back to tell me the news on the occasion that Francis had changed his mind over helping me with the book I had been asked by the publishers Macdonald to write about him. This was a disappointment, though hardly unexpected.

'Francis asked me to break the bad news,' said Peter, 'but I told him he could do his own dirty work to your face, so you'd better come up. John [Edwards] is there and couldn't be nicer.'

Francis welcomed me too, and, though he scarcely bothered to explain his change of mind, he softened the blow when he offered to make it up to me with a gift of £400. Even so, I went to see

Valerie Beston at the Marlborough the next morning to ask her advice. Should I decide to go ahead without him? She advised me not to – 'I don't think you'll regret it' – and, in her turn, sent me some Bacon reproductions as a form of compensation. Francis was in a genial mood that evening apart from some barbs at Ian Board – 'Muriel always said you were the best barman she had [pause] because you cheated her less than the others.' Ian smiled nervously, relieved that we were the only people there. Then, to my surprise for I had forgotten, Francis said it was his birthday and invited us to dinner in the upstairs room at L'Escargot. This was one of those endearing occasions which are impossible to pin down on the page. As we sat down he told us, 'I'm just a simple idiot.' It means nothing in print, but the way he said it in his sing-song voice – 'I'm just a simple *iddy-yott*' – made it witty. When the waiter put down my plate of noisettes of lamb served in a rich red wine sauce, Francis looked at it suspiciously. 'I do hope I don't have *gravy* with mine', he complained, investing the word with all the horror of the Dickensian workhouse.

# 15

# John Edwards

I'm greedy for life; and I'm greedy as an artist.
*Francis Bacon interviewed by David Sylvester, 1975*

Francis concealed it at the time, but he would have been superhuman to have emerged unscathed from the death of George Dyer. George's suicide was expected, but after the initial shock, when it is easiest to rally, the loss must have been desolating. This was confirmed by Helen Lessore: 'It affected him profoundly. Remembering the death of Peter Lacy on the opening at the Tate, Francis told me: "I feel it's like a Greek tragedy." '

Now he entered a period of calm. This was enhanced by his friendship with a young East Ender called John Edwards, whose contribution to Francis's last years has been undervalued. This is partly because John wants to maintain his privacy, and because his concern is shared by his family, who guard him so fiercely that an enquiring journalist complained to me after an abortive attempt to see John: 'The Queen and the royal family should have such people to protect *them*!'

John Edwards was working for his two elder brothers, who ran three pubs in the East End, when he met Francis in 1974. He told Barry O'Brien that they met through his older brother David, the licensee of the Swan in Stratford East, who frequently drank in the Colony and was friendly with Muriel Belcher. 'My brother used to say Francis Bacon would be coming in [to the Swan] with Muriel Belcher. She would tell my brother to get some champagne in every week – and Francis Bacon would never turn up. I was always stuck with the champagne, because even in those days people didn't drink champagne in the East End.' One day John was taken to the Colony and when he was introduced to Bacon by Ian Board remembers, he said: 'Why don't you turn up when you are supposed to for all this fucking champagne?' Francis was amused and invited him to Wheeler's, which John never enjoyed because he disliked fish, but from that day they were friends.

Ian Board recalls that 'John was hypnotised'. Francis told him "You don't want an old boiler like me," but Francis was a great seducer, and, to him, John appeared to be a tough East Ender.'

'To my amazement,' John remembers, 'when I walked into his studio about two months later, there was a picture he had painted of me. I never sat for him. He was marvellous company, good fun and a great drinking companion. He always had plenty to talk about and told me a lot of the stories about people he knew. I saw him every day. We would meet for lunch, then we would probably go to the Colony, then to a casino, after that we would have dinner and sometimes we would go on to a nightclub. We had dinner at all sorts of places – the Vendôme, Green's, the Connaught, the Ritz, the White Tower . . . the casino he most liked was Charlie Chester's in Soho. He was a very big gambler. He played roulette and he had some good wins.'

For an East End boy who could neither read nor write it was an extraordinary transition. Yet he had such self-assurance that Francis did not have to explain him away to anyone. No one ever understands what one person sees in another when it comes to love, though David Edwards, who was close to both of them, said that Francis liked his brother because he never told him lies. 'John told him exactly what he thought. Where most people would bow down to Francis, John always stood up to him. Francis respected John's judgement . . . He was always ringing John up for advice on things. He would say to John: "What do you think of that person we are having lunch with?" John would tell him. Francis was quite a good judge of character – but he used to like a second opinion.'

After a time, though, John got a bit bored by his affection and the phone calls: 'Are you coming up from Suffolk for lunch?' By now Francis wanted to be with John all the time.

Ian Board remembers: 'I noticed Francis's state when John went missing.

' "Are you in love with him?"

' "Oh no, dear! Fond of him."

'Then it was "Very fond of him". He was riddled with love.' Might have been a bit trying for John.

On one occasion when they were lunching in Francis's favourite

Italian restaurant, Mario's in South Kensington (Mario once ran the Trattoria Terrazza), John noticed Robert Fraser at a corner table. By now Fraser was one of the first English celebrities to suffer from AIDS, and looked so ghastly that at first Francis refused to go over and speak to him.

'You *must*,' John Edwards told him firmly. 'He's your friend.'

Afterwards, Francis was glad he had done so, for Fraser died a short time later. It was Francis who told me this, not John.

'I was with John the night Robert Fraser [the gallery owner] died and for some reason he was crying. I told him: 'You wait until Francis dies and you're going to shed *endless* tears. He didn't *quite* know what I was saying. I bet he does now!'

'What did the Edwards family make of it all?' I asked.

'Mum? *Delighted!* Our son has done well. East End, you know!'

David Edwards runs Seabrook Antiques in Long Melford, near John's home today, and another brother lives nearby. So does the writer Alan Hall, who runs a wine store in Melford and was able to offer advice on a more worldly and experienced level. Without such family and friends, I suspect that John might have gone to pieces when Francis died. 'He killed them all off,' says Ian Board, referring to Peter Lacy and George Dyer, but he loved John, who was strong enough to stand up to him and survives.

Many people wondered what Francis Bacon could see in a young man who was known to be illiterate. Someone remarked bitchily: 'He learned to write his name quickly enough, as soon as he got a chequebook.' Literacy had nothing to do with it. Nor had sex. John told me once with a beaming smile that they shared a bed together in Muriel's old flat after Francis passed out from drink. That was as far as it had gone.

Yet people would insist that John Edwards could not possibly provide the intellectual stimulation that Francis needed. Only someone who did not understand Francis at all would say such a thing. When he needed intellectual talk he found it easily enough in the company of David Sylvester or Michel Leiris, but he didn't want that in a close companion. John Edwards was a welcome relief after all the turbulent years. He was lively, young and street-wise, with as happy a disposition as poor George's was the opposite. Unlike George Dyer, he proved a force for the good.

John and I happened to use the same film laboratory. Once it mixed up our orders – I was given John's by mistake, or vice versa, causing considerable annoyance. Francis blamed me and, though I protested that I was blameless, he did not wish to know that. He was wholly protective.

His reply when Barry Driscoll asked him in the Colony what he would like to have been if not an artist ('A mother!') may not have been so flippant after all. He denied it vehemently when Driscoll reminded him a few weeks later, and went over to Driscoll's two sons, as nervous as church mice on their first visit to the club.

'Do you like your father?' he demanded.

'Yes, of course. . . ,' they stammered.

'Well, I *don't*!' he interrupted. 'I think he's an absolute bastard!'

Driscoll had trespassed too close for comfort.

There were times when Francis fussed over John with the beady eye of a mother hen, allowing nothing and no one to distract him. Because he was so fond of John he was more irritable with other people, as if his possessiveness made him nervous. Yet John was all he needed when they were on their own. You only have to see the opening titles of Melvyn Bragg's *South Bank Show*, as they walk side by side through the crowded streets in animated conversation, to realise the total rapport that existed between them.

Part of his dependence on John may have been due to the fact that in his old age he had begun to turn against many of his former friends. I was lucky to stay the course as long as I did, though I regret not making a greater effort to sustain our friendship. There were times when I felt inadequate, feeling he had advanced so far that there was little I could say which would interest him. While I had not fulfilled my earlier promise as a 'TV personality' – a fame that I considered spurious – and though I had stagnated for several years when I retired to North Devon, my life was far from colourless. I travelled extensively through Turkey, but even when I sailed down the Volga and climbed across the Caucasus, emulating a journey my father attempted in 1929, Francis showed no interest.

Surprisingly, his lack of interest in other people never mattered. It was due neither to snobbery nor to a sense of being superior. He may have possessed grandeur, but few people were less grand.

'Do you realise', he asked me soon after we met, 'that ninety-five per cent of people are passive, simply waiting to be entertained?' When I reminded him of this years later, he swung round with a disdainful glare: 'Did I really say that? I must have been mad. It should have been ninety-nine per cent!' Inevitably his appearances in Soho were rationed as he grew older.

One lunchtime in the French in the mid-eighties, I remarked how glorious it would be if Francis suddenly appeared through the door. Someone said: 'It's possible that he longs to come out but no one asks him. Why don't you phone?' I did so at once and, as if a taxi had been waiting, Francis arrived with considerable speed – it seemed less than five minutes.

'Where shall we go for lunch?' This had become a problem after Bernard Walsh sold Wheeler's to a consortium who, as new brooms tend to do, swept out so many things that were good. The ground floor was split, the bar was transferred, the staff no longer recognisable. The spirit of the place was destroyed, but one Saturday Francis and I braved it and were shown to an upstairs room where we were relieved to have some excellent oysters. It is hard to crucify an oyster but a lobster can be raped, and Francis looked at his with dismay as it arrived on a plate without its shell. When Francis demanded the shell, the waiter insisted that this was not what he really wanted. Ultimately, two shells were found and the pieces transferred, with an empty space on the side which should have been filled with the coral and the usual bits and pieces. Francis was so sickened he told me it was hardly worth complaining since they would not understand. I wondered how they could upset someone whose association with Wheeler's had been legendary.

On another occasion Francis suggested the Jardin des Gourmets, but it was fully booked, and so he came to the alternative decision: 'Let's go to Leoni's!' I had not been there for years and agreed enthusiastically, for it had been an old favourite and a recent mention in a food article suggested a revival. Our hopes were dampened somewhat when we were shown to an indifferent table, but at least there were noisy people around us who appeared to be enjoying themselves. Francis had become an expert on wine due, as I say, to his friendship with Baron Philippe de Rothschild and examined the list with growing interest. 'I do believe,' he confided, 'that they've made a mistake. It's the most extraordinary bargain!' He referred to a vintage which, though new to me, was, according to him, a sensational year; it seemed an expensive 'bargain' at £30.

The sardonic wine waiter uncorked the bottle with a considerable fuss and flourish and wafted the glass in front of Francis, who declined to taste it though he lavished one of his charming, disconcerting smiles: 'That's all such a lot of rubbish, isn't it? I'm sure it's marvellous.'

I sipped the nectar and flinched. I know little about red wine, but it tasted close to vinegar. But I knew my taste buds were unequal to such a special occasion and gave an appreciative nod.

Possibly because he was suffering from asthma that day, Francis was unusually *distrait*: 'I'm eighty-seven, you know,' he said at one point.

'No, you're not,' I corrected him. 'You're seventy-eight.'

'Oh yes, so I am.'

When the bill arrived he looked at it, bemused. 'I think there's some mistake,' he told the waiter, pointing at the scribbled price on the wine list. The waiter studied it too and agreed: 'Yes, you're right', but returned with a shake of the head and the information that the true amount was £130. The scribble was misleadingly illegible, but neither concession nor apology were forthcoming. It shocked me that Leoni's should be so mean when they should have been honoured to present the rare little wine to Francis with the compliments of the house. Then I realised they had no idea who Francis Bacon was. He gave a shrug and paid up without complaining, even leaving a generous tip.

'I wouldn't mind,' he declared, swinging round outside, 'except that it was such muck! Anyhow, it's taught me not to be such a bloody snob. Shall we go to the Colony for some simple champagne?'

On another occasion that was memorable for me, we continued from the Colony to the French and then the Golden Lion, where Francis was in such lively form that someone asked him what he did.

'I'm a painter.'

'That's lucky,' said the man. 'I'm doing up my house at the moment and can give you some work if you want it.'

'How very kind of you,' said Francis with his broadening smile.

Only a few days earlier one of his pictures had sold in New York for £3 million.

On 21 May 1985 the Tate Gallery honoured Francis Bacon with a second major retrospective. This time there was no drama. Nobody died. John Edwards was supportive throughout, and the Marlborough gave their usual exemplary assistance under the guidance of Valerie Beston. The only blemish was the absence of Bacon's famous *Two Figures*, better known as 'The Wrestlers' after Muybridge, though best known as 'The Buggers', which caused such alarm when it was exhibited at the Hanover in 1953 that it was kept in an upstairs room in case the gallery was raided by the police.

For me, this was a marvellous moment, remembering my tour of the gallery with Francis on the eve of his first Retrospective at the Tate. The first had the thrill of the unexpected, the realisation that this was the work of a great twentieth century artist. This time we had the confirmation. It gave me tremendous pleasure when Francis told me – 'I hope you'll be there for the second time around.' Adding, mockingly, 'I expect it will be a disaster, though I have grown accustomed to its face.'

Instead, the private view was a grand affair. I was able to talk to old friends like George Melly, whose smile equalled that of Francis in lifting the spirits; I told Melvyn Bragg that I had been the first to interview Bacon, though I doubt if he believed me; in the gents I spoke to Patrick Leigh Fermor, who beat a hasty retreat saying that his wife, Joan, had been taken ill. A few weeks earlier I had mentioned his books to Francis, who asked me: 'But they're not *really* any good, are they? Do you think he's queer? I've always thought so myself, even though he's got the reputation for being such a ladies' man. The women adore him!' He made 'adore' sound lethal. Perhaps this was typical of a generation when it was safer to keep your sexuality secret, but Francis suspected the most unlikely people.

Other guests included Geraldine Norman, escorted round the rooms by Peter Bradshaw; the Swiss financier Gilbert de Botton; and Paul Danquah. Also a woman who had not been asked but gate-crashed all the same. As she was one of my closest friends and we happened to arrive simultaneously, I knew Francis thought I had brought her. I found it annoying that he welcomed her as if she were the guest of honour while shooting me a sharp look behind her back.

The prospect of a book launch – the writer's equivalent of a private view – reduces me to an alcoholic jellyfish and invariably ends in calamity. But Francis rose superbly to such occasions. With his beatific smile, he stood beside a large table covered with catalogues as well as glasses, distinguished in a well-cut suit, sober and self-controlled. In a curious way, he was isolated. Peter Bradshaw told me afterwards that he had this impression too, that instead of being the centre of a seething throng of admirers Francis looked alone, almost vulnerable. Going over to keep him company, he asked Francis to write something special in his catalogue.

'Such as?' asked Francis.

'I don't know. Something interesting. . . . "Thank you for the trade".'

'You're not making me *cheap*!' Francis replied, scribbling his usual 'Best wishes, Francis.'

Everything went normally, even to Jeffrey Bernard asking Francis for the taxi fare back into Soho. John Edwards was outraged that he should scrounge on such an occasion, but I suspected it was a matter of principle, for 'old time's sake'.

Francis was correct to treat this occasion with the solemnity it deserved. He knew he had crossed a final frontier. He told Peter Beard that he hated nine out of ten paintings he saw, including his own. 'I don't really like most of what I see, and I think if people do one or two extraordinary things they've done a lot. . . .' He knew now that he had 'done a lot'.

She was too quick to disparage his work:

'There are an awful lot of my paintings I just don't like at all,' he told Beard. 'I really don't like those popes. I think it's an aesthetic thing really – I just don't like the form. I think I could have done it so much better. I'm always full of hope that something remarkable is going to turn up. It excites me, and hope is really quite important. I don't suppose any artist is satisfied with his work, but I think one of the terribly interesting things about all artists is they'll never know whether their work is any good because they'll be dead before time has had its terrible chance and its

214

infallible kind of judgement upon it. So they'll never know if their work is any good really because it takes quite a long time for time to really get to work on it.

Francis made the concession to Peter Beard that he did like certain things by Picasso, Matisse and, above all, Duchamp. 'But I think of any artist you can only like certain things or moments. It's impossible for people to go on creating marvellous things all the time.' Significantly, he added: 'Generally, old age makes painters better.' In this I hope he included himself. Though it was not in his nature to 'love' particular paintings, there must have been a number in this second Tate retrospective which he considered worthwhile.

He was now established beyond doubt. In his introduction to the catalogue, the then Director of the Tate, Alan Bowness, set the tone with his unqualified tribute to the artist whose 'own work sets the standard for our time, for he is surely the greatest living painter'. To substantiate this claim, Bowness explained:

> No artist in our century has presented the human predicament with such insight and feeling. The paintings have the inescapable mark of the present; I am tempted to add the word, alas, but for Bacon the virtues of truth and honesty transcend the tasteful. They give to his paintings a terrible beauty that has placed them among the most memorable images in the history of art. And these paintings have a timeless quality that allows them to hang naturally in our museums beside those of Rembrandt and Van Gogh.

This was the ultimate comparison: no artist could hope for higher praise, and it left Francis open to attack.

It came, virulently, from Bernard Levin in the *Times* on 28 June 1985, under the headline: 'A GENIUS? I SAY ROTTEN.' 'The puffing and booming of Francis Bacon,' wrote Levin, 'seems to me one of the silliest aberrations even of our exceptionally silly time.' Refuting Alan Bowness's claim that Bacon is 'the greatest living painter', Levin was wise to avoid the definition of 'greatness'. Instead he provided a short list of artists active since 1900 whose insight and feeling 'are manifestly greater than Bacon's – manifestly at any rate to anyone less silly than the director of the Tate and less *parti-pris* than the seedy throng of Bacon groupies. . . .'

His list was considerable: Bonnard, Braque, Chagall, Chirico, Derain, Ernst, Gris, Grosz, Kandinsky, Kokoschka, Magritte, Matisse, Matta, Mirò, Moore, Munch, Picasso, Rivera, Rouault, Soutine, Sutherland, Utrillo, Vlaminck and Vuillard. He added that with a generous treatment of dates he could have included Degas, Monet and Renoir, who died in 1917, 1926 and 1919 respectively.

He resented the way that 'Bodies couple in hate not love; other bodies writhe on beds, one of them swelling with the effects of the hypodermic embedded in its arm'; he was relieved that 'Disgust is kept at bay by the feeling that there is nothing sufficiently real in all this waste and folly to make disgust an appropriate reaction.'

He seized on Bacon's treatment of the Crucifixion as the final evidence in his case for the prosecution: 'What is wrong with Francis Bacon? He has not noticed that, halfway through, the Crucifixion turns into its opposite. Tintoretto noticed; so did Rembrandt; even Dali noticed.'

Levin raised a doubt that cannot be dismissed, for it worries many people that Bacon was a painter of unrelieved pessimism. Picasso, the other great painter of the twentieth century, could be optimistic, conveying his love for *Les Demoiselles d'Avignon* as strongly as his hatred of the Spanish Civil War in *Guernica*. Even in that extraordinary last self-portrait, executed in pastels shortly before his death, there is a lethal humour. But I believe that Levin's prejudice was so ingrained that he was incapable of seeing that Bacon's work, too, was rich in compassion, as expressed in the portraits of his lonely figures enclosed behind glass and George Dyer retching over the washbasin. *That* is why they are painful to look at – not because he rejoiced in violence. Michael McNay wrote that 'A bad dream by Bacon is the ultimate adjunct to any truly chic boardroom.' You could say the same of Modigliani, even Picasso, though it would need to be a very odd boardroom. The criticism becomes more serious when Peter Fuller writes that while Velasquez 'celebrated' the defiant dignity of freaks and dwarves through his handling of paint, Bacon 'applied pigment as if he hated the stuff, dragging it across raw, unsized canvas which drains it of beauty and of all semblance of life. Bacon's technical inadequacies seem to me inseparable from his spiritual dereliction.'

This was echoed by Paul Johnson after Bacon's death:

He could not draw. His ability to paint was limited and the way he laid the pigments on the canvas was often barbarous. He had no ideas, other than one or two morbid fancies arising from his homosexuality, chaotic way of life, and Irish fear of death. What he did have was a gimmick, something resembling an advertising designer's logo. In his case it was a knack of portraying the human face or body not so much twisted as smeared out of shape. It was enough. Such a logo could easily be dressed up by the scriptwriters of the industry into an image of 'our despairing century'; it fitted their favourite words: 'disquieting', 'disturbing'.

This attack, the most powerful since Bernard Levin's, drew an outraged correspondence in the *Observer*: 'The enormous tragic power of Bacon's work is there for all to see. It is not traditionally pretty. But neither is the history of our century, whence it came. Nor is most tragic art, be it Shakespeare's *King Lear* or Grünewald's altarpiece at Isenheim.' Francis would have enjoyed such a response, admiring the altarpiece as he did.

I doubt if he conceived of his paintings in the terms adopted by his critics. The rules simply did not apply to Francis, unless he reversed them, preferring abuse to praise. He told me with relish of Mrs Thatcher's exclamation when she asked the Directors of the Tate who was our greatest painter and they answered Francis Bacon: 'Not that dreadful man who paints those horrible pictures!' It has been much quoted since. Thatcher and Bacon made comic adversaries, though he was serious in his resentment of her Clause 128, intended to prevent the dissemination of information about homosexuality in schools, which he regarded as an infringement of civil liberty. Even so, he refused to sign any of the numerous letters and petitions he was asked to join. He did not feel at ease in 'groups'.

Finally, Bacon's work defies criticism. As David Sylvester told Sir Robert Sainsbury: 'You admire it for all the wrong reasons.'

From my own viewpoint, I have no reservation about his handling of paint, which I find astonishing, nor about the alleged 'violence', which is usually misinterpreted. Also artists should be allowed an off-day. Even Bacon had some days towards the end which were distinctly chilly, and had a period when he seemed to strive too hard for effect, with severed torsos wearing cricket-

217

pads. Yet as an artist Bacon knew he had left his stamp: 'I would like my pictures to look as if a human being had passed between them, like a snail, leaving a trail of the human presence and memory of the past events as the snail leaves its slime.'

Forget the 'greatest British painter since Turner', Bacon was the greatest *world* painter of the second half of the twentieth century, just as Picasso belonged to the first. The time is now, the look of the room, the clothes, the chairs, even the style of hair. His paintings have their own existence, his tension the antidote to the relaxation of the Impressionists.

Significantly, for it is intended as an introduction to art for young people, the 1992 *Art Pack* by Christopher and Helen Frayling and Ron van der Meer ends with a pull-out of the twenty greatest pictures, including the Mona Lisa and *Las Meninas*. The last are Picasso's *Les Demoiselles d'Avignon*, Mondrian's *Composition in Red, Yellow and Blue*, Jackson Pollock's *Autumn Rhythm*, and, finally, *Head VI* 1949 by Francis Bacon.

The artist Maggi Hambling wrote me a letter: 'I consider him full of love in his response to humanity – i.e., full of truth. And his paint is sensual, sensitive and consummately alive.' She referred me to a piece she wrote in the *Guardian* on his eightieth birthday, in which she said that she kept a reproduction of the second version of *Triptych 1944* pinned on the inside of her front door:

> . . . it acts as a daily reminder of my experience of the work itself: the most convincing contemporary image I have seen of life without God. For me Bacon's greatness is his ability to make me feel what it is to be alive. His paint physically, sensually, *is* pain, pleasure, humour, love, isolation and death – more intensely than anyone else's alive today.

On 14 July 1989 Francis and I were filmed together by Peter Stamford for Finnish Television (never transmitted, partly because we were too drunk even though it was only midday), and I asked him why he had never painted the happier side of life.

'I'm a very limited artist. I portray what I can. I don't try to paint despair, but after the age of thirty what is there but death?'

'What do you believe in?'

'*Nothing.*'

'Don't you believe in love?'

'I don't believe in love, really. But love is marvellous if it happens.'

'I don't mean sexual love, but love of friends, work. . . .'

'I'd say that sexual love – sexual obsession – is the strongest one. Love is love and sex is sex,' he replied impatiently. 'Sex – what is it? It is the time of coming – of coming off – that's what pleasure is, isn't it?'

'Do you bring it out in your work?'

'I don't think about it.' I started to mention the *Two Figures* and he anticipated me: 'I put two men naked on a bed. If they grapple with one another, why shouldn't they? I didn't show one putting a cock up the other's arse – I didn't think of anything like *that*!' He raised his glass of champagne – 'Comprendo?'

# 16

# Bacon Goes to Paris and New York, but Not to Moscow

France is certainly the country I prefer of all the countries I know.
*Francis Bacon in an interview with Michel Archimbaud*

Francis told me: 'I love Paris – I think Paris is the most beautiful and marvellous city in the world.' At one point he lived there, but as he grew older he felt he could not keep two places going at the same time and gave the apartment to a friend: 'I took his name so as not to pay two income taxes, as I had to pay in France and England – you know what bastards they are.' He continued to go there, taking the Underground from South Kensington to Heathrow, and managed such journeys with ease.

Francis took a perverse pleasure in telling journalists: 'No one likes my pictures in England, you know,' claiming that he was more popular in Paris and New York than he was in London. This was true in so far as the public were more aware of him than they were here. In Paris they revered him. Also, he made friends with people whose approval he respected because he found them highly intelligent, especially the critic Michel Leiris, who wrote *Francis Bacon in Full Face and in Profile*, which was highly flattering:

What, after all, is the point of a painting devoid of this ability to obsess, and which, after we have communed with it for some time, seems to be little more than an accident breaking the monotony of the wall against which it hangs? The only works which truly exist and achieve full reality are those which establish a persistent hold over us. . . .

Leiris found what he was looking for in Bacon's work, and Bacon returned the compliment by painting his portrait several times. Praise meant nothing to him unless it was tempered by intelligence, and this was of the highest.

Only six years after the triumph at the Grand Palais, Francis exhibited in the Rue des Beaux-Arts, lined with galleries and restaurants, where the crowds were so dense that the police had to close the street. Within twenty-four hours, eight thousand Parisians had flocked to the Claude Bernard Galerie; the artist himself proved a remarkable attraction as he sat in a café around the corner, instantly recognised and recognisable. Immensely gratified, Francis told Sam White: 'It is not only the most beautiful city in the world but the most artistically alert.' White commented: 'If Bacon has a spiritual home over and above any city, including his own, it is Paris. He is the first to recognise it and respond to it.'

Ten years later, in October 1987, he enjoyed a similar success at the Lelong Gallery – though only fourteen paintings were exhibited, three of which were for sale including a triptych for £2.4 million. Newspapers referred to '*le mythe Bacon*', and *Le Monde* broke precedent by running the story on its front page. '*C'est la sensation de Paris*,' said Françoise Gaillard, the gallery assistant. Francis was delighted: 'I don't know why the French seem to like me, but what I do know is that the critics in England loathe everything that I do.' It is hard to know if he believed this or wished to please the French – probably both. Michael Wishart attended the exhibition with Helen Lessore:

> In the afternoon there were just a lot of fashion models up ladders but when we went back at six-thirty, for seven, we found the Boulevard Haussmann blocked with traffic, TV and film crews. I wrote to Francis: 'Not only couldn't I get into the gallery, I couldn't get into the street. More crowds than for a royal wedding rather than a private view, though in a sense it was both.' The Parisians chanted: 'BAK-EN, BAK-EN', and when Wishart passed the home of Serge Gainsbourg he saw the sprayed graffiti on the wall: 'ONLY FRANCIS BACON IS MORE WONDERFUL THAN YOU.'

Two years later I asked Francis if he went to the art galleries when he was in Paris.

'Yaaas [deliberately exaggerated], because I want to see what's happening.'

'I mean the old stuff.'

'Oh, no! The old stuff. . . . I know it all so well it's registered in my mind. I long to see something new and exciting.'

'And do you?'

'*No*! It's a very sad period, whether it's in America or here – it's all really in a trough. . . .'

Provoking him deliberately, I asked what he thought about Gilbert and George.

For a moment he went flat like a fallen soufflé, responding suspiciously: 'What *about* Gilbert and George? I don't really *know* about Gilbert and George. Do you think they are any good? I ask *you* the question!'

'I'm not sure,' I said.

'Well, I'm certain. They want to make money, but if they were any good they would be exciting – and they're not. I just do not find Gilbert and George exciting.'

Changing the subject, I asked if he left the galleries in Paris feeling physically better, a tiresome question which snapped his patience.

'Oh, shut up you old thing – that's the way you always talk. Excitement is the pleasure!'

The favourite café which Francis went to was La Palette at 43 Rue de Seine. It is a modest place which has hardly changed over the years, consisting of a front bar with a few tables and a back room or *Salle* with twenty smaller tables. The atmosphere is probably the closest in Paris to that of the French pub in Soho, which helps to explain why Francis found it so congenial. His behaviour in each was remarkably similar though possibly more relaxed among the artists in La Palette.

The manager, Jean-François, knew him for fifteen years and remembers him with discreet affection: 'Francis loved to have a good time, and when he so decided he gave himself up to it with a joyful heart. He drank nothing but the best: champagne, old Calvados, vintage Marc Égrappé.

'Often he had lunch with the owners of galleries, leaving the restaurant very late and then coming here to drink all afternoon. On the other hand, when he came in with friends he liked to be incognito: just a quick shake of the hand and then he would take the table behind the pots of flowers with his back turned to the customers, and that pleased him – he was in the atmosphere but no one could see him, so he was relaxed.

'All the painters considered him a mountain, everyone wanted to talk to him, and he – always kind and elegant – didn't like to say

222

no. Sometimes he equivocated, answering with a smile. I will never forget one afternoon at the bar – he was leaning over it, hooked onto it with both hands – he staggered a little, and his face seemed to move, from left to right and back again: one had the impression of having one of his paintings there in front of us. He controlled himself of course, and then declared "After us the end of the world!"

'When he settled the bill he was always very generous. Sometimes he would talk of the past, that he began painting very late and never went to art school, and that: "For God's sake, when one has the will and works with all one's energy, *everything* is possible!" '

Francis enjoyed Parisian life on every level: the La Palette café as much as the great restaurants, the low life as well as the high intellectualism of Michel Leiris. One night he picked up an Algerian in Montmartre: 'He was one of the ugliest men you've ever seen, a great black brute, there was no way I could take him home to my apartment for he'd steal everything, so I rented a room in a small hotel and when he went to the lavatory I took off this Rolex watch the gallery had just given me – it was as thin as a wafer – and shoved it under the carpet before he came back.

'Well, I need hardly tell you, the brute was absolutely charming, and left in the middle of the night without a murmur and most of my francs. After he'd gone, I jumped out of bed in my boots and heard this dreadful *crunch*! I'd forgotten all about the watch.

'When I took it to be repaired they said it was useless, and I had to buy another not to offend the gallery. It was then I realised it cost an absolute fortune – it must have been one of the most expensive watches ever made.' There are several versions of this story; this is the one he told me and it rings true.

For Francis to succeed on a grand international scale, it was vital to conquer New York. This was why the charge of possessing drugs was so dangerous, for if he had been found guilty his visa would have been denied.

Francis Bacon's first show in New York was held as early as 1953 with the Durlacher Bros, a gallery which no longer exists, and comprised thirteen works. His work had been noticed by Alfred H. Barr, Jr, who recognised its stature while it was still unacknowledged in England except by the discerning few, such as Robert and Lisa Sainsbury. Barr was described by Salvador Dali in 1931 as 'a nervous young man of cadaverous paleness, but fantastic plastic culture, a veritable radar of modern art, interested in every type of innovation and disposing of a budget larger than all the museums of France combined'. By the 1950s his influence was formidable as the long-established Director of the Museum of Modern Art. Francis was fortunate to have his support, enlisted by Erica Brausen to whom Barr wrote, on 5 July 1957, with a gentle rebuke for her lack of professionalism:

> You are very kind indeed to send me the colour photos of the recent Bacons – but tantalizing, too, since you do not say if all are sold or, if not, what prices. I like the best the least expressionist, the Munch-like one with van Gogh standing still. If unsold, how much is it? How big are they? And are these really the only records? Can't you let us have some black and white photos for our files? You really ought to document thoroughly the work of England's most interesting painter! Who else will?

'England's most interesting painter'! This showed extraordinary acumen at such an early date. Francis Bacon's *Painting 1946* was sold by Erica Brausen to MOMA – as mentioned earlier, his first work to be bought by a museum.

In New York his gallery persuaded Francis to accept a luncheon invitation from a formidable hostess who was one of their richest clients. He did so under protest, arriving in a vile mood to find that he had been placed next to a pretty young man in the mistaken belief by the hostess that he would be charmed by such youthful grace, unaware that Francis would have preferred a truck driver. Taking an instant dislike to the young man, Francis interrupted the arty talk a few minutes later as he leant over and demanded: 'Who's this?', suspecting that the youth had been placed there for his benefit.

'That', preened the hostess knowingly, 'is Jackson Pollock's nephew.'

'Oh,' snorted Francis, 'the old lace-maker's niece, is she?'

His closest friend in America was Peter Beard, the American writer and photographer of African wildlife. A modern adventurer and romantic, Beard has his own wildlife reserve in Kenya, where he was jailed in 1968 after allegedly catching a poacher in one of the thirty-nine snares which protected his property. The man's screams eventually attracted his colleagues, who released him, and Beard was given twelve strokes and eighteen months' imprisonment in what he describes as 'basically a racist move'. Eventually, he won a retrial ('Francis helped to get me released,' he said, 'by writing to the top British officials') and now divides his time between Kenya and a windmill at Montauk on the edge of Long Island, perched on the cliffs overlooking the Atlantic.

Peter Beard met Francis Bacon at the Clermont Club in London for the launch of his book *The End of the Game* in 1956. It was a lucky encounter, for each man admired the other. Beard had studied art in England, Bacon was impressed by his photographs of African wildlife and particularly by those of the carcasses of elephants, telling him 'they are by far the most interesting – memory traces of life and despair'.

There were forty pages of photographs of 35,000 dead elephants. In due course, Francis painted a famous triptych with Beard's portrait on either side of a central panel, which showed a vulture descending on the carcass of a crocodile. However, a potentially sensational collaboration was aborted in New York after Bacon told Beard that he wanted to make sculptures from the carcasses, even procuring the chrome railings and latex material for the flesh to go on them. This would have been held at a Manhatten gallery until local abstract artists, including sculptors, objected to the competition. Beard remembers the lost opportunity with bitterness – 'they were not interested in art, they were interested in playing politics, a Jewish, homosexual Mafia'. This is the closest that Francis came to sculpture.

Once they became friends, Beard decided he would 'never let go, for Francis would never maintain a friendship on his own'. They were extremely close: 'though Francis knew I was not homosexual, and never made a pass at me'. Beard remembers him as 'a high-frequency person', a parallel to Ken Tynan's definition of those on 'the high wire'. He showed Bacon a page of his scrapbook which included a Bacon Pope and says that Francis 'exploded', He almost had convulsions. After an hour, when he calmed down, I asked: "What was all that about? You almost had an epileptic fit!" Francis replied that he hated the Popes knowing he could have done them so much better.' Another time, as they were walking in the early hours towards Francis's apartment in Paris, a car raced down the street and ran over his foot: 'He scurried away into the building to avoid a confrontation, limping for the rest of the week though he never referred to it. Like Andy Warhol, I never saw him flinch.'

Peter Beard also remembers having lunch with David Sylvester and Francis at L'Escargot when an American joined them, saying how much he admired their *Interviews* but it was a pity there was no colour.

'You've missed the entire point of the book,' said Sylvester, but Francis would not let it go, offering the man wine as he abused him straight to his face: 'You're just one of those unbelievable arseholes who know nothing at all' – the wine overflowing into the man's lap. 'It was just one of the most brilliant moments – the total control he had of his brain and the situation.'

When Beard told him he was writing a book on the hidden art of the Masai, Francis replied dismissively: 'I'm not interested in African art.' Beard says this was 'Bullshit! He said that because it meant so much to Picasso.'

Francis found his looks so sympathetic that he painted nine major portraits of Peter Beard. There were two versions of the triptych *Three Studies for a Portrait* in 1975; in the subsequent triptych of 1976, Beard's head is shaven following his release from prison, on either side of an astounding central panel in which vultures seem to swoop on a human carcass while a grinning monkey sits on a rail and a lavatory, its pan overflowing with blood.

When Peter Beard was married to the famous model Cheryl Tiegs, she bought one of the portraits, allegedly for 500,000 dollars, taking it with her when they divorced. Peter Beard says she sold it for two million dollars.

Though it is generally believed that no drawing by Bacon exists, I tracked down two and believe there might be two more. The first shows a corner of the studio he shared with Roy De Maistre; the second drawing, shown to me by Peter Beard, is dated 2 January 1962, made on the title page of *The Human Figure in Motion* by Muybridge. The inscription is hard to decipher with little apparent relevance to the drawing opposite, which appears to be that of *The Wrestlers*:

Portrait of Peter as opposite

_____

made on a sofa upside down as in catalogue
on setting (?) opposite

_____

figure going through door as in Eichman
photo

_____

Butcher shops hanging meat
pails (?) is opposite       (the next line is indecipherable)

_____

self-portrait as in setting per
last page –       (with an arrow pointing downwards)

Plainly, some of these comments refer to a separate page, especially as Peter Beard wrote to me of a reference to Zen: 'The ('Zen') quality of the lines is what we were talking about when he laid this on me. Zen, he said, was when you take a bucket of water from a brook and the brook doesn't change.' This was the only indication I had that Francis even thought of Zen, while his reference to Eichmann confirms that the similarity of the Bacon image to the glass box in the Israeli courtroom was not accidental.

Peter also relates a rare instance of Baconian 'chic' when Francis drew his attention to a rail in the right-hand panel in *Triptych 1976* which had the same colour blue as that of 'President Kennedy's assassination limousine'. This remark, unusually high-fallutin for Francis, could have been influenced by Beard's friendship with Jacqueline Bouvier Onassis as she signed herself in

227

her introduction to Beard's book *Longing for Darkness* about Karen Blixen and her cook Kamante.

Today, like so many others, Peter Beard remembers Francis Bacon lovingly. 'I'm a Bacon freak,' he told me. 'The most important thing in my life.'

In one of their interviews, Francis spoke more openly to Peter Beard about his interest in violence than to anyone else. This was the violence of the street accident rather than the holocaust:

If you see someone lying on the pavement in the sunlight, with the blood streaming from him, that is in itself – the colour of the blood against the pavement – very invigortating . . . exhilarating . . .

In all the motor accidents I've seen, people strewn across the road, the first thing you think of is the strange beauty – the vision of it, before you think of trying to do anything. It's to do with the unusualness of it. I once saw a bad car accident on a large road, and the bodies were strewn about with broken glass from the car, and the blood and various possessions, and it was in fact very beautiful. I think the beauty in it is terribly elusive, but it just happened to be in the disposition of the bodies, the way they lay and the blood, and perhaps it was also because it was not a thing one was used to seeing . . . It was midday, when the sun was very strong and on a white road.

There's nobody more unnatural than I am myself, and, after all, I've worked on myself to be as unnatural as I can. I can't really talk about my painting because I only work for myself and just by chance it happens that for some reason I've been lucky enough to be able to live by something that obsesses me, but I haven't got any morals to preach . . . I just work as closely to my nerves as I can, and as I'm bound up closely in my world today, perhaps it does reflect savage tensions and vacuous spaces.

I would say the photographs of elephants are naturally suggestive – what I see in this photograph is a trigger – a release action – it releases one's sensibility and one's psyche, and all kinds of images crowd into you from seeing this particular image . . . Dead elephants are more beautiful because they trigger off more ideas to me than living ones. Alive they just remain beautiful elephants, whereas the other ones are suggestive of all types of beauty.

Nietzsche forecast our future for us – he was the Cassandra of the nineteenth century – he told us it's all so meaningless we might as well be extraordinary.

It was not until 1968 that Francis crossed the Atlantic for the first time, shortly after a visit to South Africa to see his mother, who had since remarried and was ill. He came to New York to attend his first exhibition with Marlborough, New York – then called Marlborough Gerson – which comprised twenty paintings. John Russell wrote to the *Sunday Times*:

> . . . the news that the artist was in town drew a crowd of hardly manageable proportions . . . they did at least get the point that something quite exceptional was going forward and there were also several major painters who do not normally go to fancy openings and had turned up out of respect and admiration for someone who is indisputably painting better and better at a time of life when many an established artist settles for a dignified marking time.

After referring to the inevitable tag of sensationalism, he noted that 'what commanded the respect of Bacon's colleagues here was not the subject matter: it was the climate of feeling to begin with, the fastidious but quite ruthless intelligence with which ideas were being pushed farther than anyone could have expected them to go'. The paintings included the sensational central panel of the bloodstained sleeping car with the blind halfway down, suggesting that the corpse had gone through the window. This was bought by the Joseph H. Hirshorn Foundation, which owned eight other Bacons and was his foremost collector in America.

All the oils were sold in the first week for prices starting at $35,000 for the smaller pictures. *Time* magazine saw this commercial success as

> a telling comment on just how open-minded the general public has become, for Bacon's material is, to put it simply, sick. Bacon, of course, makes no bones about the fact that the obsessive subject of his paintings is homosexual despair. He argues, however, that the despair he has observed among heterosexuals amounts to more or less the same thing.

Like the Three Sisters, Francis took a long time deciding *not* to go to Moscow. I happened to be in at the beginning, when a group of us moved on from a lively afternoon in the Colony to have dinner with Francis at the Trattoria Terrazza down Dean Street. We were shown to a table in an alcove that resembled a small boiler room with exposed pipes, and when the pasta arrived it failed to lift our spirits.

229

James Birch, who ran the Birch and Conran Gallery with Paul Conran, a few doors from the Colony, tried to divert Francis by asking if he had thought of showing his pictures in Moscow. Francis gave him his telephone number and asked him to call the next morning: 'I'm really interested.' Birch could hardly believe his luck. Such a venture had been simmering for five years since he had met a Russian 'Mr Fix-It' called Sergei Klokhov in Paris, hoping to enlist his help in promoting the young artists he represented with a show in Moscow.

I have met Klokhov. The antidote to James's gentleness, the bearded Sergei would make a splendid Svengali in a Siberian production of *Trilby*. He owns a snake farm in Uzbekistan, with several scorpions as well as thirty cobras, and sells their venom commercially. He is not a man to disregard and knew his protocol precisely, advising James to send an official letter to Moscow. Nine months later James flew out after receiving a favourable reply, but within two days of meeting the members of the Union of Soviet Artists he realised they had no interest in his young artists but were desperately keen to show the works of Francis Bacon, which would blaze the way for other important Western artists.

The morning after our dinner, James phoned Klokhov and asked if he would be interested. His reaction was: 'Fantastic!' Then James made a nervous call to Francis, wondering if he had forgotten. 'Bacon remembered everything. When I insisted: "Are you sure?" he gave an impatient "Yes". He's such a humble person he thinks it's a great honour.' As of course it was – the first important living Western artist to be shown in Soviet Russia.

The exhibition took two years to arrange, during which James made five visits to Moscow. Gradually he won the trust of the Russians, but he had greater difficulty in England – not with the Marlborough Gallery, which recognised its significance at once, but with the hidebound British Council, who saw the prestige involved and started to take the show over. They were less than generous to James Birch, omitting his name from the official documents – a slight that James has not forgiven. Unaware of this, I found them helpful, offering to pay for my flight to Moscow to cover the event for the *Daily Mail* who would pay the rest of my expenses. I had a particular wish to go there, for my father and mother spent a large chunk of their lives in Russia, but apart from that I was thrilled at the prospect of being in Moscow with Francis

Bacon at such a rare moment. Everyone was excited at this penultimate stage, including Francis. Then his mood changed.

One evening in the Groucho Club, I saw Francis and John Edwards sitting in the small no-man's land which leads from the bar to the downstairs restaurant. John looked uneasy and Francis was testy. Something or someone had annoyed him, but I was taken by surprise when he told me that he doubted if he would be going to Moscow after all. Though his reasons were not entirely clear, he thought he was being taken advantage of. He had lunched with a director and his assistant from the British Council and found their complacency so irritating that he insisted on paying the bill in order not to be beholden – an inverted form of punishment which they accepted readily. 'I think James is trying to con me,' he continued.

'Oh no,' I protested gently. 'I think he can be absolved of that. He'll do anything you ask.' It was plain that the two rotten apples from the British Council were spoiling the whole barrel.

'He never warned me of all the protocol involved,' said Francis.

Seldom had I seen him look so angry, and I was thankful it was not directed against me.

I picked my words carefully, sensing it would prove calamitous if I urged him to go ahead. I sympathised over the boredom of the couple from the British Council, reassured him that James had behaved impeccably throughout and had suffered (as I had by now discovered) from the Council's machinations himself, but stressed: 'You must do exactly as *you* want to do. That is all that matters. If you don't want to go, don't.'

'Well, I don't.'

'Of course, the young Russian artists would love to see you. . . .'

'That's rubbish,' he interrupted emphatically. 'They know my work already. They send me letters. They don't need to see me.'

I laughed nervously. 'You know, you might enjoy it.'

'I doubt that greatly.'

'They'd be so glad to see you that you could do what you wanted. They could even hold the press conference without you.'

'Press conference!' he cried, as if I had forced a glass of hemlock to his lips. 'What press conference?'

Oh God, I thought, he doesn't realise that this will be part of the jamboree, already listed on the 'itinerary' sent to me by the Council. I explained that it was conceivable that the artist might be expected to say a few words, adding quickly that this would be quite unnecessary in his case. 'You must do exactly as you like.' Far from scaring him off with too much talk of protocol, the British Council had not warned him of the half of it. All those speeches! Few people welcome protocol more than the Russians as a distraction from the deadliness of their daily life, but it would be anathema to Francis.

'Anyhow,' he concluded, 'there's my asthma.' This had been worse recently and raised an understandable objection. I saw that at once.

'But Francis, if you're suffering from asthma you shouldn't go – the flight could be disastrous.' This sent him spinning into reverse.

'I don't know – it's only a few hours. Anyhow, my doctor [Dr Brass] is coming with me to see the exhibition, so if I do have an attack in Moscow there's nothing to worry about. We'll see', and he changed the subject. I could see my hope of reaching Moscow receding.

Perhaps his mind was resolved already, for I never knew him to change it after he reached a decision. In due course asthma was the official alibi, accompanied by a message of personal regret; I returned the cheque for my flight to the British Council, for my story was invalid without the presence of Francis Bacon.

James Birch believes that the decision not to go to Moscow was an unnecessary mistake. Francis's enthusiasm had been so keen that he studied Russian from a cassette for the previous six months so he would have a smattering of the language on his arrival. On the day of his flight, James had a breakfast of bacon and eggs with Francis and John Edwards at Reece Mews. 'You could tell Francis was excited,' John said. 'I bet if he'd had a visa he'd have hopped on the plane with us.' Afterwards, Francis told Geordie Greig: 'It's a great disappointment. If it wasn't for this bloody asthma I would be over there. Everything was closed after 1917. It would have been fascinating to see the country now.' Greig reported that Francis said this glumly and I am sure he did, even if his explanation was not the whole truth.

The British contingent set out to attend the exhibition which opened at the New Tretyakov Gallery on the afternoon of 22

September 1988. Sponsored by the Marlborough, this was the first major exhibition of British art to be held in the Soviet Union since the Turner exhibition in 1975. The British visitors included Lord Gowrie, the former Minister for the Arts; Henry Meyric-Hughes, the director of the British Council's Fine Arts Department; and John Edwards, who represented Francis Bacon. Roy Miles told me: 'I happened to arrive at the airport at the same moment. I was about to spend several million pounds buying Russian art but there was no one there to help me and as I struggled with my luggage I saw the Russian dignitaries bowing and scraping to that young man and I was *furious*! And do you know, he handled it superbly!'

Even without Francis's presence, the pictures caused a sensation. One woman made the poignant comment: 'Excuse us, but throughout the period of Soviet power we have been fed with a different kind of art. We have been deprived of inner freedom, perception, thought, and feelings. And a great deal of time will yet have to pass before we are capable of taking in Bacon's art.'

In London Miss Beston had asked Klokhov, casually, if homosexuals were allowed in Russia.

'Oh yes,' he smiled reassuringly, 'they are all in Lubyanka!'

A Soviet man could be sent to a labour camp for five years for homosexual sex, and eight for involvement with minors, this element giving an added *frisson* to the show. At the press conference, Grey Gowrie was at first amused, then horrified, when British journalists 'wanted to discuss Bacon's homsexuality, whereas the Russians were genuinely interested in his reputation, and in what other artists thought of him'. One British journalist asked if there was not an inherent hypocrisy in exhibiting pictures by an English homosexual in a country which imprisons its own. Charges of censorship were denied by Grey Gowrie but confirmed afterwards by Sergei Klokhov: 'We decided to leave out the triptych [writhing male figures on a bed] and I telephoned Francis Bacon and told him that, unfortunately, this painting might be misunderstood by the general public. I had to explain that what I actually meant was that it might be *understood*. He laughed. But it is not such a bad thing that this picture was left out. It was very important not to give the exhibition too much the appearance of a scandal; to include the triptych may have made the conservative elements in this country dismiss the whole show and make it an object of ridicule.' He had a point.

The critic Andrew Graham Dixon met a lady called Natasha who complained: 'I didn't understand it, and I didn't really like it. I don't think it's possible for great art to be so unpleasant.' He suggested that one trip on the Moscow Underground, a subterranean pantheon with gigantic statuary of peasants and mothers, showed why most Russians were going to find 'the British bacon hard to stomach'. His own reaction was not that different from Natasha's, though expressed more boldly and starting with the claim that 'Excrement is a subject close to Bacon's heart.' He explained that when Bacon was seventeen he looked at dogshit on the pavement and suddenly realised: 'There it is – this is what life is like.' (I should add that I never heard Francis express this foolish sentiment myself.) 'Bacon's paintings deal in prime biological fact,' he continued,

> the stink and gore and flesh of us all; man, cornered by his own mortality, blurs into meaty putrescence. In Moscow, his art – the screaming, trapped heads, the crawling things that perform for the viewer in *Woman Emptying a Bowl of Water* and *Paralytic Child on All Fours* – has never looked more ferocious or unsettling. The shit has really hit the fan.

Inadvertently, the exhibition could not have been better timed. It would not have been possible two years earlier. As Klokhov stated, it belonged 'administratively, morally, ideologically, at this particular moment in Soviet history. Bacon paints the evil in humanity, without mercy. That is new in Russia. The exhibition is a symbol of our whole concept of perestroika – now, thanks to Gorbachev, we are not afraid to show the dark side of our life, the dark side of society – *our* society.' The paintings included Eisenstein's nurse from the *Battleship Potemkin*, which was calculated to please, and the bloodstained desk where Trotsky had his skull split open by a Stalinist assassin in 1940. Tactfully, this remained unidentified, but those who recognised the image saw a significant break with past censorship.

The show also contained, on a less controversial level, one of my favourite of the later paintings – *Jet of Water*. Francis told me he had literally thrown the paint at the canvas to create a splash.

'People say it's an erection, but it's *just* a jet of water!' As usual, he laughed at such interpretations.

The 5,000 catalogues sold out, inadequate to the demand of the 150,000 Muscovites who came to the gallery during the next six weeks. Bacon's exceptionally fine portrait of John Edwards was chosen for the cover of the catalogue and the poster. At one point it seemed that no drink would be available for anyone at the private view until Edwards offered to pay for crates of champagne which he would bring himself. Humiliated, the authorities changed their mind.

Back in London Klokhov had impressed Francis at their first dinner at Wilton's. He stated his claim dramatically – if Francis gave him a picture as part of his reward, he would present it to the Pushkin Museum in Moscow where it would hang in a place of honour as the only example of contemporary art. Francis handed over the painting and was not surprised when Klokhov changed his mind in the taxi and drove straight to Sotheby's. It is hard not to admire him.

# 17

# Falling Out

Friends are people who can tear each other apart.
*Francis Bacon in conversation with Peter Beard*

Bruce Bernard was another visitor to Moscow, reporting in the *Independent Magazine* on 8 October 1988 that the Russians 'respond particularly to what is heroic and direct in art, and Bacon's work is surely both. We all felt that the occasion had been a great and historic one, and regretted not being able to toast the artist in person.' Bruce had come across Bacon's work while still at school, stimulated by the 1933 *Crucifixion* in Herbert Read's *Art Now*, 'looking stronger in a way than the Picasso 1929 *Baigneuse* that it faced, . . . I was captivated by the mysterious presence.' Unhappily, his subsequent friendship with Francis was one of those which came to grief.

I should declare a prejudice: though we have had our arguments, usually provoked by myself, Bruce Bernard is an old friend for whom I feel the highest respect. I have liked his peculiar style since we met in Soho in the fifties. Whereas his young brother, Jeffrey, exploited his charm, Bruce suppressed his. He dressed as if he had been unemployed for a very long time, entering a room defensively as if prepared for disillusion. To strangers, he seemed to exist in a perpetual state of disgruntlement, hovering in the background like a diplomatic spy in an alien regime. Most of the time he scowled; even when he smiled it was conspiratorial – though tremendously rewarding. In fact he suffers from such a surfeit of integrity that he finds it impossible to dissemble. Though he is a painter himself, few have seen his work because it fails to please him.

It took me a long time before I appreciated just how distinguished he is. He is the compiler and author of several outstanding books on art including *Van Gogh – Vincent by Himself*; *The Bible and Its Painters*; *The Impressionist Revolution*; and *The Queen of Heaven*, on the theme of the Virgin Mary. His taste is impeccable, and his art book *About Francis Bacon*, to celebrate the artist's eightieth birthday, was a culmination for which he was uniquely qualified.

Yet Francis vetoed the book, as Bruce explained in an article in the *Independent Magazine* on 2 May 1992, a few days after his death. Bruce started by stating his intention, which had been 'to make the best possible picture book of Bacon's work, with a text consisting mostly of extracts from press criticism'. As Francis told me when this was suggested, he respected Bruce's judgement – one of the very few whom he did respect, along with David Sylvester and Michel Leiris. To start with he co-operated with his usual hospitality, though this soon began to wear off. He asked a stranger in Fortnum's when it opened one morning: 'What do you give someone for breakfast – smoked salmon?' as if he had never found himself in such a position before, which may have been the case. Then: 'I have someone who insists on calling and it's becoming such a bore. He's supposed to be writing something about me, and I wish to God I'd never said yes.' By chance, the stranger saw me in the Coach and Horses that lunchtime and recounted the encounter with some amusement: 'It was the first time I've met Francis Bacon, and he seemed in a vile mood!'

Blissfully unaware of the rapids ahead, Bruce continued, lulled into complacency by Francis's graciousness when they met face to face. Francis invited Bruce and his designer, Derek Birdsall, and most of the Birdsall family to lunch where he charmed them all with his generosity and enjoyment. According to Bruce, the stumbling block came with the colour proofs, some of which were 'depressingly inaccurate' and seemed to worry Francis, 'triggering unspoken doubts'. A further lunch allayed all fears, but two days later, with less than two weeks before the book was due at the printers, Francis phoned Bruce and asked him to come round. This time the smoked salmon was replaced by an ultimatum: all the photographs and Bruce's text, apart from a brief introduction, should be removed, and no work before the *Three Studies* should be reproduced. Understandably, Bruce found this unacceptable – 'I did not stay to argue.' He wrote a letter arguing his case, but received no reply.

237

The colour proofs could have been corrected – that is the purpose of proofs – so what had gone so drastically wrong? Bruce acknowledged that several things he had written were 'unwise', and that Francis could not be expected to like 'the unavoidable sense of valediction'; but Francis was adamant, and, as I say, once he made up his mind he rarely changed it. He agreed to see the publisher, who had invested £25,000 in the production, but refused to give his permission; and as he owned the copyright for the reproductions while he was alive, he had the total right of veto. Bruce concluded: 'If our friendship was a little dented by this episode, my regard and admiration for the best he did and was will never change. I feel honoured to have known him.'

That was the truth but not the whole picture.

I can appreciate Bruce's desolation – privately, he referred to 'old man's bile'. As with the 'asthma' which prevented Francis flying to Moscow, the colour reproduction served as a pretext. There were several reasons why Francis changed his mind.

Unwittingly, Bruce had alienated John Edwards in Moscow. Edwards told me: 'It was very funny. If Bruce wanted to go anywhere or see anyone connected with the exhibition, he had to come with me. I could tell he didn't like me, but he had to pretend to be nice.' Bruce gave him scant acknowledgement, which was an error considering how important John Edwards was in his role as model for some of Francis's finest paintings in this final stage – quite apart from his value as a friend.

Someone who has asked to be anonymous told me of a curious incident one Saturday morning in the unlikely setting of a Holland Park fishmonger's where Lucian Freud spotted Francis in the queue. Knowing the owner, Lucian led Francis inside and afterwards they went for a cup of coffee at a nearby café. It was a reunion quickly to be dashed, when Lucian dropped the casual remark that he had seen Bruce's work and thought it excellent. That Lucian should have seen it led Francis to suspect that Lucian had helped Bruce throughout. For Francis this was unforgivable. No blame is attached, but anyone who knew the happy band of artists in the halcyon fifties can only grieve that such friendships fell apart.

Though Lucian Freud has warned me not to put words in his mouth, it is impossible to write about Francis and ignore him. The two of them were inseparable when I knew them in the fifties and sixties and photographed them together in the Millais studio. Lucian painted the famous small portrait of Francis on copper in 1952, which Francis admired, and the lesser-known one of George Dyer in 1965. Francis painted no fewer than twenty-five portraits of Lucian, and probably more. Twenty-five portraits – that is close to love! Together, they represented Britain at the Venice Biennale in 1954.

Apart from pictures that Francis may have given him, Lucian bought the *Head 1951* and wrote to the Curator of the Cleveland Museum, where it ended up, to correct a misstatement: 'I bought it the day he did it and quite some time later when he was looking at it in my house he said that that was the first time he thought about painting Van Gogh. I did not say it was the first in the series.'

Francis told the critic Richard Cork that at one stage he bought a Sickert of a woman standing beside a bed with a man seated next to her. 'But, like a fool, I gave it to Lucian Freud. I wish I had it now.' When Lucian sold it, Francis was displeased.

Francis told Michel Archimbaud later: 'We did have close ties, but we don't see each other anymore. It's a bit sad, but that's how it is. Our ties became overstretched.'

I doubt if there was any specific reason for their break-up – there seldom is. It was more that Lucian's work had advanced to a point where Francis's influence had diminished; and perhaps, as an artist, he wished to be free of it altogether. On his side, Francis remarked that, 'Everything Lucian does is so *careful*'. Someone has suggested that Francis was annoyed when Lucian became a Companion of Honour in 1983, having himself turned down the Order of Merit, but this sounds too petty to be credible. There were attempts at reconciliation, mainly from John Edwards who went up to Lucian at the private view for Bruce Bernard's 1984 exhibition of Deakin's photographs, *The Salvage of a Photographer*, saying, 'You must come and say hullo to Francis.' They said a few words, but by then it was too late to matter.

I was chilled to hear that a former friend of both Francis and Lucian spoke thus of a late painting: 'Here's the poor old accident standing in his stable with his head down waiting to be harnessed yet again. I wish Francis would go back to being a gentleman, which he was when we first knew him, and leave painting alone.' Such former friends are reluctant to talk about him since his death. Perhaps they cannot forgive his generosity towards them, nor forgive themselves for their forgetfulness in his final years.

Newer artists remember him with gratitude. Mark Boyle was addressing an informal group at the Hayward when he heard a voice say: 'Mark, when you have a moment could I have a word with you?' Everyone turned round and made way when they recognised Francis Bacon, who had arrived with a French dealer whom he had contacted after seeing the exhibition by the Boyle family the day before. He alerted other foreign dealers, too. 'How often I tried to thank Francis, my God!' says Mark. He describes Bacon's own work as 'one of the most heroic attempts to be truthful that's ever been made'.

Francis's endorsement of the Boyle family was instrumental in their success. It was especially welcome to Mark, who was a poet until he saw one of Bacon's *Figures* and realised that Francis was achieving with paint what he was attempting in words. 'Overnight I became a painter.' Francis respected Mark Boyle as a friend as well as an artist and went to his dinner parties at Greenwich, once bringing his sister from South Africa which was rather a dampener. 'It turned it into a genteel Edinburgh affair in contrast to the occasions when Francis Bacon might have been outrageous but was always the life and soul of the party.'

Having flinched from dinner parties when he was younger, he rather enjoyed them now. There were times when Francis was lonely, yet without the urge to throw himself into the frenzy of Soho. When he heard that the Boyle family were going to central Australia to find new soil to impress – a part of the method of their art – he was so enthusiastic that Mark instinctively asked him to join them.

'Oh, could I?' Francis exclaimed, 'I was hoping you would ask me!'

Understandably, Mark was not sure that Francis was serious and, as the time for their departure approached and the logistics grew more horrendous, he worried in case anything should happen to their elderly companion seven hundred miles from Alice Springs. Even so, he assumed Francis would come. But then a member of the family fell ill, and Francis was forgotten until

Mark Boyle found himself rushing to a waiting taxi only just in time to make the flight.

Francis was unamused. 'I'm very, very offended,' he told him afterwards.

Francis was suffering from a sense of loneliness, of being left out.

'It was very strange,' said Mark Boyle. 'Several times he almost wept in restaurants and once he accused me of being lucky to have shows in such exotic places as Japan. "That's crazy," I told him, "self-indulgent nonsense. You could have one anywhere in the world." '

'No, I couldn't,' Francis corrected him sharply. 'For one thing the owners are reluctant to lend my pictures, and in the second the insurance costs are prohibitive.' Mark mentioned this to the Japanese Foundation, and hopes it might have helped in mounting the important Bacon retrospective in Tokyo.

Others noticed Francis's loneliness. One Sunday lunchtime at the Chelsea Arts Club, when he was in his late seventies, a Danish woman who lived round the corner saw 'this little old man who looked a bit sad and left out, so I asked him to come back to my place to eat and he accepted. He seemed a bit lonely at the house – noone was talking to him – and I asked what he did. Everyone laughed at me for my mistake, but he seemed amused. Perhaps he liked being invited by someone who had no idea who he was.'

One of the more mysterious and regrettable fall-outs concerned Michael and Geraldine Leventis. At one point, towards the end of his life, they were probably his closest friends.

They met by chance. The previous night, Francis, John Edwards and Ian Board had gambled at Charlie Chester's casino, where Ian won £4,000. John advised him to stop while he was winning. Taking the proverbial advice, usually disregarded, Ian invited them to lunch the next day at the Trattoria, where they enjoyed themselves with such exuberance that when Ian beckoned to the waiter to bring them another bottle of wine the waiter produced it instantly as if he had been waiting in the wings, – 'Sent by the gentleman in the corner'. To Ian's surprise, he opened an identical wine to that which had gone before.

To Michael Leventis this was a natural thing to do, the Greek courtesy to strangers who look as if they are having fun. After Ian scurried back to open the Colony, Francis gave a wave and Mr and Mrs Leventis joined him and John Edwards. By the time they followed them up the stairs to the Colony, they were no longer strangers. Though I never had the chance to meet them, Francis told me, with that conspiratorial smile which he used when daring to praise someone, how much he liked Michael and that Geraldine was 'a really marvellous cook'. On one occasion, the Leventis hospitality was such that they all sat down to lunch at their home in Swiss Cottage at one o'clock, and rose at one the next morning. There was a strong mutual sympathy. Michael Leventis is a fine artist, though plainly influenced by his admiration for Francis. His wife Geraldine is English, humorous without being aggressive. With their love of food – they run an Italian restaurant and a coffee-bar near their home – they were hardly innocents in this respect though hoist immediately by Francis onto a higher level: 'He introduced us to a new world. We'd always gone to good restaurants but never to that extent, nor had we seen such a consumption of alcohol.'

Francis took me once to Annabel's, where he sent back pots of delicious caviare complaining to my dismay that they were too 'salty', until we were reduced to bacon and eggs, the unfailing standby of nightclub cuisine. On another occasion Michael and Geraldine Leventis had both the caviare and the bacon and eggs.

For his part, Francis found Michael Leventis attractive, a Greek Cypriot with cropped blond hair, with the advantage of the wealth of the family's Leventis Group of Companies, with worldwide interests. They were such delightful companions that the four of them went on holiday abroad. The Leventis's say they were genuinely fond of John Edwards, and when he left them in New York – where they lunched with Larry Rivers – to go his different way in the evening, they acted as 'babysitters' for Francis and kept him company. Trusting them to protect John's interests, he appointed them his executors.

And then it went wrong.

I have been given two explanations for this and it is hard to sift the truth, though I see no reason to disbelieve Mr and Mrs Leventis. One thing which is certain is the abruptness of the break.

The first version suggests that Michael Leventis bought a

242

painting from Francis 'on the side' for £400,000. In due course he was thinking of lending it or selling it to a museum in Cyprus with which his family was involved, where an eager curator inadvertently contacted the Marlborough Gallery to ask for the provenance of the picture. This was a natural thing to do but the consequence was disastrous, with the Marlborough complaining that Francis should not sell pictures behind their back. Francis was furious.

The version given to me by the Leventis's is significantly different: Michael Leventis says that Francis phoned him up to ask if he would buy a particular panel in a triptych which he was pleased with and wanted Leventis to have. Though he did not share Francis's enthusiasm for the picture, he did not wish to risk offending him and bought it through a trust for a million dollars – through the Marlborough. With the interest at 100,000 dollars, he decided a few years later that he could not afford such a luxury and made plans to sell it. Word of this reached the Marlborough and Francis reacted angrily: 'You phoned me up asking if you could have a picture . . .'

'No, Francis, Leventis corrected him, 'you phoned *me* up . . .'

Geraldine Leventis stresses that the picture had not even been sold at this point, while her husband told me: 'If I'd known it was breaking up our friendship, I'd never have done it.'

The break was absolute. When Francis entered the Colony soon afterwards, Ian asked why he was dressed in a suit and tie. 'I've just been to my solicitors to change my will,' he said, with the implication that the Leventises had been struck out of it. Alternatively, he might have withdrawn their names as his executors. In a curious way, now that Francis is dead, the truth of their appearance in his will hardly seems to matter, though it might do to them. But from that moment they were *non personae*, or so I believed until I met them.

I thought it was only fair to hear their side of the story and they invited me to their home, where I was impressed by Michael's two portraits of Francis which no one had mentioned to me before. They catch his personality so powerfully that Francis seemed to be staring at me, albeit accusingly in such circumstances.

'Strangely,' said Michael Leventis, 'I can't believe he's dead. I can't think of anyone who affected me more – more than my father.'

With his usual loyalty, John Edwards broke with them irrevocably, but over lunch at their Italian restaurant nearby, the Leventises seemed glad to talk to someone who knew Francis and surprised me when they revealed that there had been a reunion at the end. One day he came into their coffee shop with a friend and they opened the champagne. Later, they drove him and the friend to see Nureyev and as this was a private dinner they prepared to move on. 'Francis sat in the car and wouldn't get out, saying, "I'm not going in unless you two come in too." As he insisted, we went upstairs.'

This was the first I knew of their reconciliation. It took place at the end of Francis's life when the lights were dimming: 'He wasn't painting – he was very, very depressed, for if he wasn't painting, he wasn't happy. It needs tremendous strength and energy to paint in oils, but he was debilitated and sapped of energy.'

They had a final dinner at Bibendum. Michael Leventis says: 'It was the first time I had seen Francis so distant and noncommunicative, he hardly said a word and nothing seemed to register. We mentioned that to his friend of the time and he agreed, equally upset.'

Francis told Richard Cork that the afternoons were difficult: 'I get up very early and paint in here until 1 p.m. Then I'm finished, I've had it. I hate afternoons – I think they're absolutely revolting, they're a wash-out. I feel better again in the evenings.' By then Francis was eighty-one and a kidney had been removed, which made it harder to withstand punishment. No wonder afternoons seemed interminable. He was losing the strength to attack the canvas with the energy required when painting in oils, and had no wish to turn to watercolours, as Edward Burra had in the same situation. But considering his age, his stamina was remarkable. He went to dinner with Helen Lessore at her house in Camberwell, where today she lives alone at the age of eighty-five. She remembers how kind he was to her son, the painter John Lessore, who became paralysed in his teens. Francis arranged a visit to Tangier; it was a great success, Francis was angelic – looked after him marvellously.

Francis had time for the old and infirm. When Sonia Orwell was dying from cancer, he went to the trouble of renting an attractive room for her in a hotel near the hospital, and every evening when she returned from her treatment she found champagne and flowers waiting for her. He understood grief: he took my mother and myself to a strained lunch at Wheeler's after my father's death; and Robert Medley has told me how Francis looked after the widow of Ceri Richards, driving down by car with him to take her out. When Francis heard that my grandmother was agitated over a possible operation to save her sight, he arranged a consultation with the leading specialist at the time, Trevor-Roper; he paid for it himself and allayed her fears. Hating illness and the sickbed as much as I do, I find such kindnesses heroic; but with Francis they came naturally. No wonder people thought he was a gentleman.

He was also scrupulous in remembering people who might otherwise have been forgotten, like a childhood nurse known as Auntie Dorrie. 'He remained strangely loyal,' said Ian Board. 'It was one of his surprising characteristics. I'd meet him and it was either "I've just been to see the old girl" or "I'm just going to visit her", always bringing her a little box of Mr Kipling's cakes. No one else was allowed inside her flat. It was tiny, no central heating, no lav – she had to use the colander and get rid of it under the tap. One day she upset a paraffin heater and burned to death.'

Equally, he had no illusions and knew the tyranny of the weak. Writing to a close friend, he reminded him

. . . about your mother she has always been a bitter and difficult woman. If she doesn't want to see you leave her to it you have tried to do a lot for her but I think what X says is very true old age has a horrible effect on many people try not to worry too much about it If she doesn't change her attitude there's nothing you can do if she feels like she does as long as she has enough to exist on you should not worry.

When he wrote that he was seventy-six.

Few of his friends were aware of the extent of his generosity. He told Michael Wishart that AIDS was 'so ghastly and there's nothing we can do about it, but I'm going to give lots to them in my will'. Bryan Robertson told me that Francis gave him a cheque for £1,000 towards an AIDS charity.

When he presented his second version of the *Three Studies* he had a choice of several institutions but clearly had a special affection for the Tate Gallery and its new Director, Nicholas Serota, who told him that it was part of his new policy to give him a room and asked if he could show the triptych. As they were discussing a possible bequest, Francis said he would like to donate it immediately. Nicholas Serota told me that he suggested a little dinner in his honour, principally for his fellow artists and friends, but he declined. 'He felt that he wanted no fuss, no ceremony and no excitement. He was simply happy to see people enjoying the painting in the company of the original triptych and wanted it to stay at the Tate.'

When I phoned him on the morning of his eightieth birthday he said: 'It's very nice but I'm in a terrible mess. People have sent me all these flowers, but I haven't anything to put them in. I'm not the sort of person who has *vases*.'

Sir Michael Levey has described how Sonia Orwell introduced him to Francis Bacon in 1971 when he was the Director of the National Gallery, organising an appeal in the hope of buying Titian's *Death of Actaeon*. Francis offered to help in several ways – by taking part in a radio programme, by introducing Levey at dinner to people who might be able to contribute, by turning up on the dot as arranged to give his own donation of 'a substantial cheque'. Sir Michael wrote: 'My experiences do not include a comparable instance of such instinctive, imaginative, generous support for acquisition of an old master painting for the nation from her greatest living painter, but then I am not aware of having met another painter whose greatness seemed to me – seems, rather – so uncontestable.'

Helen Lessore says that not a day passed without Francis thinking about death, but when it came closer I feel he suffered more from the inconveniences of age rather than from the ambush which lay ahead and was best ignored. He told me decisively: 'My mother said, "Promise me you'll never grow old." She hated it so much. How right she was!'

Alistair Hicks reported a conversation in which Francis expressed his envy of tradition: 'From 3000 to 2000 BC the magnificent art in Egypt was being made by craftsmen. There is a lot of craft in painting. The Egyptians were attempting to defeat death.'

'Are modern artists attempting to defeat death?' asked Hicks.

'No. The difference is they believed in an afterworld. I don't.'

He told someone else: 'Man now realises that he is an accident, that he is a completely futile being, that he has to play out the game without purpose, other than of his own choosing.'

Yet he was in fact a cheerful man with a healthy disdain for the trappings of fame, the corruption of money and the mistakes of doctors. Lady Caroline Blackwood recounts the tale of a dinner when Francis joined her and Lucian at Wheeler's: 'His doctor had told him that his heart was in such a bad state that not a ventricle was functioning; he had rarely seen such a diseased organ, and he warned Francis that if he had one more drink or even became excited it could kill him. Having told us the bad news he waved to the waiter and ordered a bottle of champagne, and once it was finished he ordered several more. He was ebullient throughout the evening but Lucian and I went home feeling very depressed. He seemed doomed. We were convinced he was going to die, aged forty. We took the doctor's diagnosis seriously. No one was ever going to stop him drinking. No one would ever prevent him from becoming excited. We wondered that night if we would ever see him again.'

Similarly after Francis's operation for the removal of the kidney, Michael Wishart offered his sympathy, but it was brushed aside: 'Well, if you've been drunk since the age of fifteen, you're lucky to have even one kidney!' and Francis burst out laughing. I can hear him.

Illness and accidents were ignored, though he had the occasional fall. Bobby Hunt says that Francis was so pissed one afternoon in the Caves that when he took him next door to the Colony, he slipped on the stairs and one of the metal strips hit the right side of his eye and put it half out. Francis forced it back in and went to a hospital. 'The next day,' said Bobby, 'he had no memory of what happened, but he had a scar for some time. He never referred to it.'

Ian Board tells the story of someone who gave Francis a shove as they left – 'and Francis fell down the stairs as pissed as a fart'. Ian phoned the next morning to ask how he was and learned that one side of his nose had been pushed out of joint. 'Then I met someone who hit me on the other side and knocked it back into the right position, so I saved on the doctor's fee.' Admittedly, that sounds as if the drink had flowed too well for accuracy.

His diet of oysters, champagne and the finest wine stood him in good stead.

His stamina and powers of recovery were remarkable. After their exhausting day's filming for the *South Bank Show*, when Francis got Melvyn Bragg drunk, possibly for the first time in his life, in Mario's Restaurant, they had to continue in the Colony the next morning where the barman, Michael Wojas, says that Melvyn was an hour late and recalls 'the look on his face when he saw Francis in the corner already sparkling at eleven o'clock, having been there an hour. While Melvyn Bragg sent out for black coffee, Francis and John Edwards continued on champagne.

'Francis saw him coming,' said Ian.

'Did he get Bragg drunk deliberately?' I asked.

'Oh, *yes*! He made a particular point of topping up the drinks.'

'To get the edge,' said Michael.

'To show what idiots they are,' said Ian, with a snort.

Francis had been friendly throughout his life with the artist Rodrigo Moynihan, who admired him even though he knew that Francis could be unkind about his work, especially when he turned to abstraction. John Moynihan said that Francis was always aware that his father was half Spanish and envied him that blood, and Rodrigo was certainly attractive company. After a visit to his home in Provence after Rodrigo divorced Eleanor to marry Anne Dunn after her divorce from Michael Wishart, he wrote enthusiastically on 13 May 1967 to thank him for his marvellous hospitality in Aix. I feel if I lived in Provence I would never leave. Love Francis.' Another letter exists dated 'Wednesday morning', which indicates a later and disastrous dinner at Wilton's:

My dear Rodrigo I don't know how to apologise for last night I got so hopelessly drunk and had a sort of black-out – but I feel really awful about landing you with Nadine [the sister of his Parisian dealer, Claude Bernard] will you please let me know how much I owe you for Wilton You see why I have no friends – I have tried all morning to telephone you without success. Yours Francis.

After Rodrigo's funeral, Francis persuaded his godson to

come back to the mews where he plied him with champagne, obviously loath to see him go: 'You don't know what it's like to be eighty and alone at midnight.' By the time Francis Wishart was able to leave, it was almost light.

# 18

# Narrow Street

We all need to be aware of the potential disaster which stalks us every moment of the day.

*Francis Bacon*

Writing this book has given me the pleasure of getting to know Francis better. I had not fully appreciated just how extraordinary and many-faceted he was, with his spasmodic saintliness tempered by the swaggering panache of Cyrano and the rampageousness of Mr Hyde.

Writing about him so closely, I can see and hear him again: that unique self-mockery in his careful intonation, the cautious tread, the huge grin which swept his face when he entered a room and recognised a friend. He was a sweeter man than I had realised, but this does not diminish his capacity to hurt. On an afternoon when Lucian Freud still came to the Colony he let some information drop, saying how pleased he was that Francis liked his new home in Narrow Street, Limehouse. It took me several minutes before I realised what had happened.

In the mid-fifties, when I was starting in television, I moved from South Kensington to a small house above a barge-builder's workshop on the bend of the river at Limehouse. I loved it so passionately that I slept on the floor before the furniture arrived. Friends were dismayed by the din as workmen scraped the rust off old barges resting on the shore below, and flinched when cargo ships hooted with impatience as they waited to enter Regent's Canal Dock at night; but for me it was romance. The trumpeting of ships reminded me of animals approaching a water-hole. I did not smell the fumes from below, nor see the carpet rise because of them. I did not mind the rat in the attic and preferred the broken-down pugilist called Patsy Cokely, with whom I had the same conversation every time we met, to Cecil Beaton who had been my neighbour in Pelham Place. I arrived at the last gasp of Chinatown when Pennyfields still bore the faded Chinese lettering on blistering façades, and Lascars walked up West India Dock Road carrying brown paper parcels.

At first the East Enders thought I was 'slumming', until they recognised a genuine infatuation for the district they wished to escape from. I learned the history of the waterfront and Hackney, explored the music pubs in the evening, and above all I loved my dilapidated home. It had once been a tiny waterfront pub called the Waterman's Arms, the name I used when I took over the Newcastle Arms on the Isle of Dogs a few years later.

Friends came down to visit me and stay for Sunday lunch on the small back yard which overlooked the Thames. This was where he was photographed by Peter Beard on the roof of his house, next door to mine, a view I knew blindfold, with every detail of Cuckhold's Point opposite and the jagged shapes of the cranes nearby. The one time I returned, reluctantly, to interview David Owen in the house he converted next to the Bunch of Grapes, I went into the darkness of Booty's Wine Bar as 92 Narrow Street has become, and recognised the *smell* of the water below.

It was here that Francis spoke to Peter Beard about Conrad's *Heart of Darkness*. It is claimed that the 'rather horrid appearance' of the *Figure Study II* (1945–6) resembles 'one of the most memorable "dictators" of literature' – Mr Kurtz. It was John Russell who saw an influence on Bacon in Marlow's confrontation with Kurtz:

> His covering had fallen off, and his body emerged from it pitiful and appalling as from a winding sheet. I could see the cage of his ribs all astir, the bones of his arm waving. It was as though an animated image of death carved out of old ivory had been shaking its hands with menaces at a motionless crowd of men made of dark and glittering bronze. I saw him open his mouth wide – it gave him a weirdly voracious aspect, as though he wanted to swallow all the air, all the earth, all the men before him. A deep voice reached me faintly. He must have been shouting.

A photograph exists of myself, Deakin and Francis with two dockers at Charlie Brown's, the famous pub at the end of Narrow Street before West India Docks. Francis frequently slept on the sofa at my place underneath a painting he had given me, the small

251

head of a surgeon with a lamp on his forehead. He had been about to destroy it, having slashed the larger canvas, until a friend persuaded him to let me have it. Years later, when it hung above the fireplace in my home in North Devon, Henry Williamson, the author of *Tarka the Otter*, studied it in amazement. 'That man is a great artist!' he whispered, though he had not heard of Bacon. To my lasting shame and regret, I sold it when I was in my doldrums in Devon; I have never seen it reproduced.

When I left Limehouse in 1964 the scene had changed and the working river was dead. Prices soared as smart people moved in to convert the little houses into elegant waterfront residences. This was everything Francis and I dreaded, especially after a brief meeting with the writer Andrew Sinclair when he rented part of the house next door. It seemed to me that Francis understood that I loved Narrow Street because of its simplicity, and that when I left, the place and the people and I had changed. Still, I was heartbroken. So the news that Francis had moved there shattered me.

'Yes,' said Lucian softly. 'Didn't you know? Francis has bought this place in Narrow Street.'

To this day I shall never fully understand why. He only mentioned it once, when he said he was unable to paint there because of the 'shimmering light'. Evidently, he regarded my connection with Limehouse as irrelevant. I did not expect him to say that he hoped I did not mind him moving in. Yet I found it odd behaviour on his part – as if I was forced to part with a favourite dog and discovered that a close friend had reclaimed it without telling me. Perhaps I am the one who is odd in thinking this – I do not know. However, there was also an earlier incident.

One Christmas I went to a morning cocktail party given by the Australian Bill Stoughton and a busy little queen bustled up, all the more aggravating as the harbinger of bad news: 'Isn't it marvellous,' he purred, 'that Francis has a new friend?'

'Who's that?'

'Don't you know? It's an ex-Guardsman called Tony.'

Tony had lived with me in Narrow Street for the last year or so. A Scot with such a thick accent that few of my friends could understand, he was one of the nicest men I have known. He insisted on coming with me from London for my mother's funeral, knowing I had no relatives. At the last moment, Deakin decided it might be 'fun' to join us – though he stayed in the Grey House drinking while we went to the church service, an ordeal I remember with horror. I shall never forget Tony T.'s kindness, though this is partly because of the sensation his appearance caused in the graveyard at Georgeham. Afterwards he returned to London and his girlfriend, for the days at Narrow Street together were coming to an end.

It had been an exceptionally happy relationship, which may seem odd because we slept together but nothing more – as with the naval deserter. It must sound as if my love life was particularly unfortunate or that I was masochistic in my preference for friendship rather than the rompings of sex. I am glad to say I enjoyed both, but the friendships were stronger, lasted longer and led to real affection. To learn that he had been taken up by Francis was unbearable, as I exclaimed to Lucian Freud when he mentioned Narrow Street.

'My God, he took Tony T. and now Narrow Street. What's next?'

I never held it against Francis, yet, when I heard recently of a wild and certainly untrue story concerning a Scottish man in the mews cottage I did hope it was not my old friend Tony T!

Considering the quicksands of our relationship, I am glad I stayed the course with Francis for as long as I did, though sorry not to have been more sensitive to his moments of loneliness later on. I can vouch for Francis's generosity in private, having known it so often myself – he had a rare ability to give one money without making one feel wretchedly in his debt. He was generous with his advice, too, warning me not to buy a piece of land I had found on the Dalyan river in Turkey below some Lycian tombs: 'Myself I feel it's a bad idea as I feel Turkey could easily be the next place to be taken over – of course if you are desperately in love with someone in Turkey one throws away everything for that.' Unfortunately I was not desperately in love – how stagnant my love life sounds – and the owner of the land reneged, which was just as well for the village nearby became a tourist trap, as Francis had predicted.

Judging by his letters, I used Francis as a sounding-board: 'I have only just got back from Paris. I am terribly sorry things have gone so badly for you. I do hope they improve but one feels armageddon is around the corner for all of us.'

Shortly before Christmas 1985 he had written sympathetically: 'I am sorry things are not going well but I am sure they will. About ruining anybody's life I shouldn't worry too much most people don't have a chance of having their life ruined – the chance of going to Southern Russia sounds marvellous – I enclose £1,000 I hope it will be some help.'

Going through his letters, I see that he sent me another £1,000 on 1 May 1991. On 8 January 1992 I made a bad mistake – I paid him back. The gesture smacked of vanity, of doing 'the honourable thing', in thinking how pleased he would be that someone for once had paid. I was able to do so now because I had received the first advance for this book and it only occurs to me now that he might have suspected the source, though I cannot understand how. If he did, the repayment could have been misinterpreted if he thought I was going to publish a book while he was alive which I had promised him I would not do. Either way, my good intentions were mistaken. 'Yes,' said Bruce Bernard glumly when I told him I had repaid Francis and had not received a reply. 'That *was* an error of judgement.' Ironically, my repayment might have shadowed the last months of our friendship.

I began to reach a point when I knew that my voice irritated when I phoned Francis. I understood this, knowing that you can dread phone calls from certain people which, because they were once the closest of friends, imposes an additional guilt which can become insufferable. I found myself saying the wrong things, like one Saturday lunchtime at Green's in St James's with James Birch and Gilbert and George. I had written to Francis asking him to join us, knowing that Green's was a favourite of his and hoping to introduce them. When he failed to arrive, I phoned him and he apologised – 'You see, I didn't know where to get hold of you. I'm terribly sorry but I can't make it.' Without thinking, I told him that if he was waiting for the Spaniard he should bring him too. As the name of his new friend (to whom I shall refer throughout as the Spaniard, to save him embarrassment) had never passed between us, this was an idiotic thing to say and Francis reacted with impatience: 'Oh, don't talk such rubbish.' A few minutes later,

George phoned him and introduced himself, but Francis was adamant. Whatever he thought of their work, I believe he would have liked them.

There was no falling out, and if there was a distancing, as I suspected yet did not fully understand, I was not alone. I have one regret: that inadvertently this might have rebounded on Peter Bradshaw, and for this I blame myself. Peter and Francis had been friends since the time I introduced them, and they shared the same humour, though Peter sensed that Francis was a more serious person than I realised.

Another person's grief is like another person's dreams or dogs – a matter of indifference. Suffice it to say that Peter died of cancer, which overwhelmed him with appalling speed. With the help of Bob Keating, a friend from Devon, I was able to bring him from the Royal Marsden in Chelsea into Soho for the last time, on the day Ian Board opened the Soho Fair. Peter was able to explore the Chelsea pubs in his wheelchair, pushed by Karen, until he had to return to the hospital for his morphine. He fought the cancer with a bravery and wit that makes his loss more bearable because we remember him with pride. When they told him the worst in the Marsden, Karen said he was taking it remarkably calmly. 'You don't go screaming the firing squad, do you?' he replied.

When he left by ambulance with an oxygen mask on Tuesday morning, 27 July 1992, he wore a colourful shirt bought in the King's Road to conceal the swelling caused by the tumours, and quoted Ritso as he made his bus journey in *Midnight Cowboy*: 'I'm going to Florida!' Roy James, another close friend from Devon, had raced me up the day before, and we said we would see him the other end. Peter died in the ambulance on the way home. Karen was with him.

Peter Bradshaw could be difficult, but he was gloriously individual: funny, handsome, talented, adventurous, with a zest for travel which he shared with Karen on their journeys to the Greek islands. He was too young to die, and he knew it. 'I've been dealt a bad hand,' he told me in his only moment of bitterness. It was reassuring for us to find how popular he was with such a range of people. All the clichés of death meant more than I could have believed – the bank of flowers on his grave, including those from John Edwards and Philip Mordue, Roy Miles, and Gilbert and

George; the letters of condolence from George Melly, Valerie Beston of the Marlborough, and Keith Waterhouse – whose portrait Peter had painted the previous year which led to a memorable lunch for us all at the Ivy to celebrate the unveiling. Due to the thoughtfulness of the clergyman, the funeral at Appledore in Devon had a touching dignity, though I found it difficult to finish my reading of John Masefield's 'Sea Fever':

I must go down to the seas again, to the vagrant gypsy life,
To the gull's way and the whale's way where the wind's like a whetted knife;
And all I ask is a merry yarn from a laughing fellow-rover,
And quiet sleep and a sweet dream when the long trick's over.

That was the worst day of my life. Knowing him was the best part of it.

Francis would have been dismayed by Peter's death for they had laughed so much together, though he sat like Mount Rushmore the evening we took him and John Edwards to the first night of Waterhouse's play *Jeffrey Bernard Is Unwell*. We were in the front row of the dress circle and the entire audience turned round when an actor pranced on in a smock impersonating Francis. His expression settled into an even harder granite than before. 'Rubbish,' he whispered to me in the interval before he vanished with a diplomatic attack of asthma.

I know that Francis would have visited Peter at the Marsden, which was only a couple of minutes' walk from the mews cottage, but my regret lies in his silence earlier when I wrote to him asking if he knew a top consultant, as he usually did, who might have acted in time to stop the cancer spreading. Francis never replied. By the time that Peter reached the Marsden, it was too late. Francis himself was dead.

# 19

# The Spaniard

The Nietzsche of the football team.
*Francis Bacon's description of his ideal man*

One morning I met Francis in Soho. We had not seen each other for several months because I was still living in North Devon, a choice which still mystified him. 'The name of Appledore alone is revolting enough,' he said, though I love the place.

I asked how he was and he answered thoughtfully: 'I've got a new friend and I've been spending too much time with him. I haven't worked hard enough.' The idea excited me: if you are approaching the end of your life as an artist, which do you choose – the water lilies that had so obsessed Monet in his final years or the young man or woman?

In the Colony that afternoon, I repeated the conundrum – the lilies or the love affair? Ian Board did not understand and turned on me as if I had accused Francis, but the choice continued to fascinate me as, apparently, it did Francis. Later he met Sandy Fawkes, looking for me in the Coach and Horses. 'I'm in love,' he told her. 'What should I decide on – the young man or the water lilies?'

'What did you tell him?' I asked her.

'Have both!' Which is just what Francis did.

The young man was the Spaniard whom few people had seen, though they stayed with Baron Philippe de Rothschild in France and Francis took him to dinner with the Sainsburys in 1991. 'He was really charming,' Sir Robert told me. 'So unlike the other boyfriends that we weren't sure of their relationship.'

I learned more when I called at the mews after I had been asked to help with a programme on John Deakin which an independent TV company hoped to sell to Channel 4. It became plain that two names would tilt the balance in our favour if we

257

could persuade them to appear – Francis Bacon and Lucian Freud. Lucian had painted the portrait of Deakin of which I was the first owner and, whether he knew it or not, Francis twisted the knife when he told me this was the best painting Lucian had done since he changed to his looser style. Bruce Bernard saw Lucian, who phoned me a few days later to confirm that he would take part as promised – though he sounded reluctant. This was such encouraging news that Waldemar Janusczak decided to go ahead. But while we were filming Bruce at his home we received a phone call from Lucian to say he had changed his mind and was too 'guilty' to talk to me. This was a blow for he had spoken brilliantly on the telephone, describing Deakin as both the Ugly Sisters *and* Cinderella, and his cancellation made it all the more urgent to nab Francis.

I wrote a letter in which I was careful not to scare him off, with the usual reassurances that we would film where and when it suited him and would only take a few minutes. But when the director, John Christie, followed this up he was startled by Francis's reaction: 'I really didn't know Deakin all that well. You'd better talk to Dan.' Christie expressed his surprise, pointing out that Deakin had made him his next of kin, but Francis protested that his knowledge of Deakin was so slight as to be useless. Also, he was feeling unwell due to a course of antibiotics for his asthma.

Christie persevered and reported: 'Bacon has never actually said "No" but feels he has nothing to say.' This was at variance with the quote he gave to Bruce Bernard for the catalogue to the exhibition of Deakin's work, *The Salvage of a Photographer*, which had inspired this documentary: 'I am very pleased that the Victoria and Albert Museum has arranged this exhibition of John Deakin's photographs – because his work is so little known when one thinks of all the well known and famous names in photography – his portraits to me are the best since Nadar and Julia Margaret Cameron.' That was in 1984, and his mood had changed. Finally, we decided to set up the camera in Bibendum, which was one of his favourite local restaurants and offered the lure of a good lunch afterwards. It did not occur to us that lunching with several strangers and myself was not much of an enticement.

On the morning proposed I did not have the courage to phone Francis but bought an iced bottle of Krug and took a taxi to the mews. There was a long silence after I knocked. Suddenly there was a commotion on the balustrade above, which had always reminded me of Juliet's balcony, and Francis appeared with the indignant cry: 'I'm not being photographed!'

'Of course not,' I called back, waving the Krug like an ill-chosen Romeo. 'I want to apologise for all the trouble you've been put to.'

A moment's doubt – a glare – followed by his smile: 'All right then, you'd better come up.'

As he unlocked the door and I climbed the steep, narrow staircase for the last time, I thought I would seize the advantage with some quick volleys. 'I hear you've been to the Max Ernst exhibition. There isn't much excitement, is there?'

'Nothing at all,' he agreed.

'George Melly says it's outstanding.'

'Well, dear George is obsessed by Ernst – but he doesn't really know anything about anything, does he?' We reached the top of the stairs. Francis looked radiant: he seemed as young as he had on that first day in the French pub forty years earlier. I asked about his asthma and he explained that it left him gasping for breath, but this was one of the good days. It was now ten o'clock and, searching for something to drink, he complained that his own champagne was warm. So we opened the impressive bottle of Krug, which justified its price. With familiar relish, Francis proceeded to decimate every artist mentioned. No one was spared – which was partly for my benefit. When I made a pretentious point, he waved his glass and replied in his most mocking tones: 'Now you're our leading art critic you must be careful not to talk such rubbish! Cheerio!' This was a dig at my role as arts correspondent for the *Mail on Sunday*. Feeling that diffidence would exasperate him more than my opinions, however wrong he found them, I gave him the bait by mentioning the various exhibitions I had seen in London, and he struck.

Jasper Johns was described as 'a dainty little lady. I saw quite a lot of her in Paris. I *hated* her!' When I said I found it hard to warm to the picture of a metal coat-hanger, he dismissed it impatiently: 'That came from Duchamp.' He added: 'Did you know that Jasper Johns and Rauschenberg were lovers? [I didn't.] And, though much nicer than Johns, I can't do with De Kooning either.'

Showing him the cover for my book *With Gilbert and George in Moscow*, which they had designed, he had the grace to study it for a few seconds before throwing it dismissively on the floor. 'Oh, *yes*! There they are – why do they always have to stand like that? I did see their room in the Tate when I went to see mine, but it's not any good, is it?'

'You need to have the space to see them,' I said. 'The Tate is too cramped.'

Always curious, Francis asked if they used a stencil – 'How do they do their colours?' – and I explained that every few years they take as many as thirty thousand photographs, enlarge the details which interest them as they assemble a composition, and colour them with their startling dyes.

'They don't actually paint them?'

'No, but the technique is astonishing. More interesting than Warhol.'

'Oh, yuss,' said Francis, unconvinced. 'Do you know Warhol's early accidents? They were marvellous. Mind you, all those Marilyn's and Jackies are rubbish.'

Turning to the Bührle Collection at the Royal Academy, I knew how much he admired *Madame Moitessier* and referred to the first portrait you saw as you entered the exhibition. It was so sublime that I went back to find out the name of the painter – 'And of course it was Ingres!'

Francis gave me a basilisk stare: 'You do realise that Ingres could be *really* bad. He did some very bad things.'

We moved on to the Manets, which impressed him, and I mentioned the suicide with the man sprawled across the bed holding a revolver. He gave a snort of contempt – 'Well, of course you would mention the *worst*.' He was right.

Though he possessed early work by Auerbach, as I had done, he had turned against it. Richard Hamilton was 'technically adept', Freud's portrait of Minton was 'very, very good' but the group portrait after Watteau was 'awful'. He had doubts regarding Michael Andrews . . . and so on. I was hoping he would say: 'All right then, let's do the Deakin before we get too drunk,' but when I mentioned the film he interrupted me fiercely: 'Deakin was a horrible little man and not a very good photographer. I only used him because he was there and needed the money. Anyhow, photography is of no importance.'

It occurred to me that if he said this on film there would be no point in making the programme, which depended on the justification that Deakin was such a fine photographer that his portraits had been used by Francis Bacon – fascinating though his contemptuous dismissal would have been. Guiltily, I thought of Anna Ridley, the producer, and the rest of the crew waiting patiently in Bibendum for the great man to appear, but I realised too that Francis was in extraordinary form for a man of eighty-two and felt it would be folly to waste a moment of such a rare opportunity. This was like the old days – all the venom, all the fun. If anything should happen to him I would have this memorable occasion to look back on. So I stayed, and they waited.

If Francis had greeted me with suspicion, this had passed. For the next two hours we laughed and confided so warmly that at last he mentioned the Spaniard. I knew little except that he had some connection with a bank, and by some absurd reasoning I had conjured up an image of a dark, middle-aged, saturnine banker. Assuming that a Spaniard must be swarthy and a banker abstemious, I concluded that the Spaniard would be severe yet sympathetic. In other words, I had no idea what he was like.

Francis produced two colour photographs he had taken himself of an exceptionally nice-looking man. Not the smooth chiselled looks of a male model, nor the swept-back black hair I imagined, but a young man whose vigour was such that he seemed to be flying in mid-air though his feet were firmly on the ground. Thirty-five years old, he was one of those Spaniards with tawny-coloured hair – a great shock of it, as I remember – and blue eyes. His mouth was open, laughing with the zest of someone who enjoyed being photographed in a ski resort in brilliant weather.

'My God!' I exclaimed. 'You've done it at last.'

'What have I done?' asked Francis, evidently bemused by my reaction.

'You've found the Nietzsche of the football team.'

He looked at me with a fleeting hint of respect, and laughed: 'Oh, I have, have I?' He laughed again. 'Perhaps you're right.'

'How has everyone taken it?'

'They say he's only after my money.'

'Did that hurt you?'

261

'Not really. You see, he has money of his own. Anyhow, all my life people have only wanted to know me because of my money or my work.' He shrugged, and gave a smile of resignation. 'So there it is.'

When I produced my small Japanese Konica, he told me abruptly that he did not want to be photographed, so I put it away. I was mildly surprised, therefore, when he revealed that he was expecting a photographer from the *Sunday Times*. As he showed me out, I noticed the door to his studio, spattered with paint like a giant's palette.

'My God, I'd love that door,' I said, unaware that it was almost as priceless as a painting.

'Ask John and he'll give it to you.'

When I joined the others at Bibendum, their faces lit up assuming that, after such a long time, Francis would be in tow. I was sorry for them, yet thankful that I had dared to call at the mews. Perhaps the best aspect of this reunion was my pleasure at his happiness, which can be seen reflected in the photograph which John Christie took that lunchtime. It was not just the Krug.

Who was the Spaniard and what became of him? I have not tried to track him down; he deserves better, having given Francis so much joy.

Francis revealed that the young man wrote to him constantly after the Tate retrospective but he had not bothered to reply – 'You know how boring that can be.' But then they met at a party – 'and one night we drank so much that we came back and went to bed together'. Planting his words stealthily, Francis added: 'Now, I am afraid that the physical side of our relationship has come to an end after two years.'

'Be grateful for what you had and be thankful for his friendship now,' I said brusquely.

'I know, but I want *more*.'

We laughed again in the knowledge that Francis was eighty-two. It gave his lament a grandeur.

A few nights later I met the Spaniard for the first and only time at the entrance to the Groucho Club. Francis was with a lack-lustre man and woman who were collecting their coats; none of them seemed in the best spirits except for the Spaniard, who hurried over to shake my hand as if I were a close friend. Francis

262

glowered from the doorway like a satanic doll. 'You're always so drunk,' he muttered – which was incontestable. That was the last time I saw him. A few days later I phoned him for a quote which I could use in a competition for artists, organised by the critic Edward Lucie-Smith and myself, for the *Mail on Sunday* at the Olympia Arts Fair.

'No,' he interrupted tersely. 'I don't want to be quoted on anything. I've nothing to say to young artists and have no advice to give and no encouragement. They don't interest me in the least.'

I thought it best to change the subject, saying how pleased I had been to meet the Spaniard and how much I had liked him. His tone softened almost imperceptibly: 'Unfortunately he has to go back to Spain tomorrow. Well, goodbye Dan, I may see you when you're next up. . . .' He terminated the conversation suddenly, leaving me holding the telephone.

Against the advice of Dr Brass, Francis left for Madrid at the middle of April 1992, to see the Spaniard and presumably to comment on a show that was being prepared by the new Marlborough Gallery. Pneumonia, aggravated by a severe attack of asthma, brought him to hospital, where he died of a heart attack six days later. Apparently he was alone apart from the staff. There were no friends and no service at his cremation, except for a wreath from Noel and Leslie Botham who had taken over the French pub from Gaston Berlemont. Only a few journalists and photographers gathered round the coffin.

His ashes were brought back to be scattered at a 'chosen place' in the country. I heard that a tree might be planted there and thought, if the conditions are right, how nice it would be to start a small vineyard.

As for the Spaniard, I have the fear that he vanished from the scene because no one bothered to include him. I sent a letter, for I wanted him to know of the happiness he brought to Francis when it came like a long-lost reward, though I did not use such high-falutin' words to him. I doubt if the letter found him, but if he should read this book I hope he will realise how much he meant to Francis at a time when he was lonely.

Francis had brought the Spaniard to the Colony nine months earlier and he returned shortly after Francis's death for a meeting with John Edwards and stayed for a few words with Ian Board and Michael Wojas, who told me: 'I think he was in love with Francis, the way he talked. He was almost in tears.'

# 20

# End in Suffolk

We are born and we die and there's nothing else. We're just part of animal life.

*Francis Bacon to Melvyn Bragg*

I took the train to Suffolk, a county I hate. 'It's all so *green*,' as Francis used to say. Yet he went there frequently to see John Edwards, who is happy there, and Suffolk and Norfolk are beloved by writers and artists: Eleanor Bellingham-Smith moved there after Rodrigo left her; Elizabeth Smart had a cottage where Deakin, Colquhoun and MacBryde were such unruly guests that she found it easier to sell up and leave; even Jeffrey Bernard lived there, though I assume he was more interested in turf than grass. Bobby Hunt still lives there and James Birch escapes from London to the lodge at the gates to his father's estate. He arranged to drive me down with Paul Conran for the weekend, to stay with a fine young painter, Simon Gales, and to visit John Edwards.

The weekend started badly when I telephoned James on the Saturday morning to find he had forgotten about my lift. When I spoke to Paul Conran he said he had changed his mind; so I reported back to James, who was plainly in bed with a girl and none too pleased by the interruptions. Tersely, we agreed to meet in the Coach and Horses at lunchtime and go down by train. I was reminded of George Melly's dictum that 'No good deed should go unpunished', realising that the offer of a lift to the country is often an act of sadistic selfishness. When James phoned the Coach breathlessly to announce that Paul had changed his mind yet again and they would pick me up in half an hour, I told him: 'Oh no, you won't. I'll go by train, it's quicker.' If you are lucky enough to catch the right train from Liverpool Street you can be in Colchester in under an hour.

I sat opposite a young woman who was beautiful apart from the

265

unconcealed scar on her throat which looked as if someone had burnt her with acid. With the sudden impulsiveness of strangers, she confided that she had recently married a bank manager and had just discovered he was 'into devil worship'. She gave me intimate details of her life which I should not repeat.

At Colchester I asked the first driver on the taxi rank to stop at a pub on the way to the village I was heading for. But he looked at me stonily as if I were a devil-worshipper myself and informed me with the grim satisfaction of a Muscovite saleswoman, 'There *are* no pubs open in Colchester on a Saturday afternoon' – which seemed odd for a garrison town.

Another driver, a former football champion, was more sympathetic and stopped at a posh country pub which looked open except that it proved to be a wedding function at full tilt with ladies in mauve dresses and large purple hats who urged me to join them until the manager appeared and said it was against the law. Finally I made the village pub, which was actually welcoming. There to my infinite relief I saw Philip, John Edwards's close friend, whom I have always liked. He is cheerful and sharply aware of everything which goes on around him, with a wit that was sometimes too sharp for Francis.

Philip phoned Simon Gales to say I had been found, and contacted John Edwards who was busy at home; we arranged to meet at opening time on Sunday. I started to relax, for this was the purpose of my journey to Suffolk and John guards his home like a fortress, using his answerphone like a 'minder'. This was the first time I had seen him since Francis's death, and I hoped he realised I was on his side.

The next morning, I stared at the endless flat fields from a latticed window in Simon's quaint old thatched and gabled cottage. After Simon drove off with his girlfriend, Bobby Hunt was kind enough to join me and drive me into the village, which I shall not name out of respect for John's wish for privacy. When I arrived at a minute past twelve he was waiting for me with a smile and a bottle of chilled champagne, a welcoming combination.

I learned that we had been invited to a local barbecue. There a group of young men piled into the lounge to watch a video of the most revolting man I had ever seen prancing around on stage dressed in a skirt and a red bandeau, with a straggly beard and

266

tattoos, brandishing a guitar as if this was a send-up – though it was far from funny. Foolishly I made some comment to this effect, which did not go down well. I learned later that the horrid man is a pop idol called Axl Rose, an anagram for oral sex, and hugely popular. Seldom have I felt so old and out of touch. After some angry looks they turned back to the set, and I wandered into the back garden where John and Philip were trying to light a reluctant barbecue in order to cook some frozen sausages. Their contribution of champagne, slurped from the bottle, had run out and there was no replacement. A couple of 'Oldies' were watching, and I remarked casually to a pleasant-looking woman that it seemed an odd sort of party – 'Everyone watching that awful man on the video, and no food or drink.' 'My son is the host,' she replied and went inside to repeat my comments to a boy in his teens with a blond fringe who emerged pale with anger: 'What you been saying to my mum? I'm going to duff you up.' John Edwards, who seemed as popular as I was not, got me out in time and we drove to his home in his Mercedes.

I had been told that the house is beautiful but I was not prepared for the scale and splendour, with a barn converted into a handsome black chalet where Francis stayed, nor for the extent of the landscape gardening. Presumably the fields were flat and desolate before; now there are shades of Gatsby with young trees and banks of earth planted with exotic shrubs, a few of which I recognised, and a pipe splashing water into an artificial lake guarded by a stone heron. Recently acquired fields beyond are lined with small pines. All was protected by impressive gates and a magnificent high wall made of local flint.

There was the wistfulness of knowing that Francis would not see this when the pines are tall and strong. Otherwise I did not feel grief for him, whose life was so fulfilled, as I did for John who was so choked with emotion as he showed me around that he blurted out: 'Francis was my God, my Jesus Christ!' I tried to reassure him by saying how much he had done for Francis; but this was before Peter Bradshaw's death, which taught me more about grief than I cared to know.

'You know,' he said at one point with a self-mocking smile, 'there is one thing I really regret, that I was never able to write Francis a love letter.' He pronounces Francis as 'Frawnsis', or called him by his nickname, 'Eggs'. Later he showed me a lettter from Francis, each word printed meticulously in ink in case John could not decipher it.

'Did Francis turn against me at the end?' I asked.

'No, I don't think so. Why?'

'I have a strange feeling that he knew I was planning this book.'

'Of course he did.' John stopped walking and turned round. 'I told him.'

'Good God, why?' I knew we had discussed it together in the Groucho Club, but thought this was confidential.

'Well, I told Francis everything, didn't I?' Of course he did. How crazy I was to think otherwise.

That evening we sat and talked in the living room, joined by Philip, a perky white terrier with a parting on his back and a small affectionate cat. It is an extraordinary room, dominated by Francis Bacon reproductions and prints on every wall. I discovered Peter Bradshaw's gift to Francis, the head of the nurse from the *Battleship Potemkin*, in a place of honour – the lavatory.

'You have it,' said John, when I said it was better than I remembered, but I refused, thinking that Peter would be pleased to know it was safe and appreciated. I retrieved it after Peter's death, when John generously fulfilled his offer. At the end of the room, covering an entire wall from floor to ceiling, was the largest single painting by Francis Bacon that I had seen, a portrait of Edwards. If proof is needed, as I think it is, this confirms that Bacon's power had not diminished towards the end of his life. To describe a picture as 'great' is such a tired cliché that I hesitate to use it; but, rather than search for an alternative, I believe the term can be applied to at least twenty of Bacon's paintings, and this portrait is a 'great' finale. I had not seen it reproduced, and something about it puzzled me until I realised that there was none of the usual distortion of the face. It was portrayed with a grand simplicity, without the twist of the grimace. Alien though this was to Francis's approach to life and work, I can only assume the portrait was painted with deep affection.

Simon Gales returned from Colchester station, amazed to find us knocking back vintage wine as if it was beer. I am not a red wine drinker, having suffered from gout when I was younger, but even I could tell it was exceptional. Simon, whose father is a wine expert, *knew* it was exceptional: 'A youngish man who could hardly stand introduced himself as John Edwards . . . they were drinking a bottle of Château Mouton Rothschild and John, as carefully as he could, emptied the remnants into a fresh and sizeable glass which he handed me before staggering off, presumably for another bottle.' Simon found the evening so memorable that he wrote it up afterwards:

> Dan turned to me and said 'Follow me, there is something you must see.' I followed him down the hall into a narrow more plushly furnished living room which opened onto a conservatory. Dan pointed over my shoulder and there it was – a Bacon canvas, seven feet by five, a full size portrait of John Edwards with a startling likeness. Figures span in my mind, £1.5 perhaps £2 million of painting. It could even be worth up to four times the value of the residence in which it hangs, the strange irony was apparent.

Presumably the painting had to be carried on stretchers into the room and assembled there; at least no burglar could remove it. Simon continued:

> My concentration was broken by John as he entered with a full bottle of Mouton Rothschild, again another vintage 1970, and topped up my glass.
> 'The bastard finished all the best stuff before he died. You know . . . Francis . . . he, he was no mug.' I must have looked surprised for I thought that there was nothing better than a 1970, a fantastic vintage year apart, perhaps, from 1952 which was very rare. Yet 1970, being a twenty-two-year-old, must be now in its prime. I looked down at my glass and gently swirled the dark liquid around trying to air it.
> 'Do you want to see his eyes?' John asked us, and reached behind his chair to pull out a large folder which contained huge black and white photographs taken by himself of Francis's eyes printed as if they were suspended in air. 'Do you want to see his hands?' And his photographs of details of Francis's face, and the face itself, were handed round exuding such a stark reality that Francis himself seemed to be there as we spoke of him.

With his appreciation of the wine and Bacon's work, Simon was proving an invaluable catalyst. When he admired a signed print of Francis's *Study for a Bullfight* (1969) leaning precariously against the skirting of the wall, John said that most people looked at it for just a few seconds and turned away.

'The subject of Francis was a painful one for John,' wrote Simon,

and he often said he wanted to stop talking about him, yet he brought him up. One thing he mentioned which I found rather sad but very typical was that Dan was the only person to send his condolences on Francis's death. I sat there and looked at John, aimless and disorientated. I felt he was vulnerable and would find it difficult to uphold the responsibility for the vast inheritance that had fallen on his shoulders. Ideally he should have been left just a few million in trust with an allowance at regular intervals so that if he wanted a sports car or a holiday he could have it.

*Just a few million!* At this stage the full amount of the inheritance was undeclared, though already a talking point. At the end, after all the speculation – £60 million prophecied by *The Sunday Times*, and more by the gossips – the entire of Bacon's estate went to John Edwards, the sole beneficiary of £11,370,244. This dashed the expectations of several friends who believed they would receive a picture, *at least*. Understandably, Francis wanted his will to be as uncluttered as possible, especially as he had been so generous in his lifetime. When he heard that Helen Lessore was going to the opening of his grand show at the Metropolitan in New York, he asked Miss Beston to arrange everything – ticket and hotel, and insisted on paying for it all. When he learnt that Erica Brausen was ill and needed medical attention, he sent her a generous cheque. It was only right that the millions should have gone to John Edwards. Many people agreed that Francis had unwittingly laid John open to 'leeches, brokers, unscrupulous bankers, cowboy businessmen, and casino-minded underwriters, spongers, charities, salesmen and his own incompetence', as Simon put it later. It is a vexed point, but I believe that John will cope. He has Philip's common-sense to help him as well as his family.

Philip returned with a takeaway, emerging from the kitchen with a bottle of Lafitte de Rothschild 1970 in one hand and a plate of curry in the other. I refused the curry, but John picked at it while Philip opened the bottle and, to Simon's dismay, poured the wine into the same glasses – though I noticed him wiping out the dregs with a tissue before they were refilled. Pulling up a mock- Carolean chair and putting his feet on the table, John explained that Ian Board had given them the chair though they had to have it reupholstered.

With touching loyalty, John turned on the various former friends of Francis whom he accused of betraying him. When I felt obliged to defend them, which I did without much conviction, John resorted to 'Francis is fucking dead . . . I don't want to talk about Francis.' After telling him off for swearing, Philip rolled him a cigarette in the hope that it would help him to relax, because he was still very much stricken after Francis's death.

'I dragged on the cigarette and felt the rush of coolness sweep through to my finger-tips,' Simon remembered,

> and then handed the cigarette to Dan. With a delighted look he drew on the end briefly and blew out most of the smoke without really taking it down.
>
> 'Oh, I like these smokies!' he said as he handed it back to me, and I handed it back to Philip who asked me 'Do you like fiddling about, are you homosexual?' I replied that I was very much a heterosexual and that I was only turned on by women. 'Well,' John said, 'everyone has their own ways.' He threw up his hands. 'Each to his own.'

After this Philip put on some Mozart while John appeared with another 1970 vintage – this time Château Latour, still in its brown wrapping paper, which Philip displayed with a grin. He filled the empty glasses, then rolled another cigarette and remarked that I was somewhat of a 'virgin' as far as life was concerned.

'Dan! Breathe out, then draw on the cigarette,' he explained, and after several abortive puffs, repeated: 'No, breathe out Dan, *then* draw. No, Dan, breathe out, draw, take it all down and swallow it. *Swallow* it!'

Simon said I had a 'Churchillian look of determination' as I struggled to get it right.

> Dan proceeded to metamorphosise, firstly his eyes bulged, and then he went into a violent coughing fit shaking his head from side to side and fanning the smoke away from his face vigorously with his hand. He went bright red, then white. 'Oh God!' he gasped as he went a shade of green and threw his head back and stretched out his arms trying to regain his composure as the nicotine started to take effect. Philip and I grinned at one another. Dan's eyes began to widen and an excited smile came over his face. He jumped to his feet with a burst of sudden energy and performed a very convincing Marlene Dietrich, skipping little dance steps

271

backwards and forwards. After the entertainment ceased, Philip asked –
'What's it like, Dan?'

'Those smokies are wonderful . . . but oh,' his hand went to his brow,
'I'm not really used to this sort of thing.'

Simon says he sat back with his glass of claret and looked at
the Bacon painting and everything else in the room, listening to
the Mozart Andante No. 22.

I tried not to think of the possibility of never being in the position again of
having a private view of a £1.5 million Bacon, drinking £300 bottles of
wine and listening to music so divine, so perfect, by the best composer the
world has ever known. The situation was unreal.

'You are so relaxed, mate, I like you, you're cool man,' John
spluttered. I looked at John grinning at me, making every effort to keep
his hand straight and level as if it weighed 100 lbs. I was suddenly brought
back to reality.

John was at least genuine and despite his appalling language had a
certain amount of integrity. He himself made a self-analysis which was
endearingly heroic: 'I know I'm . . . Well, you know I can't read or write,
but at least I know the difference between right and wrong.'

'Well, if you know that, that makes you contrary to most.'

Philip tried to blow a vast amount of cigarette smoke into my
mouth, but it led to another coughing fit. As John was staring at
the floor, he went over to cheer him up and I signalled to Simon
that it was time to leave. John shook hands with Simon and
thanked him for his good company and appreciative remarks
about the portrait, while Philip gave him a peck on the cheek. As
Philip showed us out, I asked him to take care of John and help
him through a difficult period. Simon says this was exactly what he
was going to say: 'It was typical of Dan to take the initiative.'
Typically interfering and sanctimonious.

Francis insisted that if you drank only the very best wine you
had no hangover, and this was true as I gazed through the
latticed windows of Simon's cottage at the forlorn fields beyond
with a clearer head than I deserved on the Monday morning. I
recalled the details of an unusual day – Axl Rose – the stone
heron by the artificial lake – the Château Mouton Rothschild –
and the great portrait of John. One moment came back with
particular force.

'I should like to dedicate this book to you,' I told John as we walked around his property.

'And to Francis?' he asked. 'I don't know about such things, or isn't that possible?'

Of course it is and of course I do. With all my heart, this book is dedicated to Francis Bacon and John Edwards.

# Index

279